A BEGINNER'S GUIDE
TO THE Old
Testament

To John Zamoni,
Read and enjoy!

At Zamoni

COVER PHOTOS

The Jordan River.
Copyright Sonia Halliday / Biblical Archaeology Society.
> In this view of the Jordan, the river's waters are highlighted by the slanting rays of the morning sun rising over the hills of Jordan (ancient Ammon) as the river meanders toward the Dead Sea.

Moses and the Ten Commandments.
painting by James Jacques Joseph Tissot (1836–1902).
> Copyright The Jewish Museum of New York / Art Resource, NY.

The "Son of God" Fragment (4Q246).
Copyright Israel Antiquities Authority / Biblical Archaeology Society.
> In this fragment of the Dead Sea Scrolls from Qumran, the title "Son of God" is applied to a future divine savior. Moreover, both forms of the title, "Son of God" and "Son of the Most High" are used as they are found in Luke's account of the angel Gabriel's announcement of the Christ child to Mary (1:35).

Harvesting.
Copyright Garo Nalbandian / Biblical Archaeology Society.
> Biblical law (Deuteronomy 24:19) allowed widows, orphans, and strangers to follow the reapers to gather the stray stalks missed in the bundling. Such an occurrence is described in chapter two of the Book of Ruth.

A BEGINNER'S GUIDE
TO THE Old
Testament

Arthur E. Zannoni

ThomasMore®
– An RCL Company –
Allen, Texas

NIHIL OBSTAT:
Rev. Msgr. Glenn D. Gardner, J.C.D.
Censor Librorum

IMPRIMATUR:
† Most Rev. Charles V. Grahmann
Bishop of Dallas

November 11, 2002

The Nihil Obstat and Imprimatur are official declarations that the material reviewed is free of doctrinal or moral error. No implication is contained therein that those granting the Nihil Obstat and Imprimatur agree with the contents, opinions, or statements expressed.

Acknowledgments

The Scripture quotations contained herein are from the *New Revised Standard Version Bible: Catholic Edition,* copyright © 1993 and 1989 by the Division of Christian Education for the National Council of the Churches of Christ in the U.S.A. Used by permission. All rights reserved.

"The World of the Hebrews" illustration (p. 48) is reproduced with permission from *New American Bible,* copyright © 1992, 1987, 1980, 1970, Catholic Book Publishing Co., New York, NY. All rights reserved.

Send all inquiries to:
Thomas More® Publishing
An RCL Company
200 East Bethany Drive
Allen, Texas 75002-3804

Telephone: 800-264-0368 / 972-390-6300
Fax: 800-688-8356 / 972-390-6560

Visit us at: **www.thomasmore.com**
Customer Service E-mail: **cservice@rcl-enterprises.com**

Printed in the United States of America

Library of Congress Control Number: 2002109850

7525   ISBN 0-88347-525-1

1 2 3 4 5   07 06 05 04 03

ACKNOWLEDGMENTS

No BOOK IS EVER THE RESULT OF JUST ONE PERSON'S efforts; rather, many people help the author through the writing process, and they deserve to be thanked. I am deeply grateful to my publisher, Thomas More, and to John Sprague, editorial director, and Debra Hampton, acquisitions and marketing director, for their support and encouragement with the publication of these "Beginner's Guides" volumes. In addition, invaluable suggestions and support were given to me by fellow writers and friends, Bill Huebsch, Kevin Perrotta, David Haas, Jeffrey Judge, Michael Shermis, Megan McKenna, and Theresa Cotter. My lifelong friend and colleague, E. Jane Via, was a source of great inspiration and encouragement to me. Special thanks goes to Leslie Carney for typing the entire manuscript and for her attention to every detail of layout and design. Her invaluable editing and helpful suggestions improved the quality of the manuscript.

My family constantly supported me as I wrote. My son Luke sent E-mails of encouragement when the writing got tough. My daughter Laura and son-in-law Brandon supported me from afar. My young toddler son Alessandro supported me when he often patiently waited for me to finish a piece before we could enjoy each other's company. Of course, there are no adequate words for thanking my beloved spouse Kathleen, whose countless sacrifices to help finish this book number legion, and whose love for me was deeply felt. "Happy is the husband of a good wife . . . and her skill puts flesh on his bones" (Sirach 26:1, 13).

"Welcome TO A WEALTH OF MATERIAL ON THE COLLECTION of books we call the Bible! This may be called a 'Beginner's Guide,' but it's more a Primer: an in-depth introduction for novices and those more adept at reading and delving into the mysteries of the earlier books and testament of the Bible. This book is a treasure-trove of concepts, historical background that is concise and insightful and gives a sense of meaning and understanding to God's revelation over the course of centuries, yet still is vital and engaging today.

"The writer, Art Zannoni, has what is called 'eyes in the back of his head,' meaning that he writes forward and backward, looking at the material in retrospect, from the place of belief in the coming of Jesus in Incarnation and Resurrection, and forward, acknowledging the great depth that this earlier revelation sets as foundational for how God dialogues with his people for all times. Along with Zannoni's *Beginner's Guide to the New Testament,* this book completes a set of the best books for adult education, survey courses in Scripture, and foundation courses for those wanting to know the latest in exegesis and understanding of the core of our tradition as Judeo-Christians. The style is delightful, engaging, and familiar, drawing the reader into the Scriptures and imparting a love for the Word of God. No matter what your background, any reader will find intriguing material and insights that will shift the way you read the mysteries of God's revelation in the Old Testament."

—Megan McKenna
Biblical scholar, theologian, master storyteller, and author *(Prophets: Words of Fire)*

CONTENTS

INTRODUCTION

The BIBLE IS NOT A BOOK! I KNOW IT LOOKS LIKE A book, feels like a book, and is bound like a book. But it is not a book. As a matter of fact, the Greek word *biblia*, from which we derive the English word "Bible," means "books." The Bible is a library of books. As such, the books were written under the inspiration of the Holy Spirit by different people, at different times in history, addressing various audiences, and utilizing different literary genres (forms).

Opening the Bible is like entering a library. Whenever I go to a library I often make use of a guide. Sometimes the computer terminal that I turn on and read from will guide me through the library and its holdings. Other times I need the guidance of a librarian, most often a reference librarian who can help me find what I am looking for or point me in the right direction or give me the needed reference tools to help me find the resources and book(s) I am looking for.

A guide is also needed when approaching the library of books known as the Bible. Without a guide, exploring the biblical library can be frustrating, confusing, laborious, and for some, downright overwhelming. This need not be the case if you are made aware of what you need to know and look for in the Bible library.

I wrote this book to guide people, especially beginners, in exploring the wonder and marvels of the Old Testament, the first half of the Bible, which is venerated as the "Word of God" and as revealing the "Will of God." I did not write it as a replacement for reading the Bible itself but, rather, as a manual to be used alongside the Bible. Just as an owner's manual for an automobile cannot replace driving or using a car, it is nonetheless a helpful guide for safely driving and maintaining it. So the real starting point for using this book is your Bible; read it first, then this volume. Have your Bible with you and refer to it and read from it as you read this book.

This current volume is the second in a series. The first was published in the spring of 2002, entitled *A Beginner's Guide to the New Testament*. It was written prior to this book simply because I believe the reading public is more familiar with the New Testament. I thought it was best to share with the readership a guide first for the familiar, before providing the current volume on the Old Testament, which for some is less familiar and more difficult to understand.

Writing a guide for all the books of the Old Testament was a daunting task. It required prayer, discernment, discipline, and perseverance. It also required the organization of material into manageable and readable units. It proved to be a challenge of a lifetime of years of teaching, and at the same time an adventure full of surprises and joys.

If you are new to the study of the Bible or if you have studied it and want to learn more about the books of the Old Testament, I have given myself the task of guiding you through all of the books. Since I am aiming this book primarily at Catholics and your use of the Bible in the practice of your faith, I make every effort to show how the church acts as a guide for the believer—you the reader—as you

explore the Old Testament. I intend this volume to be a basic introduction that provides both information and material for your
interpretation of and reflection on the Old Testament. This book is not
intended for the scholar or specialist, but for the beginner.

As I wrote this introduction, I thought it important for you to
know up-front that the books of the Old Testament have as their
purpose the evocation of faith. They do not intend to provide detailed
and accurate scientific or historical information but, rather, to present
and proclaim revelations about God and his people that are intended
to inspire readers to appropriate a lifestyle of faith. The Old
Testament, like the New Testament, is faith literature, written by
people of faith to inspire faith. The two testaments of the Bible are not
video camera recordings of events. Rather, they are proclamations of
belief.

The books in the first section of the Bible went through three
stages of development. Put succinctly, the first stage was the actual
event; for example, the exodus of the Israelites from Egypt. There
were eyewitnesses to this event who began to pass on their stories
about the event orally. This is the second stage of development, oral
tradition. How long this oral tradition lasted is not completely known.
Finally, the oral traditions were gathered together, written down, and
edited to become the books of the Old Testament. The whole process
took centuries.

These stages of development occurred within a historical and
cultural context which influenced the writer(s). These writers made
use of a variety of literary forms, writing primarily in the Hebrew
language, a language made up of consonants and idioms.
Throughout this book attention is paid to both literary form and
various Hebrew words and idioms that might help the reader better
understand a particular text of the Old Testament.

Reading ancient documents also requires some attention to
geography. Knowing where places are located—for example, that
Samaria is north of Jerusalem, and Egypt is south of Jerusalem—as
well as where desert wildernesses, mountain ranges, and important

bodies of water are located enhance the reader's knowledge and interpretation of the biblical text. Maps have been provided in this volume to assist you in locating important places.

In chapter 1, I explore the nature and meaning of God's revelation and the Bible as part of that revelation, as well as the official list of books in the Catholic Old Testament and how to find your way around in the Old Testament. I also reflect on the issues of authorship of the Bible, the meaning of inspiration, and inerrancy as it applies to the Bible. The chapter closes with an explanation of the church as a guide to reading the Old Testament.

Chapter 2 deals with the first five books of the Bible, known to Christians as the Pentateuch. The chapter explains the meaning of the terms "Torah" and "Pentateuch," and discusses the authors involved in compiling the first five books of the Old Testament. It then explores each of the five books individually, summarizing both the book's historical context and its internal content, emphasizing certain theological themes or crucial characters. Because of its all important role in the Pentateuch, the Book of Exodus receives the most detailed emphasis in this chapter. Greater attention is devoted to key theological themes found in the Book of Exodus. The chapter ends with a reflection on Moses vis-à-vis the Pentateuch.

Chapters 3 and 4 deal with the promised land, what people today commonly refer to as the Holy Land. Chapter 3 focuses on the conquest, entering, and division of the land of Canaan—the promised land—among the twelve tribes as described in the Book of Joshua. The second half of chapter 3 looks at the life situation in the land as narrated in the Book of Judges. Chapter 4 centers on formation of the monarchy, the reigns of kings Saul, David, and Solomon, and their care for the land, as well as the division of the monarchy/kingdoms and reigns of the kings of both the northern kingdom of Israel and the southern kingdom of Judah right up to the Babylonian exile. In relationship to the entire Old Testament, this fourth chapter covers the books of 1 and 2 Samuel, 1 and 2 Kings, and 1 and 2 Chronicles.

In chapters 5, 6, and 7, I deal with the Old Testament prophets—those colorful characters who were God's spokespersons. Chapter 5 introduces the reader to the nature and meaning of a prophet in the Old Testament, as well as the relationship of the prophets to the kings. It also presents the colorful ministry of the prophet Elijah and a listing of the preexilic and postexilic prophets. Chapter 6 is devoted entirely to the major prophets: Isaiah, Jeremiah, and Ezekiel. Chapter 7 surveys the twelve minor prophets and reflects on the books of Lamentations, Baruch, Ezra, and Nehemiah.

Prayer is an essential part of every religion, and chapter 8 explores the Bible's prayer book, the Book of Psalms. After I introduce the reader to the origin, authorship, and makeup of the Book of Psalms, I give a concise explanation of the poetry of the Psalms. This is followed by a listing of the various literary forms of the Psalms, with a more detailed explanation of the hymns, laments, cursing, penitential, thanksgiving, royal, and wisdom Psalms. The chapter ends with reflections on praying the Psalms.

Chapter 9 is devoted to the wisdom literature of the Old Testament. In it, I first explore the origin of wisdom in the Old Testament, as well as its patron, King Solomon. Then I provide a succinct commentary on the books of Proverbs, Job, Ecclesiastes (Qoheleth), Song of Solomon (Song of Songs), the Wisdom of Solomon, and Sirach. I attempt to acquaint the reader with the more important themes and insights of these six wisdom books.

In chapter 10, I look at two connected themes. First, I ask the reader to reflect on the five short stories found in the Old Testament, namely Ruth, Jonah, Esther, Tobit, and Judith. Then I briefly explore some of the major Hebrew heroines of the Old Testament to show their profound import in an otherwise patriarchal (male-dominated) world.

The final chapter looks at the closing scenes of the Old Testament and the arrival of the Greeks. Stress is placed on the influence of Hellenization on the Jews and Jewish religion, and the responses to this influence as presented by the books of Daniel and Maccabees. I close the chapter with a bridge to the New Testament—resurrection.

You will note that the final item in the book is entitled "Afterword." I wrote it as sort of a homily or exhortation addressed to you the reader in which I provide a series of healthy challenges that result from reading and studying the Old Testament. I hope that you will embrace these challenges after reading both this book and the Old Testament.

Throughout this book the English translation of the Bible that I use is the *New Revised Standard Version* (NRSV). I chose it for two reasons. First, it was the translation of the Bible used in the companion volume, *A Beginner's Guide to the New Testament*, and I thought this would keep continuity between the two volumes. Second, I find it to be a good modern English version of the Bible for use in the study of Sacred Scripture because of its excellent use of the English language throughout while simultaneously attempting to remain faithful to the original language of the biblical text. However, please use the translation of the Bible that you find most helpful.

To enhance your use of this book, I provide, where needed, diagrams and illustrations. On the inside of the front and back covers (for easy access), you will find a time line to help you position personalities and events vis-à-vis the Bible. I also conclude each chapter with discussion questions to help you evaluate your understanding and a list of books for further reading. Those of you who wish to delve further into a particular topic will find ample resources.

I sincerely hope and pray that this book will help you to better appreciate, understand, interpret, and live the challenges provided by God as presented in the Old Testament. May it guide you to a deeper wisdom that comes from God. For ". . . all wisdom is from the Lord . . ." (Sirach 1:1). May it help you to pray with the psalmist: "Praise the Lord! Praise the Lord, O my soul! I will praise the Lord as long as I live . . ." (Psalm 146:1–2).

Soli Deo Gloria

1

THE BIBLE AND GOD'S REVELATION

During THE LIFE OF ANY AUTOMOBILE, THERE ARE times when it needs to be serviced. We take it off the road and into an auto shop for a tune-up and needed repairs. The mechanic or technician examines the car, often using a computer or diagnostic instrument, and then makes adjustments or repairs necessary for it to function according to fixed standards provided by the manufacturer.

The same is true of a piano when it gets out of tune. We call in a piano tuner. The trained tuner strikes a U-shaped fork which is tuned to a standard international pitch. He then tightens or loosens each string in the piano, adjusting them to the standard pitch. There are times in our lives when we need to take ourselves off the fast-moving road of life for a spiritual tune-up, so to speak; times when we need to adjust the pitch of our heartstrings to God's eternal standards.

What are the eternal standards to which we must aspire in order to achieve wholeness of life? Everywhere there are clues! We find them in the lives of other persons—our spouse, children, extended family, friends, coworkers. We find them at the deep levels of our own being. We find them in the experiences of great joy and deep sorrow. We find them when we play and pray. We find them in literature, music, art, drama, and work. Most importantly, we find them in the Word of God—the Bible. And when it is time to adjust our heartstrings, when it is time for a tune-up for the body and soul, we listen to the Word of God in Sacred Scripture for the eternal standards.

Revelation

The English word "revelation" comes from the Latin verb *revelare,* meaning "to take away the veil." It came to be understood as the disclosure of persons, events, and things previously hidden or only partially known; ultimately, "revelation" came to mean the "self-disclosure of God."

Revelation is essentially God's self-communication, a loving and utterly gratuitous invitation to enter into a dialog of friendship offered by God to humans. Human beings are called to respond in faith and not merely intellectually to God's divine self-disclosure.

God discloses (reveals) God's self in a variety of ways—through nature, through human beings, through history and tradition, and through the inspired scriptures of the Bible. For Catholics, the Bible is one of the normative channels of God's self-communication, along with sacred tradition (magisterium).

The Bible—Record of God's Revelation

The Bible records and narrates people's religious experiences. Beginning with Adam and Eve, Abraham through Moses, the kings, prophets, wisdom sages, and finally Jesus of Nazareth, these many books written over many centuries documented how some individuals and their communities experienced God in their lives. Each person had his or her personal relationship with God and then witnessed to others not only about how they understood God, but also about how God had changed their lives. All Christians turn to the Bible to help in their own personal journey with God and to God. Most of the images that today's Christians have of God, including those of Jesus and his early followers, first appeared in the recorded religious experience of the Jews as narrated in what Christians call the Old Testament.

Authorship of the Bible

For many years, Christians, including the Catholic Church, accepted Moses as author of the first five books of the Bible, and authorship of the four Gospels by apostles or disciples of apostles. Today the Catholic Church and most Christians accept Moses and the apostles as the inspiration for these books rather than as the actual authors. The books attributed to Moses were not written until some 600 or 700 years after his death. In fact, the vast majority of the books of the Bible come from anonymous authors.

Different people wrote the various books of the Bible at different times, in different places, within different contexts. Someone actually wrote the books of Ruth and Esther. Individuals were responsible for many of the prophetic books, and the Psalms, too, had a literary author(s), even if the actual writing took place after a period of fixed oral tradition. Some books had editors. Other books are compilations, such as the Book of Proverbs. All the books of the Bible come from people of faith who, inspired by God, edited or wrote them.

Inspired by God

Catholic-Christian tradition teaches that God inspired the Bible. "Those divinely revealed realities which are presented and contained in Sacred Scripture have been committed to writing under the inspiration of the Holy Spirit" (Vatican Council II, *Dogmatic Constitution on Divine Revelation*). This distinguishes the Bible from all other sacred books and gives it an authority and power as the norm for all Christian communities. But what does inspiration mean and how does this belief agree with all that has been said about the origin of the Bible? Did God actually inspire each written word? Who was inspired—preacher, writer, editor, or everyone involved?

Inspiration involves a process, under the guidance of the Spirit of God, that eventually created the Bible. Inspiration is human and not miraculous, does not prescind from the ordinary development of traditions and human procedures. The Bible has both a human and divine dimension. As a human document, the Bible was composed from the contributions of many people over a long period of time. They used their histories, talents, backgrounds, and experience as best they could. As divine, the Bible expresses the relationship of God to all people. The Bible is God's Word in human words.

The Bible makes sense only to a faith community. God blessed some individuals with a gift to interpret the meaning of events and God blessed some to communicate this meaning to others. Nourished by the faith of the community, which they shared, these authors expressed their faith in various literary forms. The Bible contains not just the record of an event, but the development and interpretation of what happened to a group of people. The individual author used his or her own genius to create the literary work from the facts commonly known. A special consciousness of inspiration was not necessary beyond the awareness of faith he or she wished to express in the actual writing. Poets, painters, or musicians are inspired to create an artistic work. They are inspired even if what they have created in reality comes from something already known. There is a community aspect in the process of inspiration as well as a full literary process with the genius of an inspired individual. Through the great words of many poets, prophets, and sages, the one Word of God became known and recorded.

The power of the Spirit guided the faith expressed by the community and raised up individuals who expressed and recorded this faith for future generations. The Holy Spirit used these individuals not as mere instruments but as human beings, each with his or her own particular talents for communication and expression.

Together, over a long period of time, they contributed a wealth of individual and communal faith expressions that achieve a unity within the completed Bible. The whole process need not have been understood at the time, and surely involved many people. Nothing essential perished, since the whole Bible expressed the faith of committed people. The Holy Spirit inspired the books of the Bible and continues to guide in their interpretation.

All of the above does not deny that God was involved in the origin of the Bible. Rather, God, who despises nothing human, uses human beings for the actual enrichment of humanity and the creation of the Bible. The medium of the message of the divine is the human. God established the context within which the human words can be seen as the extension of the divine, even as they remain very human. This process enriches the human race and manifests the goodness and power of God. Without poets, prophets, and sages, without people who could use the great words, who could reach down into the very depth of reality, the Bible would have never existed.

Just as Jesus is believed to be fully human and fully divine, so is the Bible. The name given to God becoming human in Jesus is incarnation. The name given to God becoming human in the words of the Bible is inspiration.

Inerrancy

No book on the Bible can avoid the question: Is the Bible free from errors? If God is the principal author and God does not lie, surely the Bible can never contain any errors or mistakes. But the human authors are not God. The words of the Bible are true only in the sense in which the human authors conveyed them, and surely the authors themselves were not without error. Since the Bible came from a particular time and place, no one today should presume that its authors possessed our own modern scientific knowledge. Nor did they necessarily think as Western people do today. The Catholic Church firmly teaches that: "The books of Scripture must be acknowledged as teaching faithfully, and without error, that truth which God wanted put into the Sacred Writings for the sake of our salvation" (*Dogmatic Constitution on Divine Revelation,* No. 11). Beyond that, the Bible, like any human endeavor, contains the imperfections and limitations of all things human.

Religious experience gave the world the Bible. Certain individuals had an experience of God. They lived their lives open to the possibility of accepting in faith the presence of God. Once they realized the great benefits proceeding from faith in a loving God, they wished to assist others in reaching a similar plateau in human life. From many gods and goddesses to one God in history, the Bible records the human odyssey, reaching its completion in the belief that God had entered into human history in the life and person of Jesus of Nazareth. The one Word of God expressed in many words throughout history became incarnate in Jesus. Eventually, this word in the history of Israel and Christianity became recorded in the Bible.

Vocabulary and Nomenclature

It is important to speak about a problem that arises with the use of the expression "Old Testament." It is the usual and normal way for Christians to refer to the first and largest section of their Bible. Yet for Jesus of Nazareth it was by no means an "Old Testament"; for him it was the *only* Bible, the living Word of God, that he knew. Recently, the suggestion has been made by scholars that the terms "Old" and "New" Testaments be replaced with either the terms "First Testament" and "Second Testament" or "Hebrew Scriptures" and "Christian Scriptures" or "Hebrew Scriptures" and "Apostolic Writings." If this suggestion is not accepted, then the term "Old" when applied to one section of the Christian Bible cannot mean "displaced" or "antiquated," but should be understood to mean "prior" or "earlier" or "basic." The challenge is to be respectful of and sensitive to both Judaism's and Christianity's vocabulary. For example, when we refer to an old bottle of wine or a vintage wine, we do not mean it is antiquated but, because of years of aging, it has become better with time. The Old Testament is such a fine wine, aged over a period of two millennia, its color and bouquet continuing to titillate our spiritual palates.

People usually think of the Bible as one unified book. In fact, the Bible consists of many books from different collections, various sources, and many separate literary units. The word "Bible" itself comes from the Greek *biblia*, which means "books." Christians divide these books into the Old and New Testament.

Jews and Christians disagree on precisely how many books are in the Old Testament. Jews accept books written only in Hebrew. Many of their other sacred books written in Greek or Aramaic do not form part of the Jewish Scriptures. Protestants accept this decision by the Jews. Catholics accept all of the sacred books of the Jews which form part of the Greek version of the sacred books called the Septuagint, whether they were originally written in Greek, Hebrew, or Aramaic. Both Catholics and Protestants accept the same twenty–seven books in the New Testament. The name given to the official list of books in the Bible is "Canon."

THE CANON OF SACRED SCRIPTURE

The English term "canon" comes from a Greek word that originally meant "ruler" or "measuring rod." A canon was used to make straight lines or to measure distances. When applied to a group of books, it refers to a recognized list (body) of literature. Thus, for example, the canon of Shakespeare refers to all of Shakespeare's authentic writings.

With reference to the Bible, the term "canon" denotes the collection of books that are accepted as authoritative by a religious body. Thus, for example, we can speak of the canon of the Jewish Scripture or the canon of the New Testament.

To help you further acquaint yourself with the differences in each tradition's approach to the Old Testament, the following visuals are provided.

THE CANON (OFFICIAL LIST) OF THE JEWISH BIBLE (39 BOOKS)

The Law (Torah)	The Prophets (Nevi'im)		The Writings (Kethuvim)
Genesis	**Former**	**Latter**	Psalms
Exodus	Joshua	Isaiah	Proverbs
Leviticus	Judges	Jeremiah	Job
Numbers	1 and 2 Samuel	Ezekiel	
Deuteronomy	1 and 2 Kings		**The Five Scrolls**
		The Twelve	**(Megilloth)**
		Hosea	Solomon's Song
		Joel	Ruth
		Amos	Lamentations
		Obadiah	Ecclesiastes
		Jonah	Esther
		Micah	Daniel
		Nahum	Ezra
		Habakkuk	Nehemiah
		Zephaniah	1 and 2 Chronicles
		Haggai	
		Zechariah	
		Malachi	

Jews call their Bible either "the holy scriptures" or Tanak. The consonants in Tanak come from the first letters of three Hebrew words: *Torah* (or law and instruction), *Nevi'im* (or prophets), and *Kethuvim* (or writings). These three words are the titles for the three major parts of the Hebrew Bible. Or, put more simply, Tanak is an acronym.

The arrangement of the Catholic canon is an adaptation of the Jewish Bible that was produced in Alexandria in Egypt, before the common era (B.C.E.). In the second and third centuries B.C.E., the Jewish Torah was translated into Greek by Jews in Alexandria. The reason for this translation was that following the conquest of the known world by Alexander the Great a century earlier, Jews living in Alexandria had become thoroughly influenced by the Ptolemy kings and the Greek culture that existed in Alexandria. The Alexandrian Jews consequently needed to read their sacred scriptures in their own language, which now was Greek. The name of this translation is the

THE CANON (OFFICIAL LIST) OF THE CATHOLIC BIBLE

The Old Testament (46 books)

Pentateuch
- Genesis
- Exodus
- Leviticus
- Numbers
- Deuteronomy

Historical Books
- Joshua
- Judges
- Ruth
- 1 and 2 Samuel
- 1 and 2 Kings
- 1 and 2 Chronicles
- Ezra
- Nehemiah
- Tobit*
- Judith*
- Esther
- 1 and 2 Maccabees*
- Nahum

Wisdom Books
- Job
- Psalms
- Proverbs
- Ecclesiastes
- Song of Solomon
- Wisdom*
- Sirach (Ecclesiasticus)*

Prophetic Books
- Isaiah
- Jeremiah
- Lamentations
- Baruch*
- Ezekiel
- Daniel
- Hosea
- Joel
- Amos
- Obadiah
- Jonah
- Micah
- Habakkuk
- Zephaniah
- Haggai
- Zechariah
- Malachi

The New Testament (27 books)

Gospels
- Matthew
- Mark
- Luke
- John
- Acts of the Apostles

Pauline Letters
- Romans
- 1 and 2 Corinthians
- Galatians
- Ephesians
- Philippians
- Colossians
- 1 and 2 Thessalonians
- 1 and 2 Timothy
- Titus
- Philemon
- Hebrews

Catholic Letters
- James
- 1 and 2 Peter
- 1, 2, and 3 John
- Jude

Apocalyptic Writing
- Revelation

*Indicates a Catholic deuterocanonical book, which Jews do not include in their canon and which Protestants consider noncanonical and do not include in their Bibles, except sometimes in a special section called the Apocrypha.

Septuagint. (The Roman numeral LXX is used to symbolize the Septuagint because, according to tradition, there were seventy Jewish scribes who came from Jerusalem to Alexandria in order to engage in that particular translation process.)

THE COMMON ERA AND BEFORE THE COMMON ERA

Most people are accustomed to dating ancient events as either A.D. (which does *not* stand for "after death," but for *anno Domini*, Latin for "year of our Lord") or B.C. ("before Christ"). This terminology may make sense for Christians, for whom A.D. 2002 is indeed "the year of our Lord 2002." It makes less sense, though, for Jews, Muslims, Buddhists, and others for whom Jesus is not "Lord" or the "Christ." Scholars have, therefore, begun to use a different set of abbreviations as more inclusive of others outside the Christian tradition. Throughout this book, we will follow the alternative designations of C.E. ("common era," meaning common to people of all faiths who utilize the traditional Western calendar) and B.C.E. ("before the common era"). In terms of the older abbreviations, C.E. corresponds to A.D. and B.C.E. to B.C.

If we compare the official list of the Hebrew Scriptures or Old Testament in Roman Catholic editions of the Bible with that of Jewish and Protestant editions, we will notice seven more books in the Roman Catholic list: Tobit and Judith, 1 and 2 Maccabees among the historical books; Wisdom and Sirach among the wisdom books; and Baruch among the prophetical books. Parts of the books of Esther and Daniel are also not shared by Protestant and Jewish editions of the canon. Roman Catholics call these sections that are not found in Jewish and Protestant editions the "deuterocanonical" books; Protestants use the word "apocrypha" for the same books. The term "deuterocanonical" means the "second" or "wider" canon; "apocrypha" means "concealed" or "hidden." These books were either unknown or later under dispute by some sectors of Jews and/or Christians. What is important to know, however, is that they were Jewish books.

If you have a Bible of your own that includes a separate section on what Protestants call the "apocrypha," you will note that it includes much more than the seven books mentioned above. According to widespread usage in scholarship today, "apocrypha" is a designation applied to a collection of fourteen or fifteen books, or portions of books, written during the last two centuries B.C.E., and the first century of the common era (C.E.). The following are titles of the apocrypha books as given in the *New Revised Standard Version* of the Bible: (1) First Book of Esdras, (2) Second Book of Esdras, (3) Tobit, (4) Judith, (5) the additions of the Book of Esther, (6) the Wisdom of Solomon, (7) Ecclesiasticus, or the Wisdom of Jesus son of Sirach, (8) Baruch, (9) the Letter of Jeremiah, (10) the Prayer of Azariah and the Song of the Three Young Men, (11) Susanna, (12) Bel and the Dragon, (13) the Prayer of Menasseh, (14) the First Book of Maccabees, and (15) the Second Book of Maccabees.

The books of the apocrypha represent several different literary forms and were written at different historical times. They all have their origin within the Jewish religion. Even though these extra books do not appear in the Tanak (the Hebrew Bible), they are nonetheless Jewish writings that Christians have endeared.

There are other writings that were produced around the same time as the biblical writings and the apocryphal writings, a whole collection of what is known as pseudopigrapha. Pseudopigrapha means "false writings." They are so called because these writings are falsely ascribed to Jewish leaders of the past, to the heroes of the past; for example, the Apocalypse of Daniel, the Testament of Adam, the Testament of Abraham, the Book of Enoch, the Apocalypse of Zephaniah, the Book of Jubilees, and many others. So the ancient world that produced our Sacred Scriptures that we share in common as Jews and Christians was a world that was teeming with literary products, cultural artifacts that the ancient Jews had produced. And many of these cultural artifacts became a part of the sacred canonical tradition of the Jews and also of the Christians. We share much in common.

Finding Your Way Around the Old Testament

For some people, especially beginners, finding their way around the Old Testament can be confusing, daunting, and sometimes downright disconcerting. What follows are some basic suggestions.

Like any new book you purchase, open your Bible to the table of contents and the introductory sections. Often the editor will explain where the various books of the Bible are found or have them indexed. Usually, there will be a chart or visual that lists and explains all of the abbreviations of the various books of the Bible. Become familiar with it.

In addition to these introductory materials, many modern English-language Bibles have notes at the bottom of each page. The technical name for such an edition of the Bible is an "annotated edition." These notes will often explain terms or situations, and may provide cross references to other texts (books) of the Bible. These notes are quite helpful for enhancing your understanding. Often there is also a brief introduction to each book of the Bible printed just in front of the book.

Study Bibles have time lines, maps, glossaries of terms, charts of weights and measures, and possibly an index of lectionary readings for the various Sundays of the liturgical year. These are all useful tools.

Finally, a person needs to be familiar with the way in which a biblical citation is to be deciphered.

UNDERSTANDING A BIBLICAL CITATION

Reference	Meaning
Genesis 6 (or Gen 6)	Book of Genesis, chapter 6
Gen 6:3	Book of Genesis, chapter 6, verse 3
Gen 6:3–11	Book of Genesis, chapter 6, verses 3 through 11
Gen 6:3, 11	Book of Genesis, chapter 6, verses 3 and 11
Gen 6:3–11:1	Book of Genesis, chapter 6, verse 3 through chapter 11, verse 1
Gen 6:3a	Book of Genesis, chapter 6, the first part of verse 3
Gen 6:3b	Book of Genesis, chapter 6, the second part of verse 3

The Church as a Guide to Reading the Old Testament

Whenever people go on a pilgrimage to the Holy Land (Israel) they make use of a tour guide. A guide ensures that pilgrims see all of the important biblical sites, and often his explanations improve their understanding. Without a guide it would be easy to get lost or miss something important. Catholics have a well-trained guide in the Church who helps us to better read, understand, and pray the Sacred Scriptures. (In chapter 1 of the companion volume to this book, *A Beginner's Guide to the New Testament,* I provide a short history lesson on the Church as a biblical guide.) Here we will look at how the Church can guide us through the Old Testament.

Church Teachings on the Value and Worth of the Old Testament

The books of the Old Testament provide an understanding of God and humanity and make clear to all how a just and merciful God deals with humankind. These books, even though they contain matters which are imperfect and provisional, nevertheless contain authentic divine teaching. Christians should accept with reverence these writings, which express a lively sense of God, which are a storehouse of sublime teaching on God and of sound wisdom on human life, as well as a wonderful treasury of prayers; in them, too, the mystery of our salvation is implicitly present (Second Vatican Council, *Dogmatic Constitution on Divine Revelation,* #15).

The Old Testament is an indispensable part of Sacred Scripture. Its books are divinely inspired and retain a permanent value, for the Old Covenant has never been revoked. Christians venerate the Old Testament as true Word of God. The Church has always vigorously opposed the idea of rejecting the Old Testament under the pretext that the New Testament has rendered it void ("Marcionism," *Catechism of the Catholic Church, 121, 123*).

In addition to proclaiming the value and worth of the Old Testament, the Catholic Church has provided guidelines for the interpretation of biblical texts. In a tightly packed sentence, the bishops of the Second Vatican Council (1962–1965) stated that: "Hence the exegete [interpreter] must look for that meaning which the sacred writers, in given situations and granted the circumstances of their time and culture, intended to express and did in fact express, through the medium of a contemporary literary form" (Vatican II, *Dogmatic Constitution on Divine Revelation*, 12). That sentence is quite dense. Put in simple terms, this sentence teaches that Catholic biblical study has three aspects: theological, historical, and literary.

Literary Features

We encounter literary forms daily. In reading directions for preparing food, we quickly distinguish cooking time from measurements of the ingredients; or when reading the newspaper, we easily distinguish the formal writing of a news report from the opinion column, the question and answer advice column from the obituaries, the stock market report from the basketball and baseball scores.

The Old Testament is a piece of literature. As a matter of fact, it is a library of books containing many different types of literature or literary genres. For example, the Book of Genesis contains creation narratives, legends, and sagas about the patriarchs and matriarchs, blessings, and rituals. Many of the books of the prophets contain call narratives, oracles, and, in some cases, sermons. The Book of Psalms is an anthology of 150 poems. There are even short stories in the Old Testament: Ruth, Esther, Judith, Jonah, Tobit. Paying attention to literary forms, style, and structure can help one better understand the Old Testament. Throughout this book, whenever needed the literary form of a particular Old Testament text will be mentioned and explained.

Historical Features

Every book of the Bible, including those of the Old Testament, was composed during a particular historical time and context which influences the way it was composed. Attention to the historical situations surrounding a book are important and quite helpful in determining its meaning. For example, books composed after the exodus from Egypt and during the conquering of and inhabiting of the promised land were influenced by these historical events. Those biblical books composed in relationship to the building and use of the temple in Jerusalem, like the books of Leviticus and Psalms, were affected by that event. Those Old Testament books composed just prior to, during, and after the Babylonian exile (598/87–537 B.C.E.) were influenced by that event. Military battles, natural disasters, like earthquakes, sand storms, and famines all influenced various Old Testament books. Every effort has been made throughout this book to present those historical events that have influenced whole sections of or particular books of the Old Testament. Further, the time line, which appears on the inside front and back covers, is provided to help the reader gain a better grasp of the historical situation(s) at the time of the Old Testament.

Theological Features

In addition to literary artistry and historical circumstances, Catholics reading the Old Testament must attend to the theological significance of the text. For example, knowing that people in the ancient Near Eastern world made covenants with one another is an important historical fact. Further, knowing that when covenants were made between a king and a subordinate, a particular literary form was utilized, is an important literary fact that enhances the meaning of covenant. But it is not until one reflects on how ancient Israel understood her relationship with God to be a covenant do you arrive at the theological level of meaning. This God is in a solemn pact with his people known as covenant—a solemn promise—signified either by Sabbath rest, circumcision, or the keeping of the Ten Commandments as well as certain ritual actions. These are the theological features of those Old Testament texts dealing with covenant.

Or to take another example, knowing that surrounding Mesopotamian culture had creation stories is an important historical fact. Realizing that ancient Israel may have been influenced by these is also important, as well as the fact that they used particular literary forms. But it is not until one compares the Old Testament creation narratives with those of its neighbors does one encounter the theological understanding of creation put forth in the Book of Genesis.

Looking for the theological or religious or spiritual meaning of an Old Testament text(s) is always an important aspect of interpretation and a needed one. It is central to a healthy interpretation. As the *Catechism of the Catholic Church* succinctly states: " In order to discover the sacred authors' intention, the reader must take into account the conditions of their time and culture, the literary genres in use at that time, and the models of feeling, speaking, and narrating then current" (110).

Progressive Revelation of God in the Old Testament

The Old Testament gives us a progressive revelation of a person, God. God differs drastically from all the gods of ancient Near Eastern religions in that God acts directly in the middle of Jewish history on definite men and women in definite historical situations, and reveals God's self as a person desiring intimate friendship with human persons. God alone accounts for the existence, growth, and perseverance of the Jewish people in history. Their history is impossible without their God. God has revealed himself in history in a definite way as a definite person with definite characteristics or qualities. The Old Testament is simply a record of this divinity's dealings with his chosen people. Just as we have to take a human friend as he or she is and as they reveal themselves, so we have to take God on God's own terms—as God is and as God reveals himself.

This progressive revelation is seen in God's revelation to Abraham and Sarah—God reveals himself as a God of people, a friendship God who calls and invites people to friendship with him, and who wants to seal this into a friendship pact-covenant.

God's revelation continues with Moses and Miriam—God reveals himself to them as a person who is present to his people, who is aware of their sufferings and is concerned about them, who is actively concerned and does something about it, who works through women and men to deliver them from their misery and oppression; a God of salvation.

In God's revelation to Joshua, God is revealed as a rock, someone you can rely on absolutely as a friend. God has steadfast loyalty to his people. God's promise and help can be counted on absolutely. God will never let you down. He is a faithful friend to individuals and to all of his people.

In the Book of Hosea, God is revealed as a lover who loves the people of his choice as a husband loves his beloved, the bride of his choice. Even though the people are unfaithful to God's love pact, God tries hard with a campaign of love to win God's beloved (the people) back to her first love and then lavishes his love on them when they return to their love pact. God is revealed as the living, forgiving spouse of his chosen people, Israel.

In the Book of Ezekiel, God is pictured as a shepherd who loves his sheep (his people) and cares for them with real affection, giving them good things for their happiness.

In the Book of Isaiah of Jerusalem, to whom the first thirty-nine chapters of the Book of Isaiah are attributed, God is revealed as the other, transcendent God infinitely above humans, yet a God who loves humans tenderly as a father loves his son, as a mother loves the child of her womb. God is revealed as the Creator of all that exists; God is the Lord of history who directs the course of the world's history in hidden ways; God is the Redeemer and Savior of his people.

In the section of the Book of Isaiah known as Second Isaiah (chapters 40–55), God is portrayed by a mysterious one who is to come, "The servant of the Lord." The servant who comes to save God's people, to suffer for the sins of men and women in their places, who will break decisively into human history and inaugurate a new age, a new rule of God, a new covenant between God and humans, a new law which will be written into the very hearts of the people, a kingdom of glory which will last forever.

Finally, in the books of Daniel and Maccabees, God is revealed as the one who gives everlasting life to those who are faithful to God and have a righteous life.

The Old Testament in the Liturgy and Life of Christians

The context in which most Christians today are exposed to the Old Testament is the public worship conducted in church. In the cycle of Scripture readings prepared in response to the directives of the Second Vatican Council (1962–1965) and adopted subsequently by many Protestant churches, the Old Testament has a prominent place. The three-year Sunday cycle of Scripture readings contains a passage from the Old Testament as the first of the three major selections read from the Bible. Usually, the Old Testament reading is chosen to illustrate some point in or provide the background for the reading from the Gospel. The two-year daily cycle of Scripture readings makes provision for many Old Testament selections as the first of the two major readings. In both the Sunday and daily cycles, sections from the Psalms are frequently used. Before the Gospel passage is read, the reader and congregation join in the singing or recitation of several verses from a psalm. This is referred to as the responsorial psalm.

The Old Testament in its use in the Christian community, especially the liturgy, can teach the community a great deal. For example, in many ways the New Testament is indistinguishable from the Old Testament. Though composed in Greek, the books of the New Testament reflect the vocabulary and concerns of Judaism in Palestine and the rest of the Mediterranean world during the first century C.E. The Old Testament at this time was Sacred Scripture not only of the Jewish synagogues but also of the Christian churches. Titles used in describing Jesus (Messiah, Christ, Servant, Son of God, Lord, Shepherd, etc.) all have Old Testament roots. The language used by Paul and other New Testament authors was basically the Greek of the Old Testament translation called the Septuagint. A major activity in early Christian circles was the attempt to show how in Jesus of

Nazareth the promises of the Old Testament made sense and were brought to fulfillment. The Old Testament was the Bible of the early church, the most formative document in its life, and an integral part of its worship. If twenty-first-century Christians are ever to understand the New Testament, they must not cut themselves off from the Old Testament.

The Old Testament also raises our consciousness about the social character of our faith. Even when God is presented as dealing with individuals in the Old Testament, the individual is significant only in relation to the fortunes of God's people. Abraham, Moses, and David, as well as Ruth, Esther, and Judith, are important only because through them God deals with his people. There is no cult of human personality in Old Testament faith. Furthermore, the Old Testament insists that God exercises a special concern for the marginalized of society—for widows, orphans, strangers, and others in economic need. This social concern is grounded in God's ownership of all creation and his past blessings to his people, not in a purely human imperative to share. Even the Psalms, which often form the starting point of private prayer for Christians, are essentially social documents. They were written for public worship and are still used most appropriately in that context today. When recited prayerfully by a single person or pondered meditatively, the Psalms retain their social or communal character. The individual reflects upon the documents of the praying community and stands within the community of faith, even when he or she seems most solitary.

For Christians in search of their religious and human roots, the Old Testament is the most appropriate place to begin. There we will find real human beings with great strengths and great weaknesses struggling to respond to God's presence in their lives and in the lives of their people. There we will discover that religion encompasses all aspects of human life (family, law, politics, education, culture), and is not set beside or apart from other pursuits. There we will encounter great models of faith and persons for whom the only fitting response to God is thanksgiving. This is the beginning of the great tradition of faith that has been encouraged and nurtured by the Church throughout the centuries. As we continue to pilgrimage through the twenty-first century, it becomes ever clearer that the Christian church must make every effort to keep that tradition of faith alive and hand it on to the generations to follow. Loving knowledge of the Old Testament tradition is one necessary part of that task.

For Discussion

1. What do you understand the following terms to mean? Revelation. Inspiration. Inerrancy.
2. How is the Bible both human and divine?
3. How is the Church a guide to reading the Bible?
4. Why is it important to pay attention to the historical, literary, and theological context of a biblical text?
5. How is God progressively revealed in the Old Testament? Explain.

For Further Reading

Harrington, Daniel. *Interpreting the Old Testament: A Practical Guide.* Wilmington, DE: Michael Glazier, 1981.

Lysick, David A. *The Bible Documents.* Chicago: Liturgy Training Publications, 2001.

Mueller, Steve. *The Seeker's Guide to Reading the Bible: A Catholic View.* Chicago: Loyola Press, 1999.

Newland, Mary Reed. *A Popular Guide Through the Old Testament.* Winona, MN: St. Mary's Press, 1999.

Stuhlmueller, Carroll. *New Paths Through the Old Testament.* New York: Paulist Press, 1989.

2

THE
PENTATEUCH

The FIRST FIVE BOOKS OF THE BIBLE ARE KNOWN BY two names. For Jews, they are called the Torah, for Christians, the Pentateuch. While the name for the first five books differs between these two religious groups, the content does not.

Torah is the Hebrew-Jewish term for the first five books of the Old Testament. The word *Torah*, which in English is often rendered "law," in Hebrew means not a "body of legislation" but "instruction," and can also mean "revelation" or "teachings." The term *Torah* carries with it the idea of all those things God somehow designed to give to the chosen people.

In the Hebrew tradition, the Torah was revealed by God to Moses and written down by him. Also, according to Jewish tradition, the Torah possesses a higher degree of sanctity, holiness, and authority than the rest of the canon (list of books in the Old Testament), that is, than the prophets or the writings. Eventually, the term *Torah* evolved to mean a whole "lifestyle"—a faith lifestyle based on the teaching contained in the first five books.

In addition, the term *Torah* in the Jewish mind-set also referred to the five scrolls attributed to Moses. These five scrolls or books were named by their opening words in the original Hebrew, not by their content. Pentateuch is a Greek word whose origin is founded in the Septuagint—the Greek—translation of the Old Testament. The word Pentateuch comes from two Greek words: *Penta* meaning "five" and *teukos* meaning "fold." This term *Pentateukos* should also be understood as followed by the Greek word for book, namely *biblos*. What we have then is the *Pentateukos biblos*—"the fivefold book."

The Septuagint translation didn't just translate the term *Torah,* but also renamed the first five books. In the Hebrew language they are named by their opening words, whereas the Septuagint named them for their content or principal subject matter. Our English words for the first five books of the Old Testament have come to us through the Vulgate from the Septuagint.

Thus, the term "Genesis" was given to the first book of the Pentateuch because of its concern with the origins of the world, the origins of humankind, and in particular the origin of the Hebrew people. The word *Genesis* in Greek means "origins" or "beginnings."

The second book of the Pentateuch is called Exodus, from the Greek term for "departure," because the central event narrated in the book is the departure of the Israelites from bondage in Egypt to freedom as the children of God.

The third book of the Pentateuch is Leviticus, and was given its name by the ancient Greek translators because a good part of this book consists of sacrificial and other ritual laws prescribed for the priests of the tribe of Levi. The subject matter or content of the book has to do with Levitical priesthood and the call to holiness.

The fourth book of the Pentateuch, the Book of Numbers, gets its title in our English Bibles as a direct translation of the Latin Vulgate *Numeri*, which, in turn, is derived from the Septuagint term *Arithmoi,* meaning "counting" or "numbers" or "numbering." This title for the fourth book of the Pentateuch is derived from the account of the two censuses taken of the Hebrew people, one at the beginning and the other toward the end of the journey in the desert, and this is found in chapters 1 and 26 of the Book of Numbers.

Finally, the last book of the Pentateuch is called Deuteronomy. The word Deuteronomy in Greek derives from *deutero,* meaning "second," and *nomos,* meaning "law." So the title of the fifth book means "second law," yet in reality what it contains is not a new law but a partial repetition, completion, and explanation of the Law proclaimed on Mount Sinai. Deuteronomy is in actuality Moses' sermons about the Law. It is not considered second in chronological order, but it is the second time around that Moses preaches and proclaims the Torah, the *nomos,* the Law.

Who Wrote the Torah/Pentateuch?

For centuries, when people asked who the author of the first five books of the Bible was, the answer was "Moses." The Torah stated that Moses wrote down what he was told. For the first seventeen centuries, scholars had little difficulty accepting Moses as the author of the Pentateuch.

However, as critical scholarship began to make its mark, many questioned Moses as the author of the Pentateuch. One big question that emerged was: How could Moses write about his own death at the end of the Book of Deuteronomy? Deuteronomy 34:5 reads: "Then Moses, the servant of the LORD, died there in the land of Moab, at the LORD's command."

There are clues in the Pentateuch itself that show it was not composed by a single author—variation in style, vocabulary, and grammatical structure. In addition, there are two names for the mountain of God, Sinai and Horeb. Both names appear in the Book of Exodus. The name Sinai predominates in Leviticus and Numbers. But Horeb is used in Deuteronomy. Moses' father-in-law is given two different names, Jethro and Hobab. In Exodus, he is Jethro (Exodus

3:1), while his name is Hobab in the Book of Numbers (Numbers 10:29). In the Hebrew text, two nouns appear for God, *Yahweh* and *Elohim*. A late seventeenth-century French scholar was the first to note that in Genesis 1, the Hebrew word for God is *Elohim*. But in Genesis 2 and 3, the noun for God is *Yahweh-Elohim*.

Biblical scholars also discovered that many narratives occurred twice in the text. Such narratives are called "doublets." In Genesis, there are two narratives of creation (Genesis 1:1–2:41; 2:4b–25). Abraham tries to convince foreign leaders that Sarah is his sister rather than his wife on three separate occasions (Genesis 12, Genesis 20, and Genesis 26). There are dual accounts of the covenant made by God with Abraham (Genesis 15 and Genesis 17). There are two versions of the call of Moses to lead the people out of Israel (Exodus 3 and Exodus 6). Jacob's dream is narrated twice in Genesis 32 and Genesis 35). There are two versions of the Ten Commandments (Exodus 20:1–17 and Deuteronomy 5:6–21).

The aforementioned clues or pieces of evidence coupled with generations of scholarly study began to show that Moses was not the author of the first five books of the Bible. They might be the books *of* Moses, but they were not the books *by* Moses. Equally important was the mounting evidence that the books attributed to Moses were composed at very different historical times and that more than one author was at work.

If Not Moses,
Then Who Wrote the Torah/Pentateuch?

At the dawn of the twenty-first century, most biblical scholars now agree that there were at least four or five main authors, or groups of authors, involved in the formation of the Pentateuch as religious literature. They believe these authors worked and their books were composed over a long time, stretching from some time around 1000 to 400 B.C.E. The idea that the Torah/Pentateuch evolved from a combination of various sources—at first oral and later in written form—is technically known as the "Documentary Hypothesis."

The precise identity of who wrote the first five books of the Bible is an unsolved—and most probably an unsolvable—mystery, barring an archaeological find of the most revolutionary sort. But the principal authors have been given "names" and are identified by five letters of the alphabet: J, E, D, P, and R.

J (Yahwist)

The oldest—and perhaps most celebrated—of these authors is known as "J," from the German word *Jahweh*, the source of the word "Jehovah," a mistranslation; today, properly rendered in English as "Yahweh." The biblical writer code named J constantly calls the Israelite God "Yahweh."

J probably lived some time between 950 and 850 B.C.E. in Judah (another reason he is called J), the southern half of the divided Hebrew kingdom. J is the Old Testament's best storyteller, more interesting, more humorous, and more human than the others. J's God interacts with people easily and directly. J told the more famous and most folkloric version of the two creation accounts, which begins in Genesis 2:4b. It is J's God, for instance, who is walking in the Garden of Eden in the "cool of the day" (Genesis 3:8), a lovely poetic image, and discovers Adam and Eve hiding themselves, ashamed of their nakedness.

CHARACTERISTICS OF THE J (YAHWIST) AUTHOR

1. Uses the name *Yahweh* for God.
2. Makes use of storytelling, anecdotes; many chatty little stories that have interesting and peculiar characteristics.
   - Scare-stories; for example, the incident of Zipporah (see Exodus 4:24–26).
   - Slur-stories, usually directed against surrounding nations (see Genesis 9:25, where Canaan is cursed and does not really seem to have done anything. See also Genesis 19:30ff, where the daughters of Lot conceive Moab and Ben-Ammi, the fathers of the Moabites and Ammonites).
3. Anthropomorphisms. God is described by J as having certain human features; for example, he walks through the garden, talks to primitive humans, etc. God is not degraded; this was simply a way of describing

---

God. The term "anthropomorphism" means talking about or describing God in human terms.

4. Anthropopathisms. J loves to make use of these. God is described as having certain human emotions, which is what the word anthropopathism means. For example, before the flood, God feels as if he made a mistake about making humans and is sorry for what he did (see Genesis 6:6).

5. Etiology. J loves to make use of this technique. This might be defined as cause-study or cause-explanation. It seeks to answer why things are as they are. Examples: Why do humans wear clothing? (see Genesis 3:10–21) Because nakedness had made humans ashamed of themselves. What is the meaning of birth pangs? (see Genesis 3:16) Why do people die? (see Genesis 3:19)

6. Presents God as close at hand . . . immanent.

7. Calls the holy mountain of the covenant "Sinai."

8. Calls the natives of the promised land "Canaanites."

9. Makes extensive use of imagery. For example, in Genesis 3, God is imaged as a potter and gardener, humans as living in a lush garden.

E (Elohist)

Close on J's heels is E, the Elohist, so called because this author preferred to use the word *Elohim* for God's name. E came later than J, perhaps between 850 and 800 B.C.E. E is a much less colorful writer than J, and E's contribution blossoms in earnest with the story of Abraham in Genesis 12.

The Elohist tradition is found in the call of Moses (Exodus 3:1–22). Here God is more distant than in the Yahwist. He does not speak directly to Moses; rather, he uses a medium, the bush that burns and is not consumed. There are a variety of other places in the Elohist tradition where God chooses to use a medium—such as storms, clouds, dreams, angels, voice from heaven—to communicate with the people.

The Elohist tradition shows a strong bias against foreign gods. Jacob is commanded to remove foreign gods (Genesis 35:2). In Exodus, the Elohist has God command the Israelites, "You shall have no other gods before me" (Exodus 20:3). Further, the Elohist author is interested in the experiences of Israel in the desert. Then Israel was totally dependent on God. There could be no chance of influence from foreign deities. Further, the moral exhortations of the Elohist are more strict than the Yahwist.

For the Elohist, the covenant was made with Moses on Mount Horeb. God promises to be Israel's God on the condition that Israel will be his people. There is an obligation incumbent upon Israel in the Elohist tradition. The Elohist sees the covenant and its stipulations as the logical follow-up to the saving acts of God in Exodus. This is different from J, who sees the initiative of God (Yahweh) as a gracious act which brings Israel through the Exodus and desert experiences, making her who she is.

CHARACTERISTICS OF THE E (ELOHIST) AUTHOR

1. Uses the name *Elohim* for God.
2. Tends to be abstract—less material
   - God speaks through storms, from clouds, through angels, in association with fire and dreams
   - Emphasis on God as transcendent
3. Calls the holy mountain of the covenant "Horeb."
4. Calls the natives of the promised land "Amorites."
5. Sees the covenant and its stipulations as the logical follow-up of the saving acts of God in Exodus.

D (Deuteronomist)

The third author of the Pentateuch is known as the "Deuteronomist." He most likely worked between 700 and 600 B.C.E., and was responsible for large portions of the Book of Deuteronomy, wherein he makes extensive use of exhortations and sermons. D is also thought to have shaped the later books of Joshua, Judges, Samuel, and Kings—the major "historical" works of the Old Testament that describe the conquest of Canaan and the establishment of the kingdom under Saul, David, and Solomon and his descendents. In the Book of Deuteronomy, D depicts Moses giving a series of speeches (sermons) that urge Israel to follow the Torah, but the law Moses offers in this section represents a revision of the earlier law books.

The central theological concept of the D author is really a union of the covenantal theologies of the Yahwist and Elohist authors. Covenant in D is God's living election. For the D author, on the other hand, law becomes Israel's response to God's election. The Deuteronomist sees this response as something which is incumbent on all (Deuteronomy 6:4–9). The way in which each responds to the election of God (by keeping the law) will determine God's action toward Israel.

CHARACTERISTICS OF THE D (DEUTERONOMIC) AUTHOR

1. Uses a distinctive literary style made up of exhortations and sermons.
2. Emphasizes the keeping of the law Torah.
3. Places a significant emphasis on God's love for his people and their love for God (Deuteronomy 4:37–40; 6:4–9; 7:7–8).
4. Stresses fidelity to Jerusalem as the center for encountering and worshiping God and stresses to the people the promised land as a gift from God
5. Requires obedience to the covenant and its stipulations. This obedience is exercised through keeping the laws which, for D, are a means of response to the covenant.

P (Priestly)

The texts credited to P, known as the "priestly" author, include some of the most familiar words in the Bible—"In the beginning," the creation account found in Genesis 1, and one of the versions of the Ten Commandments (Exodus 20:1–17).

P's contribution was probably written sometime between 550 and 450 B.C.E. Highly concerned with the elaborate observances of the ancient Jewish cult, ritual, worship, and priesthood, P was responsible for nearly all of the Book of Leviticus. Dry and always detail-obsessed,

P was especially interested in codifying and justifying all of the ritual laws developed by the early Jewish priesthood, including the carefully worded descriptions of the Passover ritual (Exodus 12), blessings (Numbers 6:24–26), ordination ceremonies (Leviticus 8:1–36), the vestments of the high priest, the liturgical calendar (Leviticus 23:1–44), and the sacred chest that held the Ten Commandments—the Ark of the Covenant.

The P tradition called Israel to holiness (Leviticus 19:2). It emphasized those things that would make Israel holy—worship, prayer, temple, and feasts. For P the history of Israel is told in a liturgical context. Creation emphasized God blessing humankind and the Sabbath rest. The exodus is presented by the priestly author as a great procession out of Egypt to offer worship to God on Mount Sinai (Exodus 5:3). The history of Israel for P is also a series of covenants (Adam, Noah, Abraham, Moses) which God has made with God's people. Through these covenants, P sees Israel becoming God's holy people.

CHARACTERISTICS OF THE P (PRIESTLY) AUTHOR

1. Has a concern for and interest in priesthood, worship, cult, and liturgy: blessings, Sabbath, circumcision, festivals
2. Makes extensive use of genealogies and symbolic use of numbers (see Genesis 1:1–2:4a for the use of the number 7)
3. Connects time or history together by means of the covenants made by God and his people
4. Understands worship as the means of response to the covenant

---

R (Redactor[s])

In addition to the four "writers," or groups of writers, there was another individual or group responsible for creating the Pentateuch and some of the other early books of Israelite history as they now stand. In some respects, this was a most extraordinary feat. R was the Redactor, or editor, who took the four existing strands (J,E,D,P) and spliced them together, probably around 400 B.C.E. Like the others, R's identity is a mystery. No one even knows whether there was more than one redactor. The work of the redactor is both interesting and fascinating because of the way so many different and even contradictory strands of scripture were woven together.

Clearly, then, the Pentateuch is not the product of one person, Moses. Rather, it is the result of many traditions interwoven and tied together to reflect the past and present for the people of biblical Israel. It is in that light that we must continue to view it today.

The Books of the Pentateuch

The Book of Genesis: Origins

The central theme of the first book of the Pentateuch is "origins." Chapters 1 and 2 deal with the origin of the universe and humankind; chapters 3 through 11 reveal the origin of sin and alienation from God. The remaining chapters, 12 through 50, deal with the origin of the people of Israel and are presented through the stories of the patriarchs Abraham, Isaac, Jacob, and Joseph.

Creation

The theme of creation centers on God as Creator who creates all things good and his creatures as co-curators with him of creation. It underscores the goodness of all creation, and the idea that creation is God's original blessing.

We are all quite concerned about our fragile universe and its continuation and preservation for future generations. Ecology and the ecological movement is very strong. Our challenge is to listen not only to what science tells us about the preservation of creation, but also to listen to the Bible. We creatures of God are to be co-curators with our God in caring for our planet and our universe. In the world of science, the center of the universe is the sun. In the biblical world, the center of the universe is God and God's creatures who are to care for it. In a sense, in the Bible, all of creation belongs ultimately to God: "The earth is the LORD's and all that is in it" (Psalm 24:1).

There are two creation narratives in the Book of Genesis (1:1–2:4a; 2:4b–25). These are two very different stories, that come from two different traditions. They were written by two sets of authors or compilers: the first, Genesis 1:1–2:4a, by the priestly author (P); the second, Genesis 2:4b–25, by the Yahwist author (J).

In the case of both stories, the purpose is not to teach science, in the sense of the scientific origin of the universe, nor the origin of the human species. Rather, their purpose is to teach a religious or spiritual truth about creation and humankind. We will attempt to look at the religious meaning of these stories in this section.

The Priestly (P) Account of Creation

¹In the beginning when God created the heavens and the earth, ²the earth was a formless void and darkness covered the face of the deep, while a wind from God swept over the face of the waters. ³Then God said, "Let there be light"; and there was light. ⁴And God saw that the light was good; and God separated the light from the darkness. ⁵God called the light Day, and the darkness he called Night. And there was evening and there was morning, the first day.

⁶And God said, "Let there be a dome in the midst of the waters, and let it separate the waters from the waters." ⁷So God made the dome and separated the waters that were under the dome from the waters that were above the dome. And it was so. ⁸God called the dome Sky. And there was evening and there was morning, the second day.

⁹And God said, "Let the waters under the sky be gathered together into one place, and let the dry land appear." And it was so. ¹⁰God called the dry land Earth, and the waters that were gathered together he called Seas. And God saw that it was good. ¹¹Then God said, "Let the earth put forth vegetation: plants yielding seed, and fruit trees of every kind on earth that bear fruit with the seed in it." And it was so. ¹²The earth brought forth vegetation:

plants yielding seed of every kind, and trees of every kind bearing fruit with the seed in it. And God saw that it was good. [13]And there was evening and there was morning, the third day.

[14]And God said, "Let there be lights in the dome of the sky to separate the day from the night; and let them be for signs and for seasons and for days and years, [15]and let them be lights in the dome of the sky to give light upon the earth." And it was so. [16]God made the two great lights—the greater light to rule the day and the lesser light to rule the night—and the stars. [17]God set them in the dome of the sky to give light upon the earth, [18]to rule over the day and over the night, and to separate the light from the darkness. And God saw that it was good. [19]And there was evening and there was morning, the fourth day.

[20]And God said, "Let the waters bring forth swarms of living creatures, and let birds fly above the earth across the dome of the sky." [21]So God created the great sea monsters and every living creature that moves, of every kind, with which the waters swarm, and every winged bird of every kind. And God saw that it was good. [22]Be fruitful and multiply and fill the waters in the seas, and let birds multiply on the earth." [23]And there was evening and there was morning, the fifth day.

[24]And God said, "Let the earth bring forth living creatures of every kind: cattle and creeping things and wild animals of the earth of every kind." And it was so. [25]God made the wild animals of the earth of every kind, and the cattle of every kind, and everything that creeps upon the ground of every kind. And God saw that it was good.

[26]Then God said, "Let us make humankind in our image, according to our likeness; and let them have dominion over the fish of the sea, and over the birds of the air, and over the cattle, and over all the wild animals of the earth, and over every creeping thing that creeps upon the earth."

[27]So God created humankind in his image, in the image of God he created them; male and female he created them.

²⁸God blessed them, and God said to them, "Be fruitful and multiply, and fill the earth and subdue it; and have dominion over the fish of the sea and over the birds of the air and over every living thing that moves upon the earth." ²⁹God said, "See, I have given you every plant yielding seed that is upon the face of all the earth, and every tree with seed in its fruit; you shall have them for food. ³⁰And to every beast of the earth, and to every bird of the air, and to everything that creeps on the earth, everything that has the breath of life, I have given every green plant for food." And it was so. ³¹God saw everything that he had made, and indeed, it was very good. And there was evening and there was morning, the sixth day.

¹Thus the heavens and the earth were finished, and all their multitude. ²And on the seventh day God finished the work that he had done, and he rested on the seventh day from all the work that he had done. ³So God blessed the seventh day and hallowed it, because on it God rested from all the work that he had done in creation.

⁴These are the generations of the heavens and the earth when they were created (Genesis 1:1–31; 2:1–4).

It is obvious that the author has put the story within the context of six days. The technical name for this is a hexaemeron, a six-day account. The structure ends with God resting on the seventh day. These are not seven twenty-four hour periods. Rather, they are simply a device used by the priestly author to help people remember the story. In the priestly tradition, you meditated on one aspect of creation on each day of the week. So you have a six-day account: Each day you meditate on what God created on that day, and on the seventh day you rest, allowing you time to ponder the totality of creation.

The opening phrase in the text is, "In the beginning." You might want to ask yourself: In the beginning of what? The answer, of course, is in the beginning of divine activity, not in the origin of the universe. Well, what is the beginning of divine activity? It is to bring order out of chaos.

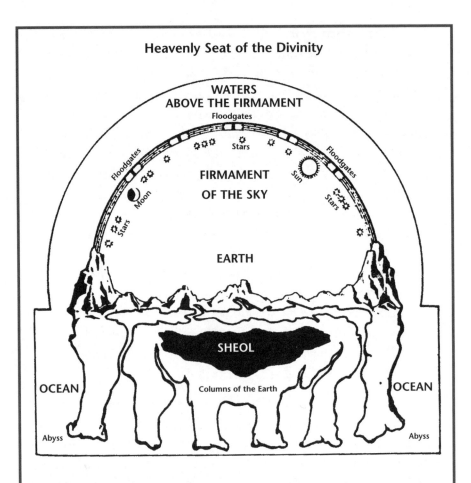

THE WORLD OF THE HEBREWS

The World of the Hebrews—Graphic representation of the Hebrew conception of the world. God's heavenly seat rests above the superior waters. Below these waters lies the firmament or sky which resembles an overturned bowl and is supported by columns. Through the openings (floodgates) in its vault the superior waters fall down upon the earth in the form of rain or snow. The earth is a platform resting on columns and surrounded by waters, the seas. Underneath the columns lie the inferior waters. In the depths of the earth is Sheol, the home of the dead (also called the nether world). This was the same prescientific concept of the universe as that held by the Hebrews' pagan neighbors.

At the beginning, the world is a disordered chaos, dark, watery, formless, and void. Then the creator God begins to subdue the chaos and to call out an ordered universe.

The image presented is that of "God's breath" or "God's wind," in Hebrew *ruach*. The idea is that the breath of God brings order to the violently moving waters, which is the story's way of talking about chaos. God's breath hovers over chaos and thus tames it.

This diverse activity proceeds through two movements or panels, corresponding to days one-two-three and days four-five-six.

STRUCTURE OF THE CREATION STORY IN GENESIS 1:1–2:4a

Panel One	Panel Two
Day 1: Separation of Light and Darkness	Day 4: Sun, Moon, Stars
Day 2: Sky (Dome) and Seas	Day 5: Birds, Fish
Day 3: Seas and Dry Land and Vegetation	Day 6: Land Animals, Humans

Day 7: Sabbath Rest

God separates and subdues Chaos	God fills creation with moving, living beings

---

The action of the first panel is one of separating. On the first day, God separates light from darkness. The power of chaos, of which darkness is a part, begins to recede before the light of the presence of God. On the second day, God calls forth a firmament (dome) which the ancients believed separated the water above—the source of rain which fell through the "floodgates" (Genesis 7:11) from the waters below—the source of seas, springs, and fountains. Thus a sort of tent of breathing space emerges. Into this would go the world we know. On the third day, God separates the dry land (earth) from the water; and from this earth vegetation of all kinds, plants, and trees, comes forth. At the end of the third day (the first panel), God has divided and conquered; the chaos has been subdued. In its place stands a universe with all of its parts in ordered harmony; the stage is set for living beings to appear.

God's action in the second panel is one of filling the spaces of the first panel with beings that move or live in them. On the fourth day (corresponding to the light and darkness of the first day) appear the sources of light (the sun, moon, and stars) which, through their movement, mark the passage of time and the festal calendar. On the fifth day, the water and air of the second day are populated with life, with birds and fishes. These receive a further call to continue God's life-giving activity. On the sixth day, those creatures who live in and off the earth make their appearance: animals of all kinds and, finally, humans—male and female—who come at the apex of creation and have a special role to play. Finally, on the seventh day, God rests, and all creation shares that rest.

This creation account is masterfully composed and carefully structured. This is further enhanced by the author's use of the word "good," which appears seven times in the text (Genesis 1:4, 10, 12, 18, 21, 25, 31). In the Bible, the number seven is the symbolic number for perfection, completion, totality, wholeness. By the sevenfold use of the word "good," the storyteller is trying to say that when God creates everything, he creates it in its perfection, totality, wholeness.

Thus, in the opening verses of Genesis we encounter God, who effortlessly, through the power of speech, invites the world into existence. God is the one who has dominion over chaos, who subdues it and brings in its place a universe harmonious and habitable, fit for life. God then appears as the source and origin of that life which fills the world. Everything that is begotten derives its life from the word of God. This is the meaning of "creation." Creation from the perspective of the biblical writers has nothing to do with science or scientific explanations; any competition here is based on misunderstanding the biblical text and is misguided. Creation is a religious statement, a statement of faith that, in order to understand ourselves and our world at our deepest level, we are to develop a response to the life-giving Word of God. "Creation" is not only a statement about temporal beginnings, but about each and every moment of our lives.

Humans As the Image of God

Genesis 1:26–28 presents humans—men and women—as the image of God. To understand this we need to note that the Hebrews were forbidden to make images of God (Exodus 20:4; Deuteronomy 5:8). Why? Because in the Bible we are told over and over again that the idols of the nations are ineffectual (see Jeremiah 10:1–11; Isaiah 40:18–20; 44:9–20; Psalm 135:15–18). They can do nothing. They have eyes but see not; ears but hear not; mouths but cannot speak. In sum, the idols are dead. The living God of Israel can be imaged only by living beings who do what God does. God creates humans to be that image.

What is involved here? In the Hebrew language the word "image" is concrete, meaning that when one looks at humans one encounters God. The only permitted "icon" of God in the Old Testament is the human person. The human person—male and female—is a transparency through whom God is seen.

You will also note in the text the notion that humans are to "subdue" and to "have dominion" over creation. It is important that we understand how to interpret this vocabulary. "Subdue" does not mean we can do anything we want with creation. A better translation would be for humans to be called to care for creation, to be co-curators with God of creation. Namely, that God wishes to share his care for creation with those who are most like him, humans. Humankind has not properly understood "subdue" and "have dominion"; basically, we thought it meant that we could do anything we wanted with all of the preserves and reserves of the universe. This is not the case at all. Rather, in the Hebrew mind, "subdue" and "have dominion" mean to reign in creation as curators of the gifts of God. As humans, men and women, we image God by sharing in life-giving and care-taking activity.

In sum, to be God's image involves two things: first, that we accept the fact that God is imaged by both men and women and not just men, and second, that we reflect God's activity in our lives by being life-giving, justice-doing, and peace-making—that is sharing dominion. To accept imagehood is an act of faith. By faith we recognize our complete dependence on God, accept ourselves and our world as gifts of our God graciously given. Being a gracious receiver of these gifts is to image God.

It is important to note in this first creation story that God is the sole creator; humans are not the creators. Rather, humans are the caretakers of creation. The Hebrew verb here for "create" is *bara*. It always refers to a divine action. It is a verb used in the Bible that has only God as its subject and that has as its direct object something new and wonderful that is made.

Let us go back now and look at some of the other insights in the text. In Genesis 1:3, you will notice that God creates light. In the Bible, light is always the symbol of goodness. The cynics say that God had to create light first because he needed to be able to see what he was creating. That is not the case at all. Rather, light is presented here as conquering darkness, which in the Bible, of course, is always the symbol for evil or death. As a matter of fact, the only thing in the entire first story of creation that is not called "good" is darkness.

You will also encounter in the text that God called or named things. For the priestly author who wrote the first creation story, to name is to exercise power and dominion over the one named; and in the Priestly author's worldview, God's naming of the various items of creation is the way in which the author shows that God has ultimate dominion over everything in creation.

The last part of the first creation story deals with the Sabbath rest. The purpose of the Sabbath rest isn't because God is tired. The purpose of the seventh-day rest is to teach humankind that work is not their God. Humans need to recognize that they need to rest from the tyranny of technology; otherwise, technology and work become their deity. The storyteller is presenting us with time for reflecting on God. Just as God did not make his work of creating what gave him meaning, but rested so as to ponder its awesome beauty, so humans are to rest so as to ponder the presence of God in creation and in one another.

"And the Lord God planted a garden . . ."

⁴In the day that the Lord God made the earth and the heavens, ⁵when no plant of the field was yet in the earth and no herb of the field had yet sprung up—for the Lord God had not caused it to rain upon the earth, and there was no one to till the ground; ⁶but a stream would rise from the earth, and water the whole face of the ground—⁷then the Lord God formed man from the dust of the ground, and breathed into his nostrils the breath of life; and the man became a living being. ⁸And the Lord God planted a garden in Eden, in the east; and there he put the man whom he had formed. ⁹Out of the ground the Lord God made to grow every tree that is pleasant to the sight and good for food, the tree of life also in the midst of the garden, and the tree of the knowledge of good and evil.

¹⁰A river flows out of Eden to water the garden, and from there it divides and becomes four branches. ¹¹The name of the first is Pishon; it is the one that flows around the whole land of Havilah, where there is gold; ¹²and the gold of that land is good; bdellium and onyx stone are there. ¹³The name of the second river is Gihon; it is the one that flows around the whole land of Cush. ¹⁴The name of the third river is Tigris, which flows east of Assyria. And the fourth river is the Euphrates.

¹⁵The Lord God took the man and put him in the garden of Eden to till it and keep it. ¹⁶And the Lord God commanded the man, "You may freely eat of every tree of the garden; ¹⁷but of the tree of the knowledge of good and evil you shall not eat, for in the day that you eat of it you shall die."

¹⁸Then the Lord God said, "It is not good that the man should be alone; I will make him a helper as his partner." ¹⁹So out of the ground the Lord God formed every animal of the field and every bird of the air, and brought them to the man to see what he would call them; and whatever the man called every living creature, that was its name. ²⁰*The man gave names to all cattle, and to the birds of the air, and to every animal of the field; but for the man there was not found a helper as his partner.* ²¹*So the* LORD *God caused a deep sleep to fall upon the man, and he slept; then he took one of his ribs and closed up its place with flesh.* ²²*And the rib that the* LORD *God had taken from the man he made into a woman and brought her to the man.* ²³*Then the man said, "This at last is bone of my bones and flesh of my flesh; this one shall be called Woman, for out of Man this one was taken."*

²⁴*Therefore a man leaves his father and his mother and clings to his wife, and they become one flesh.* ²⁵*And the man and his wife were both naked, and were not ashamed* (Genesis 2:4–25).

This story is quite different from the first one. For example, in this story, everything seems to happen in one day, whereas in the last story it took six days for things to happen. In addition, you will notice that a male human is created at the beginning and not last in the story. Further, God is imaged here as a gardener, and later as a potter, not one who brings order out of chaos.

This story belongs to the Yahwist who is a different author than the Priestly author. From verses 4 through 7, we have some interesting items. Whereas in the preceding chapter, the story of creation began with a watery chaos, the present narrative begins with an arid land that was incapable of producing any kind of growth. The mist (or flood) that went up from the earth was useless since there was no one to channel it into fertilizing courses. So the world was desolate and barren when God formed humankind, the first object of his creative activity, from clay of the ground—the Hebrew word is *adamah*. The verb "formed" representing the first of the author's numerous anthropomorphisms suggests the image of a potter molding clay, while the statement that humankind (*adam*, in Hebrew) was made from the ground (*adamah*) includes a pleasant play on words that points to an intimate bond between humans and the earth. We find the motif of people being created from clay in both Egyptian and Mesopotamian mythologies, and the Yahwist takes up this traditional imagery to express the fragile condition of human beings and their dependence on God. Creaturehood is apparent in human origins and the clay bespeaks mortality. Having come from the clay, people will inevitably return to it. Nevertheless, when the author says that God breathed into *adam's* nostrils the breath of life, he is not only saying that *adam* enjoys life as a gift from God, but he is also suggesting that human beings enjoy a share in God's own life. If this is so, then the Yahwist's teaching is not so far removed from that of the Priestly writer in chapter 1 who declared that man and woman are made in God's image and likeness. In any case, the present author—the Yahwist—will go on to show that humble and fragile man and woman were called into companionship with their Creator and enjoyed a privileged life in God's presence.

The Garden and the Tree

In the Septuagint, the Greek translation of the Old Testament, the Hebrew word rendered "garden" became translated into Greek as *paradeiosis*. This word, from which we get our English word "paradise," has connotations of abundance and pleasure. The garden was, in fact, a symbol of God's generosity in providing for the first human beings whom he had made. In Hebrew, the name Eden means "pleasure," and would have conjured up for the original readers images of bliss and contentment. To say that the garden was "in the east" could only mean to the Israelite that it was located in Mesopotamia.

The garden in Eden, paradise, is not a place but a situation. The ideal situation intended by God. It is painted in vivid colors. It is impossible to locate such a place as Eden. The names of the rivers are no real help. What is important about them is that the water flowing in Eden is so abundant that it divides into four great rivers to water a large part of the ancient Near East. The Garden of Eden is a symbol for an ideal situation.

There is more to this ideal situation. There is a "tree of life." This "tree of life" is common enough in the lands of the Bible. In Egypt, a great and ancient temple has a relief of the Pharaoh reaching out to pluck from a tree the *ankh*, the Egyptian symbol for eternal life. An ancient epic from Mesopotamia tells how its hero searched for eternal life and was given it in the form of a plant. But a serpent stole the plant from him.

The "tree of life" represents the truth that in the ideal situation intended by God, humankind was to be free from death, at least from death as a penalty, death as something to be feared. Among the abundant trees of the garden was the "tree of life." Several ancient Middle Eastern mythologies knew of a tree of life whose fruits could grant immortality, and no doubt the biblical author borrowed the idea from them. However, the tree of life has no role in the drama that was to be played out in the garden, and it is only mentioned again at the very end of the story.

Within the ideal situation was another situation, another possibility. This is symbolized in the "tree of the knowledge of good and evil." "To know" or "knowledge" in Hebrew is never simply an intellectual operation. It always involves the actual experience and possession of what is known. A common example is the phrase "to know a woman." "Knowing a woman" involves not simply recognizing or understanding a woman, but the intimacy of sexual intercourse.

As for "good and evil," other uses of this combination in the Old Testament suggest that "good and evil" equals "everything possible." Thus, "to know good and evil" is "the power to experience everything possible." "The tree" in the ideal situation is a possibility that exists for humans to make their own choices, to experience on their own terms whatever exists.

However, God tells the human that he is not to pick and choose what to do and what not to do on his own terms, but to trust God. God will keep the human being in the ideal situation if he will choose and decide according to the lines indicated by God. Of course, such a willingness to accept God's direction presumes an understanding that God loves and wishes only what is true and good for those to whom he gives directions.

According to Genesis 2:15–17, the Lord God placed the man (Adam) in the garden to "till it and keep it." This commission from God shows that from the very beginning work was an essential part of the human condition. While enjoying the fertile garden as God's gift, the man (Adam) could develop his own capacities and unfold the rich potentialities of God's beautiful world. Since in recent times we have become conscious of the scandalous way in which we waste the natural resources of the earth and of the thoughtless way in which we pollute the air we breathe and the water we must drink, commentators on our present passage often remark that the command "to till the earth and keep it" points to our responsibility as the custodians of the world, which is God's gift. We must indeed develop the world, and we must also use all the discoveries of science and technology in doing so. We cannot, however, use the world just for our own profit and convenience. We must "keep" the earth, and prudently conserve its riches; we must avoid exploitation and waste which are simply a desecration of what God has placed at our disposal.

The Creation of Woman

This section of Genesis 2:21–23 is a section which contemporary women often rightly find difficult and repulsive. In the patriarchal world in which this story was composed, women were considered a commodity and maltreated, to say the least.

God, however, is not portrayed in such a "macho" manner. In his kindness, God saw that "it is not good that the man should be alone" in the world, and that he needed a suitable partner with whom he would find fellowship. Man is, by nature, a social being who needs interpersonal relationships if he is to develop his human potential. So God, who was interested in his well-being, provided him with a "helper fit for him." This phrase appears in some other translations as "I will provide a partner for him," a rendering which seems to catch the flavor of the original Hebrew. As man's partner, woman enjoys equality with him. Of the same nature as man, yet different from him, she complements his being and enters into a relationship of mutual love and respect with him. Thus, the present narrative portrays woman as a being who is appreciated for her own worth and not just as one who is capable of satisfying man's needs and instincts.

The curious story of God's creating woman from the rib of the unconscious Adam (verse 21) is highly anthropomorphic, and may be inspired by an ancient Sumerian tale. Perhaps the extraordinary sleep that overcame Adam when God was about to provide him with a partner may suggest the mysterious nature of God's creative activity. The statement that woman was created from a rib conveys the idea that God provides the raw material from which woman is made and that she is, therefore, of the same nature or "raw material" as man. Man's reaction at the sight of his new companion was one of enthusiasm and joy, and he voiced his feelings in what are the first lines of poetry in the Bible (Genesis 2:23). Although there is no real etymological basis for the association of the Hebrew word *ishshah* (woman) and *ish* (man), the author, in typically Yahwistic fashion, uses the similarity in the sound of the words to explain that woman gets her name from the fact that she was taken from man. We may add, incidentally, that the Yahwist's play on words is reproduced in English with the words "woman" and "man."

Woman did not have an easy time in the cultural background against which this story is told. Her life was difficult. The ordinary tasks of daily life were terribly wearing: to carry water from well to home; to grind grain for flour; to gather wood for the fire; to help in the field; to tend the home and children. All these filled her day, and all were back-breaking toil.

Beyond this, a woman generally had no rights of her own. A man, whether her husband or father, was her master. If a woman had any special place of honor in the ancient Near Eastern world, it was because of her sexual role. Only her body could give a man sons; sons who could work with him in his fields, or with his flocks; sons who would carry on his name and memory when he had passed on to the emptiness of death. Further, her body could provide man with intense pleasure. Because of this, even though her individual person was treated with little dignity, her sexual role was made divine. Statues of goddesses have been found with their sexual parts exaggerated; even this divine-ising of the sexual role did little to improve the living conditions of women. But this is background. Genesis 2:20 mentions how man gave names to all the birds and animals, "but none proved to be the suitable partner for the man." Of all that God placed in creation, nothing was like man.

But when woman was created, man cried out in joy, "This at last is bone of my bones and flesh of my flesh" (Genesis 2:23). The woman, of all the works of creation, is the only equal of man. Only she is the same kind of being that he is. To a culture which put down woman, which often degraded her, this story shouts, "Not so!" Woman is like man. Woman is man's partner for life. Woman is made by God as the equal of man.

This equality is directed to a purpose the storyteller tells us. Man had been given responsibility for the created world. Now he has a helpmate, a partner in that responsibility. Man and woman together are to care for the earth which God has entrusted to them.

Once more, it is necessary to point out that the issue here is not a scientific discussion about how woman came to be. The "rib" is part of a story communicating a truth. The point is teaching about relationships. God created man and woman equal and gave them responsibility for their earth. That this teaching is to be found here does not necessarily mean that its implications were understood and lived up to then, anymore than they are now.

By way of conclusion on this, we can say that at least the storytellers in Genesis, both chapters 1 and 2, presented a notion of equality about man and woman. Subsequent interpreters may not have.

Since man and woman are complementary beings, there is a mysterious attraction between them that impels them to break the bonds that tie them to their parents' home in order to become one flesh. The concept of becoming one flesh must not, of course, be understood in the narrow sense of sexual union, but must be taken to refer to that full union of persons that enables two individuals to find fulfillment in each other. We may note, however, that it is unlikely that the author of this verse, who wrote in the polygamist environment of ancient Israel, intended to teach the doctrine of monogamous marriage or to exclude divorce. Later, Israel continued to accept both polygamy and divorce.

The assertion that "the man and his wife were both naked" (Genesis 2:25) points to the childlike innocence and to the state of bliss in which the first couple lived in the idyllic garden in which God had placed them. The statement does not refer primarily to the absence of sexual awareness or of any sexual disorder, but to the relationship of mutual trust and respect that united the first couple. Only after their sin, when this harmonious relationship would be broken, would man and woman become aware of their nakedness (see Genesis 3:7).

Theological Conclusions about the Creation Stories

There are some clear theological and religious statements that come out of these creation stories. First, everything that is created is seen as "good." Second, the God who creates shares the caring for his creation with his humans. However, this God does not force these humans to care for his creation, but rather respects their freedom to choose so. Third, the stories are an attempt to show equality between men and women and co-curatorship with God on the part of both of this fragile universe.

Sin and Alienation

In the chapters immediately following the creation narratives, the theme turns to humanity's sinful response to God's original blessing in creation (Genesis 3–11).

These chapters describe with lightning speed the snowballing effects of sin in the world. Cain is infected with sin, then Lamech

(Genesis 4), then all the world, so much so that God cleanses the world by the flood (Genesis 9) until it reaches a second climax at the Tower of Babel (Genesis 11). This time, though, instead of wiping the world clean of sinners, God decides to work within human history through one of its families. Several of the stories and images of this introductory section (Genesis 3–11) are borrowed from the folklore of neighboring peoples, but laced with a new inspired meaning. While these stories are not historically provable, nonetheless they are used as a means to explain that God is not the source of sin but, rather, humankind, whom God never abandons regardless of its continued chosen alienation from him.

Abraham

The call of Abraham in chapter 12 marks the beginning of the "history of salvation." God freely chooses Abraham and he freely responds. God promises Abraham a child (Isaac), that his descendents will become a great nation, and the land (Canaan). God enters into a covenant with Abraham and his descendents (see Genesis 15 and 17). The stories about the patriarch Abraham reveal a man of his own time, not a superman, but a man led by faith in God.

The faith of Abraham is legendary in the Bible. It is summed up in Genesis 15:6, "And he [Abraham] believed the LORD; and the LORD reckoned it to him as righteousness." In all things Abraham proves faithful and devoted to God's commands. But the ultimate test of Abraham's faith comes when God seems to demand that Abraham sacrifice Isaac back to him in chapter 22 of Genesis. This is the high point of the Abraham story, and the author(s) of Genesis maintain a high sense of drama and artistic skill in narrating the horrifying moment. Abraham is weighed down so greatly that he cannot bear to tell his son, Isaac, the truth, and Isaac, in turn, is so trusting that he never suspects what is happening. The young boy asks naturally curious questions, and the grieving Abraham can barely answer. Abraham sends the servants off to preserve the privacy of the last moments. Just when all seems lost,

God's angel stops Abraham's hand and God provides an animal to sacrifice instead.

This story often shocks modern readers. They wonder how God could ask a thing like that. But the author of Genesis wanted to make a point with this story for all later Israel. It was not uncommon in the ancient world for parents to sacrifice a son in times of great need or illness to try to appease the gods. The Old Testament records several examples, ranging from Jephthah in the Book of Judges (chapter 11) to Manasseh in the seventh century (2 Kings 21). All of these are looked upon with horror, and the story of the near sacrifice of Isaac certainly shows how God forbade any human sacrifice—he did not want human flesh but would accept animals as an offering instead, although what God wanted most was faith and trust. This whole story sums up perfectly the character of Abraham as a man of faith.

Isaac and Jacob

The stories of Abraham's son Isaac are very brief. Isaac barely stands out in his own right and serves as a bridge to the saga of Jacob. The two key Isaac stories are his marriage to Rebekah (Genesis 24:1–67) and the birth of their sons, Jacob and Esau. The drama turns immediately to Jacob, and chapters 25–36 are a series of short incidents from his life.

There are three types of Jacob stories found in this section of Genesis. First, stories about the conflict between Esau and Jacob; second, stories that center around Jacob's marriages and his adventures with Laban, an Aramean relative; and third, a number of theophanies (experiences in which Jacob encounters God).

Jacob is often portrayed as the "trickster." He tricks his brother Esau out of his birthright by feeding Esau red lentil soup when he is famished, on the provision that Esau surrender his birthright (Genesis 25:29–34). He also tricks his father Isaac into giving him the blessing instead of Esau (Genesis 27:1–45). The two brothers do eventually reconcile with one another (Genesis 32:3–21; 33:1–17).

THE JACOB STORY IN THE BOOK OF GENESIS

Conflict between Jacob and Esau

1. The twins struggle for first place in their mother's womb (Genesis 25:19–28).
2. They struggle for the birthright (25:29–34).
3. They wrestle for Isaac's blessing (27:1–45).
4. They find reconciliation (32:3–21; 33:1–17).

Conflict between Jacob and Laban

1. Jacob has to marry into Laban's family (27:46–28:9).
2. Jacob is tricked by Laban but gains a larger family (29:1–30:24).
3. Jacob tricks Laban out of his flocks (30:25–43).
4. Jacob escapes with Laban's gods (31:1–24).

Theophanies

1. God appears to Jacob at Bethel to renew the promise (28:10–22).
2. God appears to Jacob at Peniel and renames Jacob "Israel" (32:22–32).
3. God renews the promise at Bethel (35:1–15).

The story of Jacob wrestling all night with the angel of God at the river Jabbok (Genesis 32:22–32) is legendary. There he wrestled all night long to a draw with his opponent, whose name Jacob demanded, and although Jacob was not beaten, he was struck on the hip socket, an injury that resulted in a limp. As a result of this contest, his name was changed from Jacob, which means "heel-gripper," to Israel, which means "one who has struggled with God and prevailed." The name Israel, which can also mean "one who has wrestled with God," came to have unique significance for the ancient Israelites. It was not only the name given to their ancestor, Jacob, but the entire nation was eventually known by this name. A fitting name for a people who were constantly wrestling with God.

The descendents of Jacob, otherwise known as the tribes of Israel, believed that they were the chosen people of God. For God had first called their ancestor, Abraham, and had promised to make his descendents a mighty nation and to bless them with the land they could call their own. Furthermore, God had renewed these promises down through the generations to Isaac and then to Jacob. This conviction, that of being the chosen people of God, has remained with the Jews to this very day.

The Patriarch Joseph

The final chapters of the Book of Genesis (37–50) deal with the patriarch Joseph. Because of the favoritism Jacob shows to Joseph, his second youngest son, there is strife and jealousy among the brothers (Genesis 37:1–20). As a result, they plan at first to kill him, but then reverse this in favor of selling him into slavery. Sold to some traveling traders, Joseph is taken to Egypt (37:2–36), where his fortunes continue. Placed in charge of a large Egyptian household, Joseph resists the sensual advances of the owner's (Potiphar) wife. Because of her lying testimony, Joseph is sent to prison.

After two years there, Joseph begins to rise to new power and authority. Pharaoh has had a disturbing dream, and Joseph's skills at interpretation are recalled. He comes before Pharaoh and interprets his dream. In view of the dream's message regarding a forthcoming famine, Pharaoh appoints Joseph to be in charge of all of Egypt.

When the famine comes, all people from the surrounding region come to Egypt where, thanks to Joseph's wise administration, food can be found. Among those coming are Joseph's brothers. He recognizes them, tests them, and tricks them into bringing his brother, Benjamin, the youngest son of Jacob, to Egypt also. When at last Joseph makes himself known to them, his surprised and fearful brothers, he assures them of his good will. Their father, Jacob, and all the rest of their families join them and they settle and prosper in Egypt.

Throughout the story, Joseph consistently recognizes and admits his dependence on God. "How then could I do this great wickedness, and sin against God?" (39:9), he says, spurning Potiphar's wife. When Pharaoh asks him to interpret his dream, Joseph counters, "It is not I; God will give Pharaoh a favorable answer" (41:16). When he marries and has two children, Manasseh and Ephraim, both of their names acknowledge God's gifts (41:51–52). When his brothers fear him, he assures them that he is a God-fearing man (42:18). Finally, when Jacob dies and the brothers fear once again, Joseph reassures them, "Do not be afraid! Am I in the place of God?" (50:19).

Because he recognizes and accepts his place before God, Joseph is able to accomplish two things. First, he provides for the life of the land of Egypt. Second, he brings about reconciliation within his own family. Joseph the Patriarch has no delusions; he is under God and he knows it.

The Joseph story in the Book of Genesis takes the family of Abraham from Canaan into Egypt for Israel's formative experience of salvation: the scene is being set for the Hebrews' enslavement and liberation in the Book of Exodus. At the end of the Book of Genesis, they are dwelling peacefully in Egypt, and Joseph's bones are waiting for return to the land of Israel (50:25–26). But ". . . a new king arose over Egypt who did not know Joseph" (Exodus 1:8).

The Book of Exodus: "Let My People Go"

The Book of Exodus is named for the central event in the book, the going out or departure from Egypt. It centers on the Hebrews being liberated by their God from the slavelike oppression of the Egyptians at the crossing of the Red Sea.

Perhaps the most important point in the Book of Exodus is the fact that God has actively intervened (entered) in human history. The active presence of God is the central theme of Exodus. In fact, it is God's overriding force in the Israelites' preparation, departure, and journey across the desert. God is a God of deeds who saves them and makes them his people. The relationship of the Israelites in the desert to God is one of complete dependence. They must depend upon God for the bare necessities of life: for meat, for bread, and for water.

The Book of Exodus is really composed around a series of episodes. Therefore, any division of the book needs to be sensitive to the various episodes. The following is an episodic division:

DIVISION OF THE BOOK OF EXODUS

1. The childhood and call of Moses (Exodus 1–3)
2. The struggle to free Israel by plagues, climaxing in the Passover (Exodus 4–13:16)
3. The escape and journey into the wilderness of Sinai (Exodus 13:17–18)
4. The giving of the covenant and its laws (Exodus 19–24)
5. The instructions for building the Ark and the Tent of Meeting, and their execution (Exodus 25–40)

The Book of Exodus is made up of three of the four pentateuchal sources: the Yahwist (J), the Elohist (E), and the Priestly (P).

Literary Form of the Book of Exodus: "Dramatized Epic History"

The literary form proper to the Book of Exodus is that of a dramatized epic history. Within this literary form are contained other forms such as an infancy narrative and plague stories. There are three basic. characteristics of a dramatized epic history: (1) It centers around one person, in this case either Moses or God. He is leader, liberator, mediator, prophet, and priest; (2) The time elements are condensed and telescoped. An example of this is Exodus 1:6–9, which relates Joseph's death, followed by a new king coming to power who oppresses the Hebrews. Without knowing the facts, one could never tell that hundreds of years had elapsed; and (3) Facts, numbers, circumstances, etc., are embellished to highlight the underlying meaning of what is taking place. An example of this would be the number of men who departed from Egypt during the time of the exodus. The number of men is given as 600,000 (Exodus 12:37), which would imply a total of two to three million if one were to count women and children. Obviously, it is a deliberate exaggeration to enhance the importance of the departure, something the ancient people were fond of doing. Within a dramatized epic history there is a great deal of mythic heightening, embellishing a story in service of subsequent generations obtaining the meaning that the original generation had. For example, to embellish the power of God, ten plagues are mentioned; if God only unleashed one plague, no one would remember. Embellishing enhances the meaning.

Much use is made of dramatization throughout the Book of Exodus, such as the murmurings of the people, the use of direct quotations, etc. The direct quotes attributed to Pharaoh, God, etc., are not to be taken literally. They are an imaginative, not factual, sort of writing. What is being asserted is that God's will is expressed through the law. God's revelation comes through human expression and in this case through the literary mode of expression chosen by the formulators of the Book of Exodus.

Setting the Stage (Exodus, chapter 1)

⁶Then Joseph died, and all his brothers, and that whole generation. ⁷But the Israelites were fruitful and prolific; they multiplied and grew exceedingly strong, so that the land was filled with them.

⁸Now a new king arose over Egypt, who did not know Joseph. ⁹He said to his people, "Look, the Israelite people are more numerous and more powerful than we. ¹⁰Come, let us deal shrewdly with them, or they will increase and, in the event of war, join our enemies and fight against us and escape from the land." ¹¹Therefore they set taskmasters over them to oppress them with forced labor. They built supply cities, Pithom and Rameses, for Pharaoh. ¹²But the more they were oppressed, the more they multiplied and spread, so that the Egyptians came to dread the Israelites. ¹³The Egyptians became ruthless in imposing tasks on the Israelites, ¹⁴and made their lives bitter with hard service in mortar and brick and in every kind of field labor. They were ruthless in all the tasks that they imposed on them.

¹⁵The king of Egypt said to the Hebrew midwives, one of whom was named Shiphrah and the other Puah, ¹⁶"When you act as midwives to the Hebrew women, and see them on the birthstool, if it is a boy, kill him; but if it is a girl, she shall live." ¹⁷But the midwives feared God; they did not do as the king of Egypt commanded them, but they let the boys live. ¹⁸So the king of Egypt summoned the midwives and said to them, "Why have you done this, and allowed the boys to live?" ¹⁹The midwives said to Pharaoh, "Because the Hebrew women are not like the Egyptian women; for they are vigorous and give birth before the midwife comes to them." ²⁰So God dealt well with the midwives; and the people multiplied and became very strong. ²¹And because the midwives feared God, he gave them families. ²²Then Pharaoh commanded all his people, "Every boy that is born to the Hebrews you shall throw into the Nile, but you shall let every girl live" (Exodus 1:6–21).

The first chapter of Exodus sets the stage for the drama. It connects the intervening time from the patriarch Joseph to Moses, shows that the Israelites are becoming more numerous, and shows how oppression and slavery set in with the new king of Egypt. Note how immediately opposition is set up between the Egyptians and the Hebrews. It is between the "bad guys" (the Egyptians and the Pharaoh) and the "good guys" (the Hebrews and Moses). This "bad guys-good guys" setup is characteristic of the literary form of the Book of Exodus: a dramatized epic history. It is an exaggeration, but it helps to sharpen the conflict and the plight of the Hebrews.

The time that the twelve tribes of Israel spend in Egypt marks a significant part of the Exodus journey and has special significance for the spiritual journey. From the Hebrew word for Egypt, *Mitzraim*, we receive a clue to the meaning of the Israelite sojourn there. *Mitzraim* means "limitation," "bondage," or "affliction." *Mitzraim* is a metaphor for the dominant culture. Egypt is the place where the Israelites became enslaved to the dominant culture. Before these people experience freedom, they experience slavery. At one time or another, *Mitzraim* reflects the condition of every person; although we can be happy and fruitful, we can also be enslaved to the dominant culture. All religions are countercultural. Embracing the commitment of religious faith calls the dominant culture of every era into question and offers an alternative worldview—that of following God over the "pharaohs" of the culture.

The new Pharaoh, not knowing Joseph or the people, fears the twelve tribes of Israel. So the Pharaoh shrewdly orders the Hebrew midwives to put to death the Israelite male children while they are still upon the birthstool, when even the mothers do not know what is happening. He also commands his people to cast into the river every Israelite male child who escapes death at birth. He does not give these orders to his chief executioners but, rather, tells the Egyptian people to carry them out. In this manner he escapes direct blame and allows innocent people to become victims of the lawless. Conditions worsen to the point that Israelite children are no longer safe in their own homes.

Great suffering often brings forth strong, compassionate people from both the oppressed and the oppressor. We see this in the story of the Hebrew midwives, Shiphrah and Puah. Shiphrah means "brightness," and Puah means "splendid." These two women each live up to their names. Fearing God, they refuse to obey Pharaoh's orders. Through their civil disobedience, a people survive extinction. In addition, the daughter of the oppressor—Pharaoh—helps save the baby Moses.

The Early Life of Moses (Exodus, chapter 2)

¹Now a man from the house of Levi went and married a Levite woman. ²The woman conceived and bore a son; and when she saw that he was a fine baby, she hid him three months. ³When she could hide him no longer she got a papyrus basket for him, and plastered it with bitumen and pitch; she put the child in it and placed it among the reeds on the bank of the river. ⁴His sister stood at a distance, to see what would happen to him.

⁵The daughter of Pharaoh came down to bathe at the river, while her attendants walked beside the river. She saw the basket among the reeds and sent her maid to bring it. ⁶When she opened it, she saw the child. He was crying, and she took pity on him, "This must be one of the Hebrews' children," she said. ⁷Then his sister said to Pharaoh's daughter, "Shall I go and get you a nurse from the Hebrew women to nurse the child for you?" ⁸Pharaoh's daughter said to her, "Yes." So the girl went and called the child's mother. ⁹Pharaoh's daughter said to her, "Take this child and nurse it for me, and I will give you your wages." So the woman took the child and nursed it. ¹⁰When the child grew up, she brought him to Pharaoh's daughter, and she took him as her son. She named him Moses, "because," she said, "I drew him out of the water" (Exodus 2:1–10).

Here the writer makes use of the common literary form of infancy narrative, the purpose of which is to describe the origin, birth, and childhood of a great man. Ancient literature's use of this literary form often included much folklore woven around the basic core of historical fact. The truths contained here are: (1) Moses was a Hebrew, loyal to his people. (2) Moses was educated as an Egyptian. (3) God's providence is at work: God is preparing a leader for the Hebrews. (4) Moses was forced to hide in the desert. Here he meets God and hears God's call.

This scriptural text—Exodus 2:1–10—recalls the miraculous power of the Divine Presence in the miracle of birth. The parents of Moses are identified in Exodus 6:20 as Amram and Jochebed. Amram means "kindred of the most high," and Jochebed means "divine splendor." These are people touched by God. When the Divine touches creation, miracles occur: "The woman conceived and bore a son" (Exodus 2:2).

Pharaoh has ordered that all male Hebrew babies be killed. So Jochebed risks her own life and that of the whole household to save the newborn child's life. After three months, when she can no longer hide him safely in the house, she puts the newborn in God's trust, placing him in a watertight basket afloat on the Nile river. Miriam, the child's sister, stations herself by the river and waits—life waiting upon life.

When Pharaoh's daughter comes to the Nile to bathe she sees the basket among the reeds and sends her slave girl to fetch it. It is a tense moment. Will the newborn be handed over to be killed, or will it be protected to go on living?

The princess opens the basket. The cries of the child touch her heart, moving her to pity. Defying her father's orders—an example of irony on the part of the author of Exodus—she hires a wet nurse, who, unknown to her, is the child's mother. God's plan for Moses includes the selection of his mother as the wet nurse. God's will is done, even when the participants are unaware of it.

The name assigned to Pharaoh's daughter by later Jewish tradition—this name is not found in the Bible—is Lithia, which can be translated as "daughter of God." Even though this woman is Pharaoh's daughter of Egyptian origin, her obedience to the divine activity of God makes her a beloved daughter of God. She is the woman who gives the name Moses to the future lawgiver and prophet of Israel.

The drama played through women in the first two chapters of Exodus is remarkable. Israel's women are fertile; their fertility is Pharaoh's concern and target. His plans to destroy Israel are sabotaged by the midwives, Shiphrah and Puah, by Miriam and Jochebed, and even by his own daughter.

This passage commemorates for posterity not only the role of women but also the importance of a child. In the first ten verses of Exodus 2, the word "child" occurs seven times. There can be no doubt about the importance of the child and the care that is to be invested upon him. This should apply to every child we meet, including the child that is buried deep within each one of us.

The Four Key Theological (Religious) Events in the Book of Exodus

The Book of Exodus is tied together by four key theological events. The following outline describes them.

KEY THEOLOGICAL EVENTS IN THE BOOK OF EXODUS

1. The call initiated by God (Exodus 3)
2. The moment of decision (Exodus 14–15)
3. Mount Sinai and the covenant (Exodus 19–24)
4. The test of friendship—fidelity of God versus the infidelity of the people (Exodus 32–34)

---

1. The Call (Exodus, chapter 3)

You will note that in verse 10 God says to Moses: "So come, I will send you to Pharaoh to bring my people, the Israelites, out of Egypt." There is interaction between God and Moses. It is God who calls, who takes the initiative, who assures Moses that he will be with him, etc. Note also Moses' reverence, his reluctance to take on a leadership role. Moses is called to be a leader, and so to inspire us as a leader. His vocation is not just to lead his people out of the slavery of Egypt but, more important, to lead them to the promised land and in the process to be both God's spokesperson and mediator in shaping them into a people of God.

Moses' Response and the Revelation of God's Name (Exodus 3:11–18)

The structure of chapter three is rather easy. The first ten verses focus our attention on God's call of Moses, whereas verses 11–18 focus on Moses' response.

> [13]*But Moses said to God, "If I come to the Israelites and say to them, `The God of your ancestors has sent me to you,' and they ask me, `What is his name?' what shall I say to them?"* [14]*God said to Moses, "I AM WHO I AM." He said further, "Thus you shall say to the Israelites, 'I AM has sent me to you.'"* [15]*God also said to Moses, "Thus you shall say to the Israelites, 'The LORD, the God of your ancestors, the God of Abraham, the God of Isaac, and the God of Jacob, has sent me to you':*

This is my name forever, and this is my title for all generations.
¹⁶Go and assemble the elders of Israel, and say to them, 'The LORD,
the God of your ancestors, the God of Abraham, of Isaac, and of
Jacob, has appeared to me, saying: I have given heed to you and to
what has been done to you in Egypt. ¹⁷I declare that I will bring you
up out of the misery of Egypt, to the land of the Canaanites, the
Hittites, the Amorites, the Perizzites, the Hivites, and the Jebusites,
a land flowing with milk and honey.' ¹⁸They will listen to your voice;
and you and the elders of Israel shall go to the king of Egypt and
say to him, 'The LORD, the God of the Hebrews, has meet with us;
let us now go a three days' journey into the wilderness, so that we
may sacrifice to the LORD our God' (Exodus 3:13–18).

From reading the above text, one realizes that Moses' response is what he is to tell the people about this God who has sent him to them. God responds in saying from the bush that does not burn up, "I AM WHO I AM." This is the name "Yahweh." It is taken from the verb Yah, meaning "to be," which means "I am" or "He is." The threefold significance of the name "Yahweh" is as follows: (1) "He is" in the sense that he is God," he is the only God; all other Gods are nothing—no thing. (2) "He is" in the sense that he is with them or present to them. (3) "He is" in the sense that he is working for them—he is "on the ball" in their behalf. This God leads history by involving himself in it.

God's Name
The fact that God is a person comes out in the way the Old Testament emphasizes his name. Only people have names, and in the ancient world a person's name was more than just a label.

A person's name established their identity and revealed their character. So, for example, in the early stories of the Book of Genesis, Eve, which means "mother of all living" (3:20); and Cain, which means "metalworker" (4:1), are both given names that indicate something about their personality.

NAMES FOR GOD IN THE OLD TESTAMENT

NAME	BIBLICAL TEXT
Elohim (a plural noun of majesty)	Genesis 1:26–27
El Elyon ("God most high")	Genesis 14:18–19
El Olam ("Eternal God")	Genesis 21:33
El Berith ("Covenantal God")	Judges 9:46
El Roi ("God of Seeing")	Genesis 16:13
El Shaddai ("God Almighty")	Genesis 17:1; 49:25; Exodus 6:3
YHWH ("I AM WHO I AM")	Exodus 3:13–14

Biblically speaking, knowing a person's name, or giving a name to someone, is often a way of gaining authority over that person. God gives the stars their names because he is their Creator (Psalm 147:4). He gives the people of Israel their name, and in doing so asserts his authority over them (Isaiah 43:1). Similarly, when Jacob wrestles with an unknown angel, he wants to know the angel's name so that he can establish a proper relationship with him (Genesis 32:29–30). To know the name of a god could therefore be very important, for a god's name gave the worshipper access to his power. By calling upon or blessing in a god's name, his presence could be assured.

The Old Testament attitude to God's name is distinctive. Using God's name in this semimagical way is expressly forbidden in the Ten Commandments (Exodus 20:7). God's name is not something to be discovered and manipulated by men and women: it is something that God himself reveals in his love to his own people.

Because of this there is an extraordinary reverence for God's name throughout the Old Testament. The reticence to mention the name of God is so widespread that we do not even know for certain how his personal name was pronounced. Hebrew has no vowels, and this name for God revealed at the burning bush was written down *YHWH*. It is technically referred to as the sacred tetragramatton. Vowel sounds are needed to pronounce it, of course, but we do not know precisely which sounds were used. When the Old Testament was written down in its present form, Jewish religious teachers regarded the personal name of God as too sacred to say. Whenever they found it they would substitute the Hebrew word *Adonai*, which means "my lord." In this way, the vowels of Adonai came to be pronounced with the consonants of God's name *YHWH*, to produce something like the English term "Jehovah." Nowadays it is customary to write this name as "Yahweh."

IMAGES FOR GOD IN THE OLD TESTAMENT

Image	Biblical Text
King	Psalm 95:3
Judge	Genesis 18:25
Shepherd	Psalm 23
Wind/Breath	Genesis 1:2
Rock	Deuteronomy 32:4; 1 Samuel 2:2; Psalm 18:2, 31
Light	Psalm 27:1
Sun	Psalm 84:11
Shade	Psalm 121:5
Dew	Hosea 14:5
Lion	Jeremiah 25:38; Hosea 13:7, 8
Leopard	Hosea 13:7
Bear	Hosea 13:8
Eagle	Exodus 19:4 Deuteronomy 32:10–13
Father	Psalm 89:26
Warrior	Exodus 15:3
Mother	Isaiah 49:15; Numbers 11:12 Deuteronomy 32:18
Husband	Isaiah 54:5
Redeemer	Isaiah 41:14
Midwife	Psalm 29:10; Isaiah 66:6–9
Lady Wisdom (Sophia)	Proverbs 1:28, 3:13–18, 8:22–25, 30–31 Wisdom 10:17
Strength	Psalm 28:7
Refuge	Psalm 46:1
Shield	Psalm 18:2
Fountain	Jeremiah 2:13

It would be incorrect to conclude that Yahweh is the only name for God in the Old Testament; in fact, there are many names for God. And in addition to multiple names for God, the Old Testament provides a variety of images for God (see previous page). "To whom then will you liken God, or what likeness compare with him?" (Isaiah 40:18).

God's Call to Be His People (Exodus 3:16–22)

16Go and assemble the elders of Israel, and say to them, 'The LORD, the God of your ancestors, the God of Abraham, of Isaac, and of Jacob, has appeared to me, saying: I have given heed to you and to what has been done to you in Egypt. 17I declare that I will bring you up out of the misery of Egypt, to the land of the Canaanites, the Hittites, the Amorites, the Perizzites, the Hivites, and the Jebusites, a land flowing with milk and honey.' 18They will listen to your voice; and you and the elders of Israel shall go to the king of Egypt and say to him, 'The LORD, the God of the Hebrews, has met with us; let us now go a three days' journey into the wilderness, so that we may sacrifice to the LORD our God? 19I know, however, that the king of Egypt will not let you go unless compelled by a mighty hand. 20So I will stretch out my hand and strike Egypt with all my wonders that I will perform in it; after that he will let you go. 21I will bring this people into such favor with the Egyptians that, when you go, you will not go empty-handed; 22each woman shall ask her neighbor and any woman living in the neighbor's house for jewelry of silver and of gold, and clothing, and you shall put them on your sons and on your daughters; and so you shall plunder the Egyptians" (Exodus 3:16–22).

Thus far we have been focusing our attention upon Moses and God. God's message to Moses is also meant for all of the Israelites. Through Moses God is likewise calling them. Their (the Hebrews') vocation is to leave the slavery of Egypt and become God's people by worshipping in the desert. ". . . the LORD your God has chosen you out of all the peoples on earth to be his people, his treasured possession" (Deuteronomy 7:6).

Moses and the People's Reluctance (Exodus, chapters 4 and 5)

Here Moses expresses a lack of confidence. God grants Moses another to help him, his brother Aaron, who becomes a mouthpiece for Moses. In Exodus 4:30 and 31 we see that the people believe when Moses and Aaron call the people together and address them. But with hard times in chapter 5, they lose confidence and will have nothing to do with Moses (Exodus 5:20–21). Then Moses again turns to God to complain about being sent upon such an impossible mission (Exodus 5:22–23).

God's Assurance and Promise of Success (Exodus 6:1–8)

Notice the various use of anthropomorphisms, such as "a mighty hand," "outstretched," "will drive" etc., and how they might mean "power," "might," and "protection." Throughout the Book of Exodus, notice other forms of anthropomorphisms, such as God's anger, etc. Still, the Israelites in their slavery will not listen to Moses (Exodus 6:9). Slowly their confidence and belief will be built up, and only with the tenth sign (plague) will they have enough faith and courage to follow God through Moses.

2. Moments of Decision (Exodus, chapters 7 through 15)

The Plagues (Exodus 7:14–12:36)

The signs and wonders of the plagues are not to be interpreted as miracles as we presently understand the term "miracle." Many of the plagues, in fact, the first nine, seem to have been natural phenomena—the fact, these were natural phenomena does not mar their sign value of pointing to the presence and activity of God, and this of course is the most important element in any of the wonders worked by God. God can work in many ways. What is remarkable is that he does work through these phenomena to accomplish his purposes. Also, what is significant is that Moses, God's spokesperson interprets these phenomena as God's interventions in behalf of the Hebrew people. The people saw beyond these natural phenomena to a God working in their behalf because they never would have risked their necks to follow this man Moses. On the other hand, Pharaoh, while impressed, reacts in disbelief, and so hardens his heart.

We must remember, signs do not prove in the sense of forcing our assent. They lead us to investigate and search further. For their full meaning, one must turn to God. Only in faith do we come to the fuller value and significance of what the sign points to. It should be noted that the signs and wonders which are taking place in the Book of Exodus are worked for the benefit of the Israelites so that they will make the decision to follow Moses and therefore God. Thus, the plagues are more for the benefit of the Israelites than for the punishment or threat of Pharaoh and the Egyptians.

No one of the three traditions found in the Book of Exodus (J, E, P) lists all ten plagues. Sometimes these ten plagues are called the ten fingers of God, perhaps because of the designation in Exodus 8:19 of the gnats as "is the finger of God."

PLAGUES IN THE BOOK OF EXODUS

1. The pollution of the Nile River and all other Egyptian water supplies (Exodus 7:14–24)
2. Frogs (Exodus 8:1–15)
3. Gnats (Exodus 8:16–19)
4. Flies (Exodus 8:20–30)
5. Pestilence (Exodus 9:1–7)
6. Boils (Exodus 9:8–12)
7. Hail and thunder (Exodus 9:13–35)
8. Locusts (Exodus 10:1–20)
9. Darkness (Exodus 10:21–29)
10. The death of the firstborn among the Egyptians and their animals (Exodus 11:1–10; 12:29–36)

These plagues affect not only the Egyptian people (8:28–29; 11:29) but also their water (7:19), land (8:2, 9, 20; 9:25b; 10:14, 22), crops (9:31; 10:15), and animals (7:21; 8:13; 9:3, 9, 10, 25a, 29).

The plagues have a theological rather than historical function in the Book of Exodus. Together they are a means of divine chastisement; an acknowledgment of the divine power (Exodus 8:15) and sovereignty (Exodus 8:18; 9:29); and an attestation that God is a God of liberation who does indeed hear and answer the cry of the oppressed (Exodus 3:7–8). They also provide an opportunity for one to acknowledge one's sinfulness, to ask forgiveness (Exodus 9:27–28; 10:16–17), and to experience a change of heart (Exodus 10:10).

Now the fact that these happened at a particular time and were interpreted by Moses and the Israelites as the mighty acts of God would give these their sign and wonder value. However, we must not think that these signs and wonders all happened overnight. Remember that one of the characteristics of a dramatized epic history, which is the literary form of the biblical Book of Exodus, is the condensation of time.

There is a recurring theme in these plagues, the theme of "the hardening of Pharaoh's heart." Here we must understand the mentality of the Hebrews. For the Hebrews, God is the one who causes all things; if Pharaoh is obstinate, then it is God who causes him to be so.

The final sign and wonder, the tenth plague, the killing of the firstborn (see Exodus 11:1–10; 12:29–30), is really a difficult one to interpret. It is mentioned by J, E, and P. What sort of phenomena this is poses a problem that cannot be solved. The portrayal of God directly planning and executing humans is repulsive. From our present viewpoint it is hard to see how it could be since we have no rational explanation for it. Such a catastrophe so central to the action of the exodus seems more than ordinary. This is not to say that it might not be heightened and exaggerated in the telling. (Remember the characteristics of a dramatized epic history.)

Passover (Exodus 12:1–28)

Passover is really the birth of God's people. As yet the Hebrews are a motley group of dispersed individuals. Only with their passing through the Red Sea do they begin to become God's people. Becoming God's people, however, is not something which takes place automatically. When God calls them to become his people, there is required a decision on their part. Certainly, they wanted to leave the slavery of Egypt and become free, but this also means that they must leave the fleshpots of Egypt for the hardships of the desert, that they must leave the known for the unknown, the sure for the unsure. This decision can only be made through faith and trust in God and under the leadership of Moses, God's representative.

The Passover account consists of two parts: (1) the Passover ritual (Exodus 12:1–13, 24–28; 13:1–10); and (2) the passage through the Red Sea (Exodus 13:17–14:31).

Let us begin by talking about the Passover ritual. Slaying and eating a lamb was part of the ritual described in Exodus 12. The Israelites were spared the visit of the destroying angel of the tenth plague by smearing the lamb's blood on the lintels and doorframes of their homes. The Passover ritual is a sacred family meal, later commemorated annually to remind the Hebrews of God's action on their behalf; the bitter herbs (similar to a salad) symbolized their period of slavery and oppression; loins girded, sandals on their feet, and staff in hand bring out that a journey of departure is an essential aspect of the sacred meal. Because of the blood of the lamb they were saved. The first meaning of Passover, then, is the passing over of the angel of the Lord who spares the Israelite's firstborns and then makes possible their departure from Egypt. (Exodus 12:13, 27).

In the narrative of the passage through the Red Sea (Exodus 13:17–14:31), we have dramatized in the crossing of the waters of chaos the universal human experience of facing up to the moment of decision. Throughout the course of history the crossing of water has always been symbolic of decision. Caesar crossing the Rubicon, Leif Erickson the Atlantic, Washington the Delaware, the allied forces during the Second World War the English Channel. In each case, once the decision is made there is no turning back.

Here the Israelites want to give up and turn back, but steeled by the leadership of Moses they do what must be done. But is this not just a fairy tale like George Washington chopping down the cherry tree? No, George Washington chopping down the cherry tree is a story with

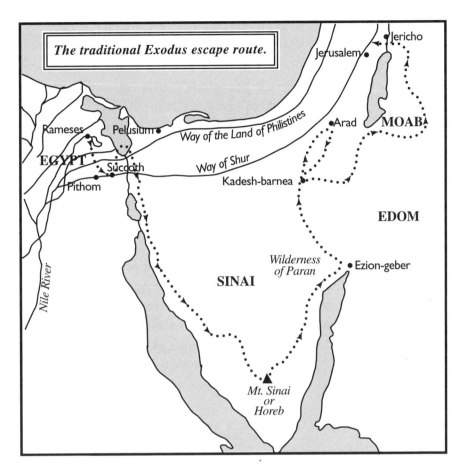

The traditional Exodus escape route.

a purpose. No doubt George was a very truthful person. The story is used to remind us of his truthfulness. This is different. This is sacred history, but a special kind of history, namely, dramatized epic history. This is more like George Washington crossing the Delaware. Some paintings have dramatized the crossing depicting him standing up holding a flag in the prow of the boat and dressed in a clean uniform. In actuality his uniform was most likely tattered; perhaps he was crouched over in the boat, etc. The basic fact, however, remains. He did cross the Delaware. So with the crossing of the Red Sea, the Israelites under the guidance of Moses crossed over and so escaped the Egyptians. Did it take place exactly as depicted in the Book of

Exodus? No, for this is a dramatized epic history. What does the Israelite's passage through the waters involve? The decision of the Hebrews involved two things: a turning away from something in order to turn to God. Recall the whole notion of "conversion"— leaving the known for the unknown. Choice always involves a negative and a positive side. When one chooses something one has to give up something else. What does their decision achieve? It achieves freedom from slavery and freedom for becoming God's people—only now do they begin to be the people of God. Only now are they free to worship God as they wish. The process of shaping them into a people will be a long process, but it has begun.

3. Mount Sinai and the Covenant (Exodus 19 through 24)

The covenant is central to the whole of Sacred Scripture since it unifies the very notion of the Bible as a record of God's dealings with humans. Now at Mount Sinai, God makes more explicit the fuller meaning of this alliance, especially the roles of himself and humans in this covenant.

The Covenant Making Them a People
(Exodus 19:1–8, 16–19)

¹On the third new moon after the Israelites had gone out of the land of Egypt, on that very day, they came into the wilderness of Sinai. ²They had journeyed from Rephidim, entered the wilderness of Sinai, and camped in the wilderness; Israel camped there in front of the mountain. ³Then Moses went up to God; the Lord called to him from the mountain, saying, "Thus you shall say to the house of Jacob, and tell the Israelites: ⁴You have seen what I did to the Egyptians, and how I bore you on eagles' wings and brought you to myself. ⁵Now therefore, if you obey my voice and keep my covenant, you shall be my treasured possession out of all the peoples. Indeed, the whole earth is mine, but you shall be for me a priestly kingdom and a holy nation. These are the words that you shall speak to the Israelites."

⁷So Moses came, summoned the elders of the people, and set before them all these words that the LORD had commanded him. ⁸The people all answered as one: "Everything that the LORD has spoken we will do." Moses reported the words of the people to the LORD . . .

¹⁶On the morning of the third day there was thunder and lightning, as well as a thick cloud on the mountain, and a blast of a trumpet so loud that all the people who were in the camp trembled. ¹⁷Moses brought the people out of the camp to meet God. They took their stand at the foot of the mountain. ¹⁸Now Mount Sinai was wrapped in smoke, because the LORD had descended upon it in fire; the smoke went up like the smoke of a kiln, while the whole mountain shook violently. ¹⁹As the blast of the trumpet grew louder and louder, Moses would speak and God would answer him in thunder (Exodus 19:1–8, 16–19).

After reading the above text, notice the following:

God is responsible for the covenant; he takes the initiative. "I bore you on eagles' wings and brought you to myself" (19:4).

The covenant is conditional. The people must listen and keep their part of the covenant. "If you obey my voice and keep my covenant" (19:5). The whole purpose of the covenant is to make the people God's people. "My treasured possession . . . a holy nation" (19:5–6).

Moses remains the mediator, the go-between; nevertheless, the people themselves must ratify the covenant. "Everything the Lord has spoken, we will do" (19:8) This is the healthiest response to God in friendship. Note the I/you/Thou relationship throughout this passage. Friendship, here depicted under the notion of being God's people, is and must be a two-way street.

In the second passage, Exodus 19:16–19, there is a theophany on Mount Sinai. Here the smoke and fire are a sign of God's presence and power. (This most likely belongs to the Elohist—E—tradition.) The storm theophany is used throughout the Old Testament for the awesomeness and power of God. The theophany is usually a part of the Elohist tradition which stresses the transcendent character of God.

The theophany is an appearance or manifestation of God in character and attributes which reveal his divinity and power.

The People's Response (Exodus 20:1–17; 24:1–11)

The people respond to the covenant in terms of law and worship. In Exodus 20:1–17, we have the Ten Commandments. The Decalogue, literally ten words, are humankind's ten-word response to God. The first three deal with humans' relationship with God and the last seven deal with humans' relationship with one another. The whole purpose of the commandments is to bring about union with God and union with our fellow humans.

The Ten Commandments and the Sinai Covenant

According to the Sinai covenant, the linkage between God and people is lived out by keeping the Ten Commandments. In the original Hebrew text they are referred to as the "ten words" (Decalogue). They are words of commitment to the promises of God and to the quality of relationships people have with one another.

These "ten words" apply to believers who are committed to the covenant even today. In brief, we commit ourselves to have God as our god, not our work or our culture. We promise to take time out for God—that is what Sabbath is all about, for if we always work and never stop and reflect, we cannot nurture our relationship with God, with one another, and with creation.

The remaining seven commandments relate us both to one another and to God. We care for and respect the elderly, for they have nurtured us in the faith tradition. We do not kill, for we realize that we are all made in God's image and likeness, and that to kill another human being is to kill a piece of God. We do not adulterate our human relationships or our faith. We respect the property of all and refrain from stealing. We do not go around falsifying our witness to one another or coveting each other's property or with persons with whom we are in loving and committed relationships.

The Ten Commandments are the backbone of the Sinai covenant. Taking the covenant seriously requires all of us to examine the way we have attempted, or failed, to live the commandments in our own lives. Expressed positively, the commandments challenge us to believe

These modern-day tablets of the Ten Commandments carved in Hebrew depict God's covenantal laws handed down to Moses. They are on display on a wall of Rachel's tomb, located on the road between Jerusalem and Bethlehem.

THE TEN COMMANDMENTS: MANY VERSIONS

The Old Testament provides more than one version of the Ten Commandments. The two best-known versions are found in Exodus 20:1–17 and Deuteronomy 5:6–21. They are quoted below. In addition, there are five other "decalogues" or lists that loosely follow the lists in Exodus and Deuteronomy. These are found in: Exodus 34:14–26; Leviticus 18:6–18; 20:2–16; Ezekiel 18:5–9; and Psalm 15:2–5.

EXODUS 20:1–17

[1]Then God spoke all these words: [2]I am the LORD your God, who brought you out of the land of Egypt, out of the house of slavery; [3]you shall have no other gods before me.

DEUTERONOMY 5:6–21

[6]I am the LORD your God, who brought you out of the land of Egypt, out of the house of slavery, [7]you shall have no other gods before me.

⁴You shall not make for yourself an idol, whether in the form of anything that is in heaven above, or that is on the earth beneath, or that is in the water under the earth. ⁵You shall not bow down to them or worship them; for I the LORD your God am a jealous God, punishing children for the iniquity of parents, to the third and the fourth generation of those who reject me, ⁶but showing steadfast love to the thousandth generation of those who love me and keep my commandments.

⁷You shall not make wrongful use of the name of the LORD your God, for the LORD will not acquit anyone who misuses his name.

⁸Remember the sabbath day, and keep it holy. ⁹Six days you shall labor and do all your work. ¹⁰But the seventh day is a sabbath to the LORD your God; you shall not do any work—you, your son or your daughter, your male or female slave, your livestock, or the alien resident in your towns. ¹¹For in six days the LORD made heaven and earth, the sea, and all that is in them, but rested the seventh day; therefore the LORD blessed the sabbath day and consecrated it.

¹²Honor your father and your mother, so that your days may be long in the land that the LORD your God is giving you.

⁸You shall not make for yourself an idol, whether in the form of anything that is in heaven above, or that is on the earth beneath, or that is in the water under the earth. ⁹You shall not bow down to them or worship them; for I the LORD your God am a jealous God, punishing children for the iniquity of parents, to the third and fourth generation of those who reject me, ¹⁰but showing steadfast love to the thousandth generation of those who love me and keep my commandments.

¹¹You shall not make wrongful use of the name of the LORD your God, for the LORD will not acquit anyone who misuses his name.

¹²Observe the sabbath day and keep it holy, as the LORD your God commanded you. ¹³Six days you shall labor and do all your work. ¹⁴But the seventh day is a sabbath to the LORD your God; you shall not do any work—you, or your son or your daughter, or your male or female slave, or your ox or your donkey, or any of your livestock, or the resident alien in your towns, so that your male and female slave may rest as well as you. ¹⁵Remember that you were a slave in the land of Egypt, and the LORD your God brought you out from there with a mighty hand and an outstretched arm; therefore the LORD your God commanded you to keep the sabbath day.

¹⁶Honor your father and your mother, as the LORD your God commanded you, so that your days may be long and that it may go well with you in the land that the LORD your God is giving you.

[13]You shall not murder.

[13]You shall not commit adultery.

[15]You shall not steal.

[16]You shall not bear false witness against your neighbor.

[7]You shall not covet your neighbor's house; you shall not covet your neighbor's wife, or male or female slave, or ox, or donkey, or anything that belongs to your neighbor.

[17]You shall not murder.

[18]Neither shall you commit adultery.

[19]Neither shall you steal.

[20]Neither shall you bear false witness against your neighbor.

[21]Neither shall you covet your neighbor's wife. Neither shall you desire your neighbor's house, or field, or male or female slave, or ox, or donkey, or anything that belongs to your neighbor.

in one God and reverence the sacred; to take time off for prayer and play; to support family values in changing times; to cherish everyone's life; to be known for our fidelity; to be trustworthy and respect each other's rights; to tell the truth; to avoid covetousness; and to replace greed with the joy of giving.

With the commandments God seals the covenant between himself and his people; they are now one. Whereas with Abraham the covenant was a personal thing, between God and Abraham and his descendents, here in the Exodus the covenant takes on a social or community dimension: it is between God and "a people." God called an entire people out of slavery; the people had to decide whether or not to follow. The decision was not an easy one. They must leave the "fleshpots" (the easier) life of Egypt for the desert and unknown hardships. This decision to leave Egypt and respond to God's invitation is finally ratified on Sinai. On Sinai Moses carried up the peoples' decision: to accept God as their God. The commandments are seen as a way of life; a way of living in friendship with God.

The whole of the Old Testament is a record of how God's people either accepted and lived the covenant "friendship pact" or rejected it. We will see that the Old Testament is an account of God's fidelity and love, and humans' attempt at faith as well as their infidelity and lack of love.

The Covenant Ratification Ceremony

In Exodus 24:1–11, the covenant is sealed in the holocausts and communion sacrifice and in the ceremony of the sprinkling of the blood upon the altar and the people. Notice that these are elements of worship in the text.

The passage begins with the people going to meet the Lord. Once again the people as a community give their response to God. They all answer with one voice, "All that the LORD has spoken we will do . . ." (see Exodus 24:7). This is followed by the erecting of an altar and the offering of a sacrifice. A sacrifice is the offering of a gift which stands for the people giving of themselves to God.

Sprinkling of blood. Blood is a symbol of life. For the Hebrews blood was a sign of life—since without blood a person cannot live; for them blood was a source of life. Blood here symbolizes God, and the life he wants to share with his people (Exodus 24:6). Blood, therefore, symbolizes union which God has with his people.

The communion sacrifice or peace offering—the meal—is where the people sit down and eat a meal in the presence of God (Exodus 24:9–11). The sharing of a meal in common was another way of expressing the bond of union and friendship between God and the people. The symbolism involved here is universal. A meal eaten together has always been a sign of friendship and life shared together. The one time when the family is all gathered together is for the main meal each day. If someone invites another person over to their home for dinner, it is a great compliment. Sitting down to the same table with them, a visitor is made to feel as one of the family; the visitor feels at home as one of them. Here in the account of Mount Sinai, God, of course, does not partake in the meal. The Israelites eat in the presence of God. However, usually in the communion sacrifices throughout the Old Testament, part of the offering would be burnt for God and the rest would be eaten by the people as their share in the sacred meal.

Thus, through these ceremonies of worship, the Israelites made their response to God and sealed their covenant with him.

Summing Up the Covenant

God's role as we have seen in the Exodus covenant is one of abiding presence with the people, active concern in their behalf, and the shaping of this people into his people. The human person's role in turn was to respond to the divine initiative of God's presence and activity through worship and the living of the Ten Commandments.

4. The Test of Friendship—The Fidelity of God versus the Infidelity of People (Exodus, chapters 32–34)

Chapters 32 through 34 of the Book of Exodus deal with the themes of apostasy and renewal of the covenant, better expressed as the infidelity of the people and the fidelity of God.

Infidelity of the People

Friendship with another is something freely given, it is never forced. As with Adam and Eve and with Abraham, so now the Israelites too must prove their willingness to live with God. The hardships of the desert gave the Israelites the chance to prove their loyalty to God and to the covenant of friendship which they had made with him. Unfortunately, however, they did not always rise to the occasion. The incidents of the golden calf (Exodus 32), the revolt against the leadership of Moses on the occasion of their refusal to go into the promised land (Numbers 13–14), and the Israelite's numerous complaints and grumblings are examples of this. They were punished for their infidelities, but in each case they were the recipients of God's enduring patience and unending mercy. This theme of God's fidelity and mercy in contrast to the Israelites' infidelity and fickleness is an ever-repeating one throughout the Old Testament.

The Fidelity of God

God, unlike the human person, is not fickle and therefore remains ever faithful to his part of the covenant. The Hebrews, in fact, had a word to express this: *emeth*, which literally meant "rock" and which came to stand for God's fidelity. God as a rock is firm and unchanging. He is the rock upon which everything is firmly based and founded. He is also rock as eternal and unchanging as the mountains. He never goes back on his promises: He always fulfills them.

The word "Amen" also comes from the word *emeth*. "Amen" is meant to express our response of fidelity to God, our so-be-it, our steadfastness, and our covenant with God.

The remainder of the book of Exodus, chapters 35 through 40, deals with building and furnishing the sanctuary as well as the tent of meeting. Because of space constraints, they will not be discussed here.

The Book of Leviticus: Worship and Holiness

Leviticus, the third book of the Pentateuch (in Hebrew, *Vayikra,* "and he called") is written in a different style from Genesis and Exodus, which were primarily story books. Leviticus is concerned with the laws given by God on a wide range of religious, liturgical, and other matters.

The elaborate laws outlined in Leviticus cover sacrifices and burnt offerings; the consecration of priests; the distinction between what is clean and unclean, including elaborate discussions of dietary laws (Kosher laws); skin diseases such as leprosy; rules regarding purification rites after childbirth and menstruation; the ceremony for the annual Day of Atonement *(Yom Kippur);* and laws governing Israel's life as a holy people; and the liturgical calendar.

Biblical scholars believe that Leviticus was compiled by priests of the Jerusalem temple in the fifth century B.C.E. Most likely composed as a training manual for the priesthood, the book intricately details how to sacrifice animals and the appropriate ceremonies for ordaining priests. The ancient Jewish practice of animal sacrifice, described in precise and elaborate detail in this book, was the centerpiece of Jewish worship for centuries. (That practice ended with the destruction by the Romans of the temple in 70 C.E.)

DIVISION OF THE BOOK OF LEVITICUS

I. **Description of sacrifices from the people to God (1:1–7:38)**
    A. Burnt offerings (1:1–17)

    B. Cereal offerings (2:1–16)

    C. Sin offerings (3:1–6:30)

    D. Guilt offerings (7:1–27)

    E. Peace offerings (7:28–38)

II. **Consecration of Aaron and the priesthood (8:1–10:20)**

III. **Laws of purity (11:1–16:34)**
    A. Individual purity (11:1–15:33)

    B. Atonement ritual (16:1–34)

IV. **Laws of holiness (17:1–27:34)**

While Leviticus is the shortest book of the Pentateuch, it is a very difficult book for moderns to relate to, divorced as we are by time, space, and culture from its world of concerns. There are, however, two themes in the book that need comment: the call to holiness and the celebration of the Sabbath.

The Call to Holiness

In every religion, holiness is central. Properly speaking, holiness belongs to the divine; only God is holy. "Holy, holy, holy is the LORD of hosts" (Isaiah 6:4). The threefold repetition of the noun "holy" is one of the ways in ancient Hebrew of expressing the superlative degree. The notion of God's holiness is found not only in Leviticus but also in Isaiah and the Psalms (see Psalm 93:3, 5, 9).

The claim of this holy God calling Israel to be holy is heard in "You shall be holy to me; for I the LORD am holy, and I have separated you from the other peoples to be mine" (Leviticus 20:26). In the Exodus, God chose Israel to be "a kingdom of priests, a holy nation" (Exodus 19:6; Deuteronomy 7:6). Israel does not in any way win, or merit, or achieve holiness for itself. It is completely the gift of God.

91

Israel is then enjoined to be as holy as its God: "You shall be holy, for I the LORD your God am holy" (Leviticus 19:2). The Hebrew word for "holy" is *kadosh*. It means to be cut off from the secular or profane, to be set apart for a specific purpose—service to God. Persons, places, and things are considered "holy" in the Old Testament, for they are set apart for service to God.

We can discover that holiness has a twofold aspect, one positive and one negative. Positively, holiness involves attachment to God, sanctification, living in a holy way. This involves our worshipful recognition that God alone is the Holy One, and our living it out in our relationship with others in our lives: "You shall love your neighbor as yourself" (Leviticus 19:18). Negatively, holiness involves a "separation from" what is unholy, unclean, impure, and sinful, "for I the LORD . . . have separated you from the other peoples to be mine" (Leviticus 20:26). The call of the Lord to the Israelites that they be holy echoes throughout the book.

Holiness of Time

In addition to its concern for holiness expressed in cereal offerings and animal sacrifices, Israel also had its calendar of feasts to help it recognize the holiness of time. The most important of the annual feasts are listed in Leviticus 23: Passover/Unleavened Bread (23:4–14); Feast of Weeks (Pentecost) (23:15–27); New Year (Rosh-Hashanah) (23:23–25); Day of Atonement (Yom Kippur) (23:26–32); Feast of Tabernacles (Booths) (23:33–43). In addition to these was the especially important weekly celebration of Sabbath.

Keeping the Sabbath Holy

If one starts with the question of why Israel celebrates the Sabbath, two answers can be discovered. The command to keep the Sabbath holy is the longest of the Ten Commandments (Exodus 20:8–11; Deuteronomy 5:12–25), and the two accounts are quite similar until the reason for the commandment is given. In Deuteronomy 5:15, Israel keeps the Sabbath to remember how God had redeemed them from the slavery of Egypt. Thus, the Israelites remember that all their freedom is the gift of the redeeming God. When we look at Exodus 20:11, we find a completely different reason. Israel rests to share in God's Sabbath rest of creation (Genesis 2:3). The Sabbath is holy because God has blessed it, set it aside for a specific purpose as a time to remember God and the goodness of all creation. Keeping the Sabbath is a very sacred obligation (Exodus 31:12–17) because in this way Israel remembers God, the Creator of the universe and the Redeemer of Israel. Keeping Sabbath is an act of memory.

Who celebrates Sabbath? Well, according to the Bible, everyone does: "You, your son or daughter, your male or female slave, your livestock, or the alien resident in your towns" (Exodus 20:10; 23:12; Deuteronomy 5:14). All share the Sabbath rest. All those people whose lives are intertwined with mine—family, household, even aliens are involved. Our Sabbath rest expresses an awareness of the interconnectedness of our lives, with other people, with animals, with the natural world. Keeping Sabbath is an act of faith that our lives, our work, our time are, and continue to be, in the hands of the creating, saving, loving God. Keeping Sabbath is countercultural, for it calls us to be liberated from the tyranny of technology and in so doing we will become holy.

The Book of Numbers

The English title of the Book of Numbers refers to the census of the twelve tribes that opens the book and again closes the book in chapter 26. The Hebrew title, *Ba-Midbar* ("In the Wilderness"), is more accurately descriptive, because the book begins with the decision to leave Sinai and cross the desert toward the promised land. The Israelites finally reach the oasis of Kadesh-Barnea, where they spend most of the forty years in the wilderness.

The Book of Numbers is easily divided into two parts: Chapters 1 through 25 relate how the entire first Exodus generation, which murmured against God in the wilderness and refused to take the promised land, died off, except for Moses and the two faithful spies,

Joshua and Caleb. The second part of the book, chapters 26 through 36, begins with another census and then deals with the new generation that God led toward the promised land under Moses' leadership.

Three important themes are found in the Book of Numbers: the metaphor of forty years of wandering, the actual wandering in the wilderness with its symbolic meaning, and a series of blessings.

For Forty Years

Since, according to Numbers 13 and 14, the people refused to (take) enter the promised land, they are to wander in the wilderness for forty years. The number forty is a very familiar one in the Old Testament, and is rich with meaning. In the story of Noah and the flood, it rains forty days and forty nights (Genesis 7:4, 12, 17; 8:6). After ratifying and sealing the covenant, Moses is with God on the mountain forty days and forty nights (Exodus 24:18). It is during this time of absence that the people get restless and make the golden calf (Exodus 32). After the covenant is renewed, Moses once again spends forty days and nights with God on the mountain (Exodus 34:28). When Elijah is being pursued by Queen Jezebel, he flees for his life and travels forty days and nights until he comes to the mountain of God at Horeb (Sinai) (1 Kings 19:8).

In the Bible, numbers are often not meant to be taken literally, but serve a symbolic function. What would be the symbolic meaning of the number forty? On one level, forty represents a longer period of time. Here in the Book of Numbers (13–14), all the present generation over twenty years old must die off (14:29). But there is more. The longer time has a content: It is a time of need, of struggle, of testing.

In the Old Testament, a third level of meaning appears. The number forty denotes a period of preparation for some special action of the Lord, maybe a theophany, maybe a response to prayer; regardless, it is a time of grace. After the flood in Genesis, a new creation begins; after Moses' conversation with God comes the renewal of the covenant. After Elijah's journey, God comes to him and enables him to return, strengthened, to his prophetic ministry. After the Israelites

94

wander in the wilderness, they will cross over at last to the promised land, "a land flowing with milk and honey" (Numbers 13:27), the land promised by God to their forefathers. It will be a grace-filled time.

The Wilderness

Since the time of the wandering—the forty years—is by and large symbolic, what about the place? Ancient Israel certainly knew the Negev desert and the Sinai desert. But by the time the author of the Book of Numbers wrote it, it had acquired metaphorical proportions. The desert is a place of extremes, where choices have to be made in order to survive. It is also a place of temptations, the first being to stop, to settle down, and not continue. The Israelites did not travel on the Sabbath; they spent almost a year at Mount Sinai, and a good while at an oasis named Kadesh-Barnea (Numbers 13:26; 20:1). But the time comes to move again at the bidding of the Lord.

The second temptation in the wilderness may be even worse than the first. The people complained to Moses (see Exodus 14:11–12). This is a typical response of the Israelites in times of danger (see Exodus 16:3; 17:3; Numbers 14:2–3; 20:4–5), or even in times of inconvenience: "We are tired of manna all the time! We wish we had a tastier diet as we did in Egypt!" (see Numbers 11:4–5). "Why did you bring us here? We were better off in Egypt!"

They do not want to stop the journey; they want to reverse it. It is nostalgia for the past. In nostalgia, the Israelites want to bring the present into the past in order to avoid the future.

Well, the wilderness is not only a place of temptation, it is a place of encountering God and of covenant. In the wilderness the Israelites entered into covenant with God, who freed them from oppression and called them to a whole different view of reality, a new set of values, for example, to worship only this God and to be concerned for the rights and needs of others.

In addition, the wilderness is a place of testing, where the Israelites' fidelity to God was tested and often failed. This is often described as the "murmuring" or "rebellion" in the wilderness, and it started right away, according to the Book of Exodus. What is it that the Israelites murmured for or about? God provides them with wonderful water from the rock (Numbers 20:1–13). They have no food; in their hunger they pine for the "fleshpots" of Egypt. The Hebrew word makes the meaning quite clear: in Egypt, they had pots of meat to eat. God sends manna to feed them. Later they grow tired of the monotony of the manna, so God sends quail (Numbers 11:1–35). The people wanted another leader, one who would take them back to Egypt; Moses and Aaron were the prime forces reminding them of their covenant and challenging them to fidelity (see Numbers 12:1–16; 14:1–4; 16:1–35).

In sum, the Israelites failed the test of the wilderness. They refused to be gracious receivers of God's graciousness. This generation shall not enter into the land, "not one of you shall come into the land . . ." (Numbers 14:29–30); they did not pass their test.

Yet the wilderness is also a place of presence. The Israelites wandering in the wilderness had tangible and concrete symbols of God's presence in their midst. When Moses was "too long" on the mountain conversing with God where he had received detailed instructions for the building of two objects: the Ark and the Tent (see Exodus 25–27).

The Ark was an ornate, portable, wooden box. Its original symbolism was that of a portable throne for God. Israel was forbidden to make images of God (Exodus 20:4–5), no God was conceived as invisibly hovering over the Ark. For example, when the people went out to war, God above the Ark went before them (Numbers 10:33–36). Similarly, it has been suggested that the Ark may have been used in worship services as a "portable Mount Sinai." Just as God had been present there, with smoke and thunder (Exodus 19:16–19), so God was present hovering over the Ark, surrounded by smoke (incense) and thunder (the blowing of the ram's horn or trumpet, Exodus 19:16, 19).

Another understanding of the Ark developed later. It was the place wherein the tablets of the covenant law were preserved (Deuteronomy 10:1–9). Because of this, it is called, at times, the Ark of the Covenant or the Ark of the Testimony (to the Covenant).

The other symbol of God's presence was the Tent of Meeting, also called the Tabernacle. It too was a portable shrine, set up outside the camp. There Moses would go to encounter God, to seek an oracle, to discuss problems, to speak "face-to-face" with God (Exodus 33:11).

Each of these objects reflected a theology of presence in the wilderness; the Ark, more God's presence to lead and fight for the people; the Tent, the place where God was present for purposes of revelation. At the beginning of the Book of Numbers, after the census of the people, the tribes are to encamp, deployed around the Tent. When they are on the march, they are to continue to be, each in its own proper place (Numbers 2:17). Thus, the march through the wilderness took on the character of a solemn, liturgical procession. Both Ark and Tent are visible reminders of the continuing presence of God in the midst of the people. Whether encamped or on the march, they should not be afraid, because God was with them.

In sum, Israel's time in the wilderness was a profoundly important time. It is where they covenanted with God, and where they were tested in their faithfulness to that covenant. The wilderness is a place of extremes in which the basic questions are posed in clear and urgent ways. It is essentially a hostile place, made friendly only by the presence of God and the promise of what is to come. Will Israel be seduced by the idolatry of the past, preferring to return to Egypt, or will they recognize that their whole life is in the hands of God, who cares for them and continues to be faithful to his promises?

Blessings

Another theme found in the Book of Numbers is that of blessing. To bless, biblically speaking, was to set persons, places, or things apart from the secular or the mundane for spiritual or religious purposes. The most famous personal blessing in Numbers is known as the "Aaronic benediction," given by God to Aaron:

"The LORD bless you and keep you; the LORD make his face to shine upon you, and be gracious to you; the LORD lift up his countenance upon you, and give you peace" (Numbers 6:24–26).

Blessings also look to the future, as does the last section of the Book of Numbers. This is marvelously portrayed in the story of Balaam (Numbers 22:2–24:25). Balaam was a renowned international professional wizard, seer, prophet. His fame is mentioned in archaeological discoveries dating back to 700 B.C.E. Balak, king of Moab, is afraid of the power of Israel and summons Balaam repeatedly to come and curse Israel.

But Balaam, though a pagan, speaks for the God of Israel and is completely obedient to the word of the Lord (Numbers 23:26). A pagan prophet ignoring the wishes of his king-employer and rejecting offers of wealth and honor is completely obedient to the word of God.

When Balaam finally comes to Moab, despite some resistance from his donkey (see the hilarious story of the talking donkey in Numbers 22:22–30), he attempts to speak four curses, but they all become blessings on Israel. Balak the king becomes so frustrated with Balaam that he asks him to neither curse nor bless Israel (Numbers 23:25). This does not work, and the content of all four of Balaam's oracles is the same: God has and will continue to bless Israel.

According to Balaam's oracles of blessing, Israel is a unique people that lives apart and has become numerous (Numbers 23:9–10); no harm can come to them because God is with them (Numbers 23:21–23). The third oracle speaks of the fullness of God's blessing, which brings with it life, prosperity, and power. Israel is like a well-watered garden or like the mighty cedars (Numbers 24:6–9). Finally, Balaam describes Israel's coming victories over the surrounding peoples (24:14–25).

In these oracles, God shows that he can even use a non-Israelite to purvey his blessings. The promises that stand out to Israel in the blessings are: numerous people, presence of God, and possession of the land. Throughout all the wilderness period, God has been faithful to these promises, not because of, but in spite of Israel's behavior. God remains a blessing to them.

The Book of Deuteronomy

The Greek name for the final book of the Pentateuch literally means "second law"; it is derived from the Greek translation of the words "copy of this law" in Deuteronomy 17:18. The book does not present new laws so much as reiterate earlier ones.

Modern biblical scholarship views most of the contents of the Book of Deuteronomy as material that was passed down orally until it was recorded most likely in the seventh century B.C.E., lost, then rediscovered, as reported later in the second Book of Kings, chapter 22. A "book of the law" was discovered in the first temple in 621 B.C.E., during the reign of the Judean king Josiah. With the discovery of this book, Josiah realizes that his people have not been following the laws properly. He sets the country on a rigorous period of religious reform in which strict Mosaic law is again enforced. It seems that Josiah's discovered "law book" was some form of the Book of Deuteronomy, probably the middle sections that run from chapters 4 through 28.

Internally speaking, Deuteronomy is essentially Moses' farewell address—actually three addresses—in which he rearticulates the acts of God, solemnly warning of the temptations of the ways of Canaan. Moses pleads for loyalty to and love of God as the main condition for life in the promised land.

Two theological themes emerge from these speeches/addresses of Moses: worship of and belief in one God, and the keeping of the covenant (which will be discussed in the next chapter).

Worship of and Belief in One God

Hear, O Israel: The LORD is our God, the LORD alone. You shall love the LORD your God with all your heart, and with all your soul, and with all your might (Deuteronomy 6:4–5).

This is the Shema, the most commonly spoken prayer in Judaism, and also traditionally called the "Great Commandment." Many Christians may know it in the form that Jesus uses (Mark 12:29), when he is asked which commandment is the first. They may not realize that Jesus is quoting the Old Testament.

In the first line of the Shema stress is placed on listing something Israel rarely practiced. Failure to listen has led to the recurring temptation for Israel to worship other gods. For the Book of Deuteronomy, idolatry, not atheism, is the greatest sin against God and his covenant. The second line of the Great Commandment stresses love. The only response to God is love. Over and over again in Deuteronomy, Israel is called to wholehearted loving response, a response that flows from the very center of their persons, and is manifested in their whole lives (see Deuteronomy 6:5; 10:12; 11:1; 13:4).

Israel is to respond to God with wholehearted love. But what does it mean to love the Lord? In Deuteronomy, love is always a verb, an action, never simply an inner emotion. God's love toward Israel consisted in his deliverance of her out of Egypt, his guidance of her through the wilderness, and his gift to her of the promised land. So, too, Israel's love toward God was to be active obedience in response to his love. But what is the content of that obedience? Concretely, what does God command? All the laws in Deuteronomy are intended to spell out the answer. Obeying the laws is how you love God.

Postscript: Reflections on the Death of Moses, Servant of God

Before leaving our treatment of the Pentateuch, it seems appropriate to reflect on its patron, Moses, who, after God, is the most important character in these five books.

"The Lord said to Moses, 'Your time to die is near' . . ." (Deuteronomy 31:14). Joshua is appointed to lead the people into the land (31:23). Moses then hands on two songs to the whole assembly of Israel; one is a song of judgment and warning (32:1–43), the other, one of blessing on the tribes (33:1–29). Going up Mount Nebo, Moses gazes out across the Jordan to the promised land, a land he may not enter, and dies (34:1–5). He was buried there in Moab, but no one knows where (34:6).

God is, of course, the dominant actor in the Pentateuch, but among human figures Moses is clearly the most important. More important than doing dramatic deeds—like bringing on the plagues or splitting the sea in two (Exodus 14:16), or bringing water from the rock (Numbers 20:8)—is Moses' role as a prophet. Deuteronomy in fact considers him the greatest of all the prophets (34:10–12). A prophet in the Bible is not primarily someone who foretells the future, as in our popular English usage. Rather, a prophet is one who is called to speak for God. This is made profoundly clear in Deuteronomy 18:18, "I will raise up for them a prophet like you [Moses] from among their own people; I will put my words in the mouth of the prophet, who shall speak to them everything that I command." Moses speaks on God's behalf to Pharaoh, to the Egyptians, to the Israelites. Unfortunately, the people do not always listen. They also murmur and rebel. When this happens, Moses experiences another prophetic function. As an intermediary, the prophet speaks on behalf of God; but at times, the prophet must speak to God on behalf of the people. The prophet is also an intercessor. Moses intercedes for the people after the golden calf incident (Exodus 32–34; Deuteronomy 9:7–29; 10:10–11) and frequently during the wilderness murmuring (see Numbers 14:10b–20).

And yet this man, who had a stutter, this prophet, teacher, intercessor, leader, wonder-worker, perhaps the greatest figure in Israel's history, died before entering the promised land! How could this be explained? There was only one possible explanation: Moses was being punished for sin. The only question is: Was he being punished for some sin of his own or for the sins of others?

Deuteronomy offers an answer: "Even with me the LORD was angry on your account, saying, 'You also shall not enter there'" (Deuteronomy 1:37; 3:23–28; 4:21–22). Moses was the Lord's faithful servant (Deuteronomy 3:24; 34:5), but he was not allowed to enter the land because of the sins of the people. He suffered on their account. In this, Moses is very much like another prophet, the suffering servant of Isaiah 53:4–5: "Surely he has borne our infirmities and carried our diseases . . . he was wounded for our transgressions, crushed for our iniquities."

"Then Moses, the servant of the Lord, died there in the land of Moab, at the Lord's command. He was buried in a valley in the land of Moab, opposite Beth-peor, but no one knows his burial place to this day" (Deuteronomy 34:5–6).

For Discussion

1. Now that you know that a variety of authors were involved in composing the Pentateuch, what is your reaction?
2. Which one of the books of the Pentateuch is your favorite and why?
3. How do you react to the all-important role that women played in the early life of Moses?
4. How do the four key theological events of the Book of Exodus pertain to your practice of faith?
5. In your own life pilgrimage, have you ever felt called to holiness or been blessed or involved in a wilderness experience, or called to love God? Describe your response.

For Further Reading

Achtemeier, E. *Deuteronomy, Jeremiah*. Philadelphia: Fortress, 1978.

Bailey, L. *The Pentateuch*. Nashville: Abingdon, 1981.

Bailey, L. *Leviticus*. Atlanta, GA: John Knox, 1987.

Binz, Stephen J. *The God of Freedom and Life: A Commentary on the Book of Exodus*. Collegeville, MN: Liturgical Press, 1993.

Brueggeman, Walter. *Genesis*. Atlanta: John Knox Press, 1982.

Sarna, N.M. *Exploring Exodus*. N.Y.: Schocken, 1986.

3

JOSHUA, JUDGES, AND THE PROMISED LAND

While THE FIVE BOOKS OF THE PENTATEUCH COVER the period from creation to the end of the forty years of wandering in the desert by the Israelites, the books of Joshua and Judges cover entry into and division of the promised land among the tribes of Israel. The Book of Joshua describes Israel taking and moving into the promised land—the land of Canaan. The Book of Judges narrates settling down in the land. What was this land like? How did it look? What did it have to offer?

The Land of Canaan:
A Land Flowing with Milk and Honey

According to the Bible, the promised land was promised to Abraham and his descendants by God (Genesis 15:18–21). Canaan was a very attractive land. The Book of Exodus calls it, ". . . a good and broad land, a land flowing with milk and honey" (Exodus 3:8), and a little later on God describes it, saying: "I declare that I will bring you up out of the misery of Egypt, to the land of the Canaanites . . . a land flowing with milk and honey" (Exodus 3:17). To the spies who were sent to scout it out, it appeared as "an exceedingly good land" (Numbers 14:7). The ancient land of Canaan is what is today the whole Mediterranean seacoast down to Egypt (the modern nations of Syria, Lebanon, Jordan, and Israel). Its cities carried on extensive trade with Egypt in the south and the countries of Lebanon and Syria in the north. In fact, in the Semitic language, the word "Canaanite" means "trader," and captures in a name how other ancient peoples saw them.

The material wealth and architecture of ancient Canaan could be seen in its walled cities with impressive buildings situated along the trade routes. Documents discovered by archaeologists in Elba in north Syria testify to the existence of many important towns there as early as 2300 B.C.E., and the city of Jericho—one of the most thriving cities in ancient Canaan—is believed to be the oldest city in the world, going back perhaps as far as 9000 B.C.E. This thriving economic culture also brought with it religious beliefs, beliefs the seminomadic Israelites did not share. They clashed almost entirely with Israel's unique faith in one God, who had declared that no other gods or images were to be before him. The Hebrews, whose name means "wanderers" or "caravaners," were about to be lured by the religion of the Canaanites who were "traders." The nomads—the Israelites— were about to be lured by the city dwellers—the Canaanites—toward the religion of Canaan.

The Religion of Canaan

Canaan had a rich set of religious beliefs as it had economic prosperity. The basic principle that shaped the religious system of Canaan was the worship of gods who controlled the forces of nature, especially those that affected the climate and annual cycle of rain and drought in the coastal areas along the Mediterranean. In this area of the world there is almost no rain from April until October, so the year is made up of two real seasons, the dry season and the wet season, during which the storms bring rain from the west across the Mediterranean. Almost all of the gods who were important to the Canaanites were gods involved in this rhythm of nature. Typically, their religion pictured the gods as the personified power of the storm, the drought, the growing crops, sexual fertility, and the like. Around these gods and goddesses myths and rituals developed. This can be loosely labeled a "nature religion," with a pantheon of deities.

Yet there is also a cosmic aspect of the religion of Canaan. The gods act on a cosmic scale, directing the fates of the entire created world. The task of human religion then became the need to win favor and bring a favorable blessing and order on creaturely existence. All kinds of elaborate myths and cultic practices developed to ensure the gods acted favorably toward the people of the land of Canaan. Chief concerns centered around fertility of the soil and of the animal and human population—birth rates had to remain high to offset the terrible infancy and childhood mortality rate. Naturally, then, emphasis was centered on performing sexual actions that would bring about fertility by human imitation of divine powers that bestowed fertilizing seed and life on the land.

For Canaanites, this often meant intercourse with a cultic prostitute, many of whom were identified with Canaanite cultic sanctuaries located at Shiloh, Gilgal, and Mizpah. This behavior on the part of Israelites is strongly condemned. Deuteronomy 23:17–18 makes this clear:

> *[17]None of the daughters of Israel shall be a temple prostitute; none of the sons of Israel shall be a temple prostitute. [18]You shall not bring the fee of a prostitute or the wages of a male prostitute into the house of the LORD your God in payment for any vow, for both of these are abhorrent to the LORD your God.*

The author of Deuteronomy, like many of the prophets (see Hosea 4:12–13; Jeremiah 2:7–8; 2:23–24; Micah 1:7), is expressing disgust with those people who had turned away from singular devotion to the

God of Israel to go after the delights and attractions of the fertility cults of Baal, Asherah, and the other gods of the Canaanites.

The Canaanite Pantheon

Archaeologists have discovered tablets listing hundreds of gods worshipped by the Canaanites. A few of these gods are cosmic deities, having responsibility for major forces of nature all over the world. The rest are local gods of a single place. We will turn our attention to the more important ones:

El, the father of the gods and creator of all creatures. He appears as the highest god and final judge in all disputes among the divine beings. He lives at the source of two cosmic rivers that make up the ocean on a sacred mountain far away.

Baal, the god of the storm, who is the day-to-day king of the gods. He controls the annual rainstorm and fertility cycle of the earth, and on him depends the yearly agricultural success. His titles include "king," "eternal one," and "lord of heaven and earth." Above all he is *Alijan Baal*, "Baal the prevailer," and he is often portrayed with an arm upraised holding a war club, the symbol of thunder, and with a twisted staff in his other hand, symbolizing the forked lightning.

Asherah, the goddess over the sea, and wife of El. She does not have a large role in the fertility rights, but she has an important role in influencing El's decisions and needs to be won over to Baal's side.

Anat, the sister and wife of Baal. She seems to be both sister and wife of the god. She certainly acts as a warrior in her bloodthirsty battles on behalf of Baal, but can also be identified with sexual charms. She combines the dual role of a goddess of love and war at the same time.

Astarte, a third goddess, is also identified strongly with fertility rites. Her cult was widespread in Canaanite areas. She shares many aspects in common with Anat.

The three goddesses manifest the feminine side of Canaanite religion, combining the roles of mother goddess, protectors of childbirth, givers of fertility to women, and helpers with sexual charm. Though each goddess has some warrior traits, more often they are depicted as sacred prostitutes looking out of their windows to entice passersby.

The Story (Myth) of the Gods of Canaan

Archaeologists excavating ancient Canaan discovered a series of clay tablets that have on them texts about the role of Baal, the storm god. These texts (tablets) contain what scholars refer to as the *Epic of Baal*.

The story opens with some kind of conflict between Yamm, the god of the sea, and Baal, god of storm and vegetation, over which one should be king of the earth. Yamm seems to gain the upper hand at first and is challenged by Baal to battle; Baal wins. This phase of the story (myth) symbolizes the victory of divine order over the chaotic rampages of the untamable ocean (this may have influenced the writer of the first creation story in Genesis 1:1–2:4a where the first action of God is to tame the unruly waters).

Now that Baal has won kingship he wants a palace to dwell in. He gets his sisters (or wives), Anat and Astarte, to win over Asherah, the wife of El, to his cause. She persuades El, the father of gods and men, to grant Baal's request. El grants it and the blacksmith god builds a fine palace of gold and silver. To celebrate its completion, Baal holds a great feast for the gods in which his kingship is acknowledged. Now order and peace prevail on the earth.

But this is short lived, for soon a major threat looms in the person of the god Mot, the personification of death. He is unhappy that Baal got the kingship and believes he should have it instead, for he is more powerful. He demands that El and the assembly of gods hand over Baal to his power. This happens and Baal descends to the netherworld to battle Mot; but unfortunately Baal eats the bread of death and is overcome. As a result, the earth wilts and fades for lack of rain and the gods go into mourning over his death.

At this point, Baal's sister Anat goes in search of her brother, and with the help of the sun goddess, Shapash, she locates him and somehow frees him from Mot's kingdom of the dead. Meanwhile, back on the sacred mountain, the god of artificial irrigation (cisterns and canals), Ashtar, tries to take Baal's place as king. But his feet are not long enough to reach down to Baal's footstool, and so he is found inadequate. The canals and cisterns will never replace natural rains.

Anat now does battle with Mot and slays him, winnows his remains like wheat, and sprinkles them like seed across the fields. As Baal revives and returns to his kingship, the earth once again flourishes and lives.

A separate incident in which Baal himself fights against Mot ends with both of them still battling fiercely when night falls. Shapash, the sun goddess, begs El not to let death rule the earth, and so El forces Mot to go back to ruling the realm of death (the dead). This symbolizes the triumph of the rains and life-giving forces over the killing heat and dryness of summer and early fall. Baal may disappear each year from April to October, but he always returns.

Whether it is Anat or Baal who actually defeats Mot is less important than the significance of the story as a whole. It dramatizes the conflict between the "wet" and "dry" seasons. For civilization to survive, it is absolutely essential that Baal triumph in the end.

Canaanite Religion and Ancient Israel

The Baal myth and cult of Canaan had its influence on ancient Israel as it entered the promised land, and for a long time after settling down in the land. The fertility rites in honor of Baal and his wives were elements of Canaanite religion that most horrified the Israelites, who had a very strict idea of the sacredness of sex and its connection to marriage. Yet many other practices were shared by both peoples. *Sacrifice* played a large role in both religions. Leviticus 1–8 details the rules of sacrifice for Israel. *Altars* were often similar in shape: the altars found in Canaanite cities had four sharp projections at the corners called "horns," and the Bible describes Israelite altars the same way (Exodus 27:2; Leviticus 9:9; Psalms 118:27). These "horns" prevented the animal being sacrificed from rolling off the altar. Both religions had altars for incense. Both had *temples* made up of three parts: a porch, a sanctuary, and a special inner sanctuary which in Israel was called the "holy of holies."

But Israel condemned other practices they found disgusting. One was child sacrifice, widespread in ancient Canaan. Apparently, parents offered up a small child to be burnt before a cult statue of the god in payment for the deity's aid or in fulfillment of a vow made to the deity. Israel also condemned what the Bible referred to as *massabah*, a Canaanite pillar which was shaped as a phallus or used as a memorial stone for the dead (see Hosea 3:4; 10:1–2; Exodus 23:24; 34:13; Deuteronomy 7:5). Along with these pillars, the prophets of the Bible often condemned Israel's use of "high places," which were raised outdoor altars (see Isaiah 15:2; 16:12; Jeremiah 19:5; Hosea 4:13). The Canaanites had worshiped on these altars.

Other practices condemned by the Israelites from their pagan neighbors included the burning of incense before a female goddess and offering baked cakes (Isaiah 17:8; Ezekiel 6:4), burning incense to the storm god Baal (Jeremiah 44:3), or worshiping the sun, moon, and stars as gods (Deuteronomy 4:19; 17:3; Jeremiah 8:2; 2 Kings 23:5).

In sum, ancient peoples lived with a great deal of uncertainty about the power of the gods, always celebrating their return from powerlessness, as when Baal escaped from the hands of death. They relied on magical recitation of prayers and rituals, and indulged in degrading sexual practices in hope of achieving union with the gods. Israel, on the other hand, with its strong faith in one God who stood above all natural forces, saw through the weaknesses of Canaan's desperate search for security in life and rejected any worship of nature.

The Book of Joshua

The Book of Joshua is the sixth book of the Old Testament. In broad outline, the book tells of Israel's conquest of Canaan under Joshua, after the death of Moses. The book falls naturally into two major sections. Chapters 2 through 12 describe the miraculous conquest of the land by the tribes under Joshua's leadership, and chapters 13 through 22 tell how Joshua divided the land among the tribes and settled all the boundary and territorial disputes. Chapter 1 functions as a preface and chapters 22 through 24 as an epilogue which sets the meaning of these events in a theological context. In chapters 23 through 24, Joshua gives his final words, his last will and testament, in which he exhorts Israel to remain faithful after his death, and has the people solemnly renew their covenant promise to God.

OUTLINE OF THE BOOK OF JOSHUA

I.   1:1–18, introduction: describes the power and authority of Joshua
II. 2:1–12:24, the conquest of the promised land
III. 13:1–21:45, the division of the conquered lands among the twelve tribes
IV. 22:1–24:33, Joshua's farewell address and the renewal of the covenant

---

The "invasion" or "conquest" described in Joshua would lead one to believe that all twelve tribes acted together in a saturation bombing fashion and subdued the land. In the Book of Judges, however, we find that the "invasion" or "conquest" was more like a gradual encroachment by some tribes into Canaanite areas, and that the Israelite "victory" was hardly divine. What's more, the newly settling tribes lived in almost constant peril of being uprooted and dispossessed by the surrounding people—Canaanites.

Since it thus appears that the Book of Joshua was not intended to be scientific history, what was it intended to be? This is best answered by looking at the different traditions in the Book of Joshua and the theology that is being taught.

The settlement of the twelve tribes in Palestine.

Sidon

DAN

Dan

Tyre

ASHER

NAPHTALI

ZEBULON

Bashan

ISSACHAR

Machir

Taanach

MANASSEH

Samaria

Shiloh

EPHRAIM

GAD

(Dan)

Bethel

BENJAMIN

Ashdod

Jerusalem

JUDAH

REUBEN

Hebron

Gaza

Philistia

SIMEON

Moab

Beersheba

You may think that the authors of the Book of Joshua are the same J,E,D,P that authored the Pentateuch. This is not the case. Actually, J and E do not have anything to do with Joshua; P makes a slight contribution; but it is D who makes the greatest contribution. In addition to P and D, scholars posit two other writers contributed to the Book of Joshua. For convenience we will call one G, for Gilgal, the shrine where he likely wrote his account, and the other B, short for "boundary-setter," which describes his principal contribution to the narrative.

G is the oldest source. G could have possibly been an eyewitness to the Israelites crossing the Jordan and entrance into Canaan. As G remembered things, the man Joshua was the prime mover of events, and the former desert tribes jointly accepted Joshua as their new leader. G's contribution to Joshua is the core narrative found in chapters 2 through 9, which describe who did what, when. G is also greatly interested in explaining how various places in the promised land received their names (see 7:26).

B, on the other hand, wrote later than G. His purpose was to establish the validity of Israelite claims to the land in Canaan. As a result, he wrote an encyclopedic real estate record minutely describing the boundaries of land apportioned to the various Israelite tribes. B's account is narrated in chapters 13 through 19.

P, the priestly author, was interested, as usual, in matters concerning ritual, worship, and cult. He contributed the story in Joshua 22 about the "rival altar" built by the tribes living in the east Jordan area. P contributed a few other miscellaneous notes as well to the Book of Joshua.

What about D? D was not a single writer, but a particular school or guild of writers who compiled a general history from the Book of Joshua through the second Book of Kings—a period roughly six centuries in length. The fingerprints of D's writing are found in Judges, 1 and 2 Samuel, 1 and 2 Kings, and the Book of Deuteronomy. The D tradition began writing in the mid 600s B.C.E., and the last D editor wrote in the mid 500s B.C.E. The name often ascribed to this body of literature is the "Deuteronomic History."

D's primary theological interest was to stress the conditional nature of the Sinai covenant. D was the proponent of the "great if": "If you obey God's commands, then you will prosper; if you don't, then you will succumb to your enemies." He ascribed wholeheartedly to God's statement: ". . . if you obey my voice and keep my covenant, you shall be my treasured possession out of all the peoples" (Exodus 19:5). The final D editor, who was writing nearly seven centuries after the time of Joshua, wanted to set the stage for the reader of the Joshua/Kings history which was the concern of the D tradition. D wanted to establish from the beginning that the reason for Israel's success was fidelity to God's covenant; the reason for failure, infidelity.

Thus, right from the start of the Joshua/Kings saga, D sets out to establish the "iffiness" of the Israelites' relationship with God. The two central D chapters in Joshua (1 and 23) are filled with this message. For example:

> [12]*For if you turn back, and join the survivors of these nations left here among you, and intermarry with them, so that you marry their women and they yours,* [13]*know assuredly that the* LORD *your God will not continue to drive out these nations before you; but they shall be a snare and a trap for you, a scourge on your sides, and thorns in your eyes, until you perish from this good land that the* LORD *your God has given you* (Joshua 23:12–13).

The Book of Joshua and the Teaching of Theology

The D editor has carefully woven basic themes of his school's theology into the scenes of the Book of Joshua. We will now look at these themes and compare them with the theological statements in the Book of Deuteronomy, a book D also composed. So with one finger in our Bibles at Deuteronomy and the other at Joshua, we will look at four aspects of D's theological thinking.

God of Heaven and Earth

Turn to the story of Rahab and the spies (Joshua 2:8–21). D took this story from the older G tradition and used it to present one of his favorite themes. In Joshua 2:11, Rahab says to the spies: "The LORD your God is indeed God in heaven above and on earth below." Now turn to Deuteronomy, the fullest articulation in the Old Testament of D's theology. In Deuteronomy 4:39, D writes: "So acknowledge today and take to heart that the LORD is God in heaven above and on the earth beneath; there is no other." We see that D has used the story of the harlot Rahab to teach a core concept of his theology: God is Lord of the universe. He is greater than any "nature god" of the Canaanite pantheon.

The People of Israel Set Apart for God

Now return to the Book of Joshua, this time to 6:17–21. There we read about God's instructions about putting Jericho "under the ban." (The "ban" was a primitive practice of declaring persons or objects as dedicated to the deity and then destroying them.) The reason for the institution of the ban appears in Deuteronomy 7:6:

> For you are a people holy to the LORD your God; the LORD your God has chosen you out of all the peoples on earth to be his people, his treasured possession" (Deuteronomy 7:6).

Thus, D presents the theoretical basis of the ban in Deuteronomy, and then gives a historical application of it in Joshua. D did this in order to teach his people (readers) that the Israelites had to be a people set apart, undefiled by pagan ways. To achieve this, D sanctioned the deplorable and extreme method of killing all captives taken in battle, lest some Israelites should be tempted to intermarry with the captives and be converted to their pagan ways.

Look at All the Lord Has Done

A third example of how D historicized his theology occurs in Joshua 23. There, Joshua begins his farewell address to his countrymen in these words:

And you have seen all that the LORD your God has done to all these nations for your sake, for it is the LORD your God who has fought for you (Joshua 23:3).

In a parallel passage, found in the Book of Deuteronomy, Moses called the people together in the desert to give his farewell address:

²Moses summoned all Israel and said to them: You have seen all that the LORD did before your eyes in the land of Egypt, to Pharaoh and to all his servants and to all his land, ³the great trials that your eyes saw, the signs, and those great wonders (Deuteronomy 29:2–3).

D is telling us here that Joshua, like his predecessor Moses, emphasized that it was God who had won the people's battles for them. D constantly stresses this message. The people had to understand that it was God who was in control of their destiny and not they themselves, and least of all the "nature gods" of the Canaanites.

God Keeps Promises
A final theme that D especially emphasized in the Book of Joshua was that God had kept all of the promises which he made to the people in the desert. Here is a marvelous summary:

⁴³Thus the LORD gave to Israel all the land that he swore to their ancestors that he would give them; and having taken possession of it, they settled there. ⁴⁴And the LORD gave them rest on every side just as he had sworn to their ancestors; not one of all their enemies had withstood them, for the LORD had given all their enemies into their hands. ⁴⁵Not one of all the good promises that the LORD had made to the house of Israel had failed; all came to pass (Joshua 21:43–45).

This summary, which in effect says, "And they all lived happily ever after," is hardly historically accurate. As we will soon see, the Book of Judges depicts a situation that was nothing like D's idyllic description in Joshua. To explain the discrepancy between the accounts given in Joshua and Judges, it is important to remember D's motive in editing Joshua. He wanted to establish the central premise of his theology—conformity to God's covenant laws and reliance solely on God's guidance results in peace and prosperity. He thus presents the time of Joshua as a "golden age" in which the Israelites lived by God's laws, relied wholeheartedly on him, and consequently received abundant blessings.

The Assembly At Shechem and
The Covenant Renewal Ceremony
There is one final matter in Joshua to consider. It concerns Joshua 24, which deals with the assembly at Shechem. The subject matter of this chapter reveals much about Israelite life at the beginning of the period of the Judges. Notice that Shechem appears for the first time in this chapter. In the preceding chapters of Joshua, we found that first Gilgal and then Shiloh were the centers of the Israelite invasion force. Then, suddenly, Shechem appears. What is the significance of this?

We receive a clue by reading Joshua 24:14, 18.

> "Now therefore revere the LORD, and serve him in sincerity and in faithfulness; put away the gods that your ancestors served beyond the river and in Egypt, and serve the LORD" (Joshua 24:14).

> ". . . and the LORD drove out before us all the peoples, the Amorites who lived in the land. Therefore we also will serve the LORD, for he is our God" (Joshua 24:18).

In 24:14, it appears that Joshua is telling the assembled people for the first time about the need to "put away the gods that your ancestors served beyond the river." Why was this necessary? Moses had already taught this to the Israelites in the desert. Was Joshua addressing people who had not been in the desert with the other Israelites? Notice that in 24:18, the assembly says, "We, too, will serve God." "Too" implies here that Joshua's audience is joining the faith of other Israelites who already believed in God.

What is occurring at Shechem is this: A number of Hebrew tribes descended from Abraham, whose ancestors had not gone down into Egypt, are for the first time pledging themselves to keep the covenant, which their "desert relatives" had entered into years before. The biblical, historical, and archaeological evidence indicates that not all of the tribes descended from Jacob crossed the Jordan with Joshua and his band of nomadic followers, because not all of them had entered Egypt in the first place.

Thus, when Joshua and the tribes affiliated with him entered the promised land, they encountered their long-lost cousins from centuries before. These stay-at-home tribes welcomed the opportunity to join forces with Joshua and their other relatives who were now settling in Canaan, and who brought with them the marvelous story of God's actions at the Red Sea in the desert. The native tribes were especially impressed by the ideal of social equality, which grew out of the Sinai covenant. They wanted to be freed from the rule of tyrannical Canaanite despots; thus, they gladly accepted the radical political, religious, and social ideas which Joshua and his comrades imported from the desert.

An important social and political tradition evolved out of the Shechem assembly. According to this tradition, the various tribes were independent, autonomous units of equal stature and rank before God, owing no allegiance to any earthly ruler. "The LORD our God we will serve," the tribal leaders affirmed at Shechem, "and him we will obey" (Joshua 24:24).

The Book of Judges

The Book of Judges recounts the history of Israel from the death of Joshua to the time just before the birth of the Hebrew prophet Samuel, roughly a two-hundred-year span stretching from the end of the Israelite conquest of Canaan, the "promised land," to the beginning of the monarchy, about 1000 B.C.E. This creates a slight chronological problem because the Book of Judges seems to cover four hundred years of history. The book combines a series of tales of the exploits of various tribal leaders. Although called "Judges," they didn't sit around in black robes and decide legal cases. These "judges" may be described as "warrior/rulers," but even that description doesn't quite fit them all. The most notorious of the judges is Samson, among the most famous yet least understood of the Israelite "heroes," whose behavior makes the term "judge" very questionable.

The Hebrew word used here for "judge" is *shofet*. It has been variously translated by scholars who seek to convey a modern impression of what the word actually means. The translation that enjoys the greatest scholarly consensus is that of "deliverer." This word suggests that the true role of the "judge" was not to dispense justice in a legal proceeding, as judges do today, but rather to "deliver" the Israelites from a situation of dire distress.

The judges were ad hoc leaders; that is, they ruled only as long as needed in order to resolve a particular crisis. They were never considered by their followers to be permanent, absolute sovereigns, like the despots and petty kings of the Canaanites. Rather, they were charismatic leaders chosen and appointed by God.

Significantly, no judge ever led *all* of the Israelite tribes during his or her tenure of leadership. Instead, each judge mentioned was a leader in one small area of the land, often at the same time as another judge was leader in a different area.

What is recorded in Judges is a collection of various stories—some from the northern tribes and some from the southern tribes. When the final editor put all of these stories together, the completed version made it appear as if each judge ruled the entire land.

It is important to remember that these deliverers were "charismatic" leaders; that is, they were given the "charism" or gift of leadership by God himself. God imparted some measure of his own spirit to them in order to empower them for leadership. Thus, it was really God himself—acting through his handpicked judges—who saved the people from the various crises recorded in Judges.

The true judge was quick to point out that it was God who had brought success. Such was the case with the judge Gideon, for example:

²²Then the Israelites said to Gideon, "Rule over us, you and your son and your grandson also; for you have delivered us out of the hand of Midian." ²³Gideon said to them, "I will not rule over you, and my son will not rule over you; the LORD will rule over you" (Judges 8:22–23).

In other words, Gideon was saying, "I didn't rescue you from the power of the Midianites, God did. Therefore, he must rule over you." This concept of charismatic leadership was based on Israel's belief that God insisted on relating directly to his people and not through intermediaries, even when, as we shall see soon, he allowed them to choose kings as their earthly rulers. God insisted on personal relationship with his people. He had shown this at the Red Sea, repeatedly in the desert, and now in the promised land. He was a God who was in history with his people. He wanted to be present in his people's lives, not distant, like the gods who were the nature deities of the Canaanites.

Thus it was that the D editor of Judges constantly asserts the leading role that God played in recorded events:

Whenever the LORD raised up judges for them, the LORD was with the judge, and he delivered them from the hand of their enemies all the days of the judge; for the LORD would be moved to pity by their groaning because of those who persecuted and oppressed them (Judges 2:18).

Alas, however, after a particular judge died the people fell quickly back into apostasy: "But whenever the judge died, they would relapse and behave worse than their ancestors, following other gods, worshiping them and bowing down to them" (Judges 2:19).

The core story of Judges is the cycle of infidelity by the people, consequent attack from their enemies, God's sense of pity, his appointment of a judge, and relapse by the people into infidelity after the judge's death. This core story is woven around the life and time of the various judges from Othniel through Samson.

OUTLINE OF THE BOOK OF JUDGES

I.   1:1–2:5, general introduction
II. 2:6–3:6, prologue to the tales of the judges
III. 3:7–16:31, the stories about the judges
    3:7–11, Othniel
    3:12–30, Ehud
    3:31, Shamgar
    4:1–5:31, Barak and Deborah
    6:1–8:35, Gideon
    9:1–57, Abimelech
    10:1–16, Tola and Jair
    11:1–12:7, Jephthah
    12:8–15, Ibzan, Elon, Abdon
    13:1–16:31, Samson
IV. 17:1–18:31, the tribal history of Dan
V.   19:1–21:25, the tribe of Benjamin

What conclusion shall we draw about the message of the Book of Judges? Is it that kingship was the solution to the discord and disunity which permeated tribal life? As we will see in 1 Samuel, many people thought that it was. Yet that, as we will find out, was too facile a solution—one fraught with peril.

At the conclusion of the era of the judges, we find that Israelite life was no different than it had been at the beginning of the period. Enemy armies still attacked on one front and Baalism still threatened on another. No lasting solutions had been found to the problems raised by either peril. Conquest of land by pagan armies and conquest of hearts by Canaanite gods were both still constant threats.

The Theological Significance of the Land for Israel

Before leaving the books of Joshua and Judges, we must pause and consider how important the receiving and taking of the land is to biblical theology.

Israel always understood the land to be a gift from God. Before the conquest, the patriarchs in Genesis are regularly portrayed as landless: Abraham the sojourner from a distant country, Jacob and his family settling in Egypt by special grant of the pharaoh. The patriarchal narratives stress the hope of land as a promise given by God. Yet, as God guides them toward the promised land after the exodus, the conditional nature of this gift is brought out. People must choose between slavery in Egypt or wandering in the wilderness (see Exodus 16–18 and Numbers 11–20).

Again when they are poised at the edge of the new land, the Book of Deuteronomy insists that they must choose their course carefully. The land will be a gift of God, sacred, blessed, and made fruitful, but it will also be a source of temptation to forget God and follow Baal and other pagan deities when the people prospered there. The land would also be a sacred responsibility of stewardship under God. It is the land of the covenant, so that possession of the land and obedience to God's covenant law go hand in hand. Sabbath rest, care for the poor, protection of the widow and the stranger, and keeping the whole body of law found in Deuteronomy chapters 12 through 25 come with the right to the land.

While what has been described above as the ideal understanding of the land as a gift from God, it is important to realize that from the moment that Israel entered the land, the actual history was seen as a story of greed and progressive betrayal of God, who was the owner of the earth and the gift-giver. The D editors remember the time of the judges, for example, as a period of petty strife when tribes refused to bear the burdens of the covenant. The dismal picture of the other tribes warring against Benjamin closes the Book of Judges, and the author adds as a final, very negative summary: "In those days there was no king in Israel; all the people did what was right in their own eyes" (Judges 21:25).

But the same judgment would be leveled against the rule of the kings in the books of Kings, and against the landowners, prophets, and priests in the prophetic books.

In sum, it is not farfetched to say that the patriotic American song "This Land Is Your Land, This Land Is My Land," if sung by the ancient Israelites, is a summary of the theology. For in truth, the land belonged to both God and the Israelites, and while God always kept his promises, the people did not always keep theirs.

According to the Old Testament, the gift of the land was never truly graciously received by the people. It was eventually lost for a while during the Babylonian exile (597/87–537 B.C.E.).

For Discussion

1. How were the Israelites tempted by the culture and religion of Canaan?
2. How does the Book of Joshua teach theology?
3. In the Book of Joshua, why did the covenant have to be renewed at Shechem?
4. Explain the biblical understanding of the term "judge." In what ways are the exploits of the judges of Israel more edifying than historical?
5. What is the theological meaning of God's gift of the land to the people?

For Further Reading

Auld, A.G. *Joshua, Judges and Ruth*. Philadelphia: Westminster, 1984.

Brueggeman, Walter. *The Land*. Philadelphia: Fortress Press, 1977.

Cross, F.M. *Canaanite Myth and Hebrew Epic*. Cambridge: Harvard University Press, 1973.

McKenzie, John L. *The World of the Judges*. Englewood Cliffs, N.J.: Prentice Hall, 1966.

Miller, J. Maxwell, and John H. Hayes. *A History of Ancient Israel and Judah*. Philadelphia: Westminster, 1986.

Soggin, A. *Joshua*. London: SCM Press, 1982.

THE BIBLICAL KINGS: THE MONARCHY AND THE BABYLONIAN EXILE

Shortly AFTER THE ISRAELITES HAD SETTLED IN THE land of Canaan, after the exodus and Sinai experiences, they faced governmental structural problems. Enemies on all sides were attacking. Israel's most ardent wish was to be like the surrounding nations, which had centralized governments. The people cried out for a king.

When the Hebrew people occupied the land of Canaan, they settled in every region. As Joshua, who had succeeded Moses as leader, began to grow old, there was no real successor appointed for him. Leadership in the tribes fell to local chieftains—the judges. Only in times of crisis did these charismatic leaders call the tribes together to fight. When the crisis ended, the tribes went back to their own territories to care for their own needs.

An Experiment in Monarchy

The first movement toward monarchy began in the time of Abimelech, son of Gideon, one of the judges. When Gideon died, Abimelech assembled his tribesmen, suggesting it would be better for one person to rule over Israel. When he received approval for this suggestion, he hired assassins to murder his brothers. Afterward, the people gathered in Shechem to make Abimelech king. Jotham, the only surviving brother, spoke against it. He expressed his objection in a parable. The trees searched for a ruler for all the trees. None of the strong trees wanted the position. Only the bramble was willing to take the job (Judges 9:7–15).

Applying the story, Jotham concludes that Abimelech is not fit to serve as king because he has executed his brothers. If the people make him king, it will be very bad for them. Jotham's conclusion was soon established. The men of Shechem found themselves in disagreement with Abimelech. They began to distrust him because he murdered Jotham's brothers. Revolt soon followed. Shechem was burned to the ground and, ultimately, Abimelech was killed. The first experiment in monarchy failed.

Samuel, the People, and the King:
The Books of 1 and 2 Samuel

Later, the Philistines, a new and crueler enemy, attacked Israel. They came from the north armed with iron weapons and chariots. They settled along the eastern coast of the Mediterranean, west of the Israelite settlements. While Samson and Samuel judged Israel, Philistine attacks became more frequent. Many began to see the need for a more central and unified government.

As Samuel grew older, the people approached him at Ramah with the demand, "You are old and your sons do not follow in your ways; appoint for us, then, a king to govern us, like other nations" (1 Samuel 8:5). Scholars have isolated two sources, which were used by the final editor of the narrative of the foundation of the monarchy. One source (1 Samuel 7:3–8:22; 10:17–27; 12) contains material which expresses opinions *opposing* the monarchy. The other source (1 Samuel 9:1–10:16; 11) favors a monarchy for Israel.

The antimonarchy source reveals that Israel has begun to worship foreign gods. As a result, she has been overcome by the Philistines. Samuel, portrayed here as a judge, urges the people to return to God. They will then crush the Philistines. The people repent, Samuel offers a sacrifice, and the Philistines are routed.

As a result of this victory over the Philistines, the people demand a king as ruler. Samuel's response interprets that request as a rejection of God as king. In return for all the good God has done for Israel, they reject his sovereignty over them by demanding a human king. Samuel continues describing the rights of the human king. He will conscript. He will tax. He will make them serve on building forces and in armies. They will no longer be free. Samuel's words cannot dissuade the people. They want a king to govern them and to lead them in battle.

Having no alternative, Samuel assembles the people to choose their king. They make their choice by drawing lots. The first lot fell for the tribe of Benjamin. The second lot fell for the Benjaminite family of the Matrites. The third and final lot fell on Saul, the son of Kish. Upon hearing this, Saul ran and hid. When found, he was brought before the people, who proclaimed, "Long live the king!" (1 Samuel 10:24).

In the promonarchy source (1 Samuel 9:1–10:16; 11), Samuel is portrayed as a seer or a prophet. A Benjaminite, Saul is sent by his father to search for his asses. When the journey proves unsuccessful, Saul remembers there is a man of God in the land of Zuph named Samuel. So he sets out to enlist Samuel's help.

Samuel received a vision from God telling him that Saul was coming to him. He would become prince over Israel. He would be anointed "ruler over my people Israel," and "he shall save my people from the hand of the Philistines" (1 Samuel 9:16). When Saul arrived, Samuel invited him to dine. During the meal, he informed Saul that his father's donkeys had been found.

The next morning, as Saul was leaving, Samuel took olive oil and poured it over Saul's head, declaring that he shall reign over Israel. (For the ancients, just as the olive oil penetrated into the skin of the one being anointed, so too it was believed did God's spirit penetrate him as well. The one anointed was called messiah, which means "anointed one of God.") Further, Samuel announced the signs that would occur to verify that the Lord had chosen Saul as prince over Israel. As he traveled homeward, Saul received the spirit of God.

There are differences in the two narratives on the institution of the monarchy. The promonarchy source shows that the monarchy is initiated by Samuel, with the approval of the Lord. The antimonarchy source stresses the displeasure of the Lord at the thought of a human king. Therefore, the king was selected by lot, which allowed the choice to fall to chance. Both stress a theology of kingship, which realizes God is king of Israel. Therefore, any human king must represent God's will for the people. He reigns as vice-regent under God, not as God. In ancient Israel, kings were never deified as they were in Egypt.

The two books of Samuel are the primary narration of the appointing and anointing of a king over Israel and the reigns of kings Saul and David. (Another version is found in the books of Chronicles.) The first Book of Samuel centers on the life of the prophet Samuel and the reign of King Saul, while the second Book of Samuel centers on the reign of King David.

OUTLINE OF THE BOOKS OF SAMUEL

1 Samuel 1–3	The call, dedication, and childhood of the prophet Samuel
1 Samuel 4–6	Stories surrounding the Ark of the Covenant in battle
1 Samuel 7–12	God, Samuel, and Israel's decision to have a king
1 Samuel 13–31	The reign of Saul and David's rise to power
2 Samuel 1–8	David's reign as king over all Israel
2 Samuel 9–20	The "succession narrative" of David's sons
2 Samuel 21–24	An appendix containing other David traditions

Israel's Rustic King, Saul (1 Samuel, chapters 13–31)

In the early years of Saul's reign, the spirit led him to serve faithfully as "prince" over Israel. He was faithful to God's commands. As Saul became more accustomed to his position, he began to follow his own will. He interfered with the priests and their activities (1 Samuel 13:8–15), ordering a sacrifice to be offered, rather than waiting for Samuel, as he had commanded. During the war with the Amalekites, Saul explicitly violated the command of God. According to the *harem,* every living being must be put to the sword as a thank offering to God. (This is hard to understand, since God had commanded, "Thou shalt not kill." In this period, the commandments of the decalogue apply only to those bound by the covenant. Enemy nations were outside the limits of the covenant.)

After conquering the Amalekites, Saul spared Agag, the Amalekite king, and the best sheep, oxen, fatlings, and lambs. He would not destroy them (1 Samuel 15:8–9). He kept the animals apart in order to offer sacrifice to God. Acting as a prophet, Samuel spoke God's will to Saul. Samuel told him, "God wants obedience, not sacrifice." Because he had rejected the word of the Lord, the Lord now rejected him as king.

God now commanded Samuel to go to the house of Jesse in Bethlehem to choose a successor to Saul (see 1 Samuel 16:1–13). Samuel obediently filled his horn with olive oil and proceeded to Bethlehem. As Samuel was entertained by Jesse, his elder sons appeared. None of them are the chosen of the Lord. Finally, Jesse's youngest, David, who was out in the fields tending sheep, appeared. Immediately, Samuel recognized that David, a red-haired, fair-faced young man, a shepherd and musician, was the one chosen by God and poured the oil over his head. This anointing with oil marked the elevation to kingship. For this reason, the kings in Israel were called "the anointed of God" or "the messiah of God."

Although David is anointed king, Saul remained. However, the spirit of God had left Saul to rest on David. The remaining chapters of the first Book of Samuel tell of the struggle between David and Saul and the friendship that developed between David and Jonathan, Saul's son.

Saul and David: An Awkward Relationship

Ancient Israel's first king, Saul, had been called by God to be a religious as well as a political and military leader of his people. Scripture maintains that Saul failed his religious mission because of his lack of faith. God then called the prophet Samuel to go and anoint David.

There are two accounts of how Saul came to know David. Hearing of David's masterful skill with the harp and his gift of singing poetry, Saul invited David to his court to play for him whenever he felt depressed. David charmed away the king's sadness and lightened the king's depression (1 Samuel 16:14–21).

The second story is the well-known account of David and Goliath (1 Samuel 17). The little shepherd youth, relying on God's singular protection, used a stone and a slingshot to kill the huge, experienced Philistine warrior. David's fearlessness and courage attracted Saul, who hired David as one of his military leaders.

The brave and handsome David was quite appealing to women. They danced and sang in merriment: "Saul has killed his thousands, and David his ten thousands" (1 Samuel 18:7). The emotionally unstable Saul was consumed with jealousy at such an unfavorable comparison.

From this point on, the relationship between Saul and David was strained and deteriorated. One painful episode followed another. On one occasion, while David was playing the harp for Saul, the king suddenly picked up his spear and hurled it at David. The agile young officer evaded the shot (1 Samuel 18:10–11). Next, Saul promoted David to more responsible military leadership, but at the same time ordered him to go on more dangerous, even life-threatening missions.

Further, Saul embarrassed and humiliated David by first offering him the great honor of his eldest daughter's hand in marriage. Then, shortly before the wedding, Saul arranged for her marriage to someone else. When Saul's younger daughter, Michal, said she loved David and wanted to marry him, Saul saw it as yet another opportunity to control David (1 Samuel 18:20–29). Luckily, Michal really loved David and protected her new husband from continued and sometimes lethal attacks by her father.

Saul's constant erratic behavior also intruded on David's deep friendship with Jonathan, Saul's son. "Then Jonathon made a covenant with David, because he loved him as his own soul [self]" (1 Samuel 18:3). Saul could not bear to see this deep commitment and love between his son and David. The king concluded he must kill David. Jonathan informed David and helped him escape (1 Samuel 19:1–3).

David went into exile in the area of Engedi. In that situation, David meditated on God and deepened his faith. This is powerfully narrated in Psalm 57. Saul, however, would not settle for an exiled David; instead of attending to affairs of state, Saul exhausted his energies in pursuing his rival to destroy him.

At the same time, David never raised a hand against the king and did nothing to actively gain the crown. One day, Saul entered a cave "to relieve himself"—a euphemism for urination or defecation— (1 Samuel 24:3) and then went to sleep. David and his men were in the deeper recesses of the cave. David discovered Saul asleep there. He was tempted to kill the king and put an end to Saul's animosity toward him. But David rejected the temptation, for, by the rules of war, no soldier should murder a sleeping man. He simply settled for snipping a piece of the royal garment as a trophy. He even felt guilty about his action, for one should not touch the "Lord's anointed" messiah without permission.

David retreated to a safe distance outside the cave and yelled to wake the king and tell him how he had spared his life. Saul experienced a temporary pang of remorse and thanked David for his mercy. He made David promise that if he became the next king he would spare Saul's descendants. David readily agreed.

But Saul soon forgot his momentary reconciliation and again vowed to eliminate his presumed enemy. Just before his last campaign, Saul disguised himself and consulted with the witch of Endor about his prospects (1 Samuel 28:1–25). He asked her to conjure up the spirit of Samuel for him. She summoned Samuel from the dead. Samuel said Saul was wrong to have disobeyed the Lord. Samuel predicted that Saul and his sons would die in battle the next day and the enemy would be victorious (1 Samuel 28).

This came true in Saul's last battle at Mount Gilboa. Saul, realizing his imminent defeat and knowing capture was at hand, committed suicide by throwing himself upon his sword (1 Samuel 31). An alternate account (2 Samuel 1:1–16) of his death maintains that Saul asked an enemy soldier to finish him off since he was not yet dead, but in great pain from his self-inflicted wound. Because Jonathan and Saul's other two sons had also been killed that day, he knew his dynasty was finished.

David deeply mourned the deaths in his eulogy, "The Song of the Bow" (2 Samuel 1:17–27). "O daughters of Israel, weep over Saul, who clothed you with crimson in luxury. . . . I am distressed for you my brother Jonathan; greatly beloved were you to me" (2 Samuel 1:24, 26).

David: King of All of Ancient Israel
(2 Samuel, chapters 1–8)

Though David had already been anointed by God through Samuel to be the new king, the thirty-year-old leader realized he must gain support for his crown. David did this in four stages.

First, he went to the venerable ancient city of Hebron, Israel's capital. Among his own people he was acclaimed as king. There, he built a solid foundation for his monarchy amid the clans who clung to the traditions of the nomadic life. Around the cave of the patriarchs, their memories and traditions stretching back to Abraham, David ruled from Hebron for seven years and six months (see 2 Samuel 5:1–5).

Second, David needed the allegiance of all the tribes in Israel. They needed to be organized under one king who would lead them in victorious campaigns against the Philistines and other neighboring tribes. In a series of small wars, the remaining descendants of Saul were killed. Though David was not involved in these deaths, they were to his benefit. He soon emerged as the undisputed leader of a unified kingdom.

Third, David realized he needed a more central capital for its strategic and symbolic value. He envisioned a fortress city that would link the southern tribes with the north. He found exactly what he wanted in the fortress city of Jerusalem, inhabited then by Jebusites. Towering over the midpoint between north and south, the city was protected by the Kidron Valley to the east, and the Kinnon Valley to the west, each valley meeting the other in the south. Heavy walls protected the northern exposure.

The Jebusites were so confident about their invincibility that they remarked to David: "You will not come in here, even the blind and the lame will turn you back . . ." (2 Samuel 5:6). In other words, it scarcely needed to be protected. But the tireless Joab, David's military commander, and his trained scouts found the inner vertical shaft and cut through the rock that connected the city above with the water supply below. Thinking the shaft would never be discovered by an enemy, the Jebusites had left it unprotected. Through it, David and his soldiers entered the city and conquered it. Thus, Jerusalem became the capital of Israel. It became the political, spiritual, and moral center of David's empire, and of the people of Israel, and it remains so today. David ruled from Jerusalem for thirty-three years (2 Samuel 5:5).

David's fourth and final strategy was to bring the Ark of the Covenant—a box made of acacia wood containing the two tablets of the Ten Commandments, and above which it was believed God invisibly hovered—to Jerusalem. The transfer of this most sacred symbol of Israelite religion to Jerusalem legitimized the kingship of David, and spiritually united all of the tribes of Israel. Since the glory of God had often settled on the Ark in a shining cloud, the Ark was the most precious historic link to God's presence among the Hebrew people. God had spoken to them from the Ark. Its arrival in Jerusalem symbolized God's presence in the city of David (2 Samuel 6:1–15).

The Ark had been secured in the tiny village of Baale-Judah. The procession of the Ark of God's glory in the Holy City of Jerusalem was marked by religious pageantry. "David and all the house of Israel were dancing before the LORD with all their might, with songs and lyres and harp and tambourines and castanets and cymbals. . . . David danced before the LORD with all his might; David was girded with a linen ephod" (2 Samuel 6:5, 14). Thus was God enthroned in Jerusalem.

King David had Phoenician architects build him a suitable palace and government buildings. He entertained the idea of building a temple for the Ark, but God revealed to him the singular beauty of preserving the Ark in its ancient style, linking it to the origins of Israel's ancient faith (2 Samuel 7).

As the king aged, reigning over his national state, his military leaders advised him to stay at home, protected from the danger at the front where a variety of small wars expanded his kingdom's territory.

But two events spoiled David's senior years. David committed adultery with Bathsheba, lied to her husband Uriah about it, and conspired to have him killed in the front lines of a battle (2 Samuel 11). The prophet Nathan confronted David with his sin, of which he repented (2 Samuel 12:1–25). David's sorrow is memorialized in Psalm 51, a profound act of contrition.

Second, David's son, Absalom, betrayed him and mounted an insurrection against him. At one point, David was forced to flee for his life (2 Samuel 15:1–23). Eventually, the revolt was suppressed and Absalom was brutally killed. David, a loving father, mourned the loss of his son with gut-wrenching grief, despite the filial betrayal. "The king covered his face, and the king cried with a loud voice, 'O my son Absalom, O Absalom, my son, my son!'" (2 Samuel 19:4).

David had hoped to build a temple, but the prophet Nathan told him that was not God's will for him, but the son who would succeed him (Solomon) would build the temple. At the same time, Nathan assured David of the fidelity of God's promise, "Your house and your kingdom shall be made sure forever before me; your throne shall be established forever" (2 Samuel 7:16). This promise is referred to as the Davidic Covenant.

In the seventieth and final year of his life, the old king's bones were very cold. His attendants brought a beautiful young woman, Abishag, to sleep with him and warm him, but David accepted her only as a nurse.

His final decision on his deathbed was to ensure that Solomon would succeed him to the throne. Of the psalms attributed to David, it is likely that Psalm 23, with words that today console many, would have comforted the dying king. "The Lord is my shepherd, I shall not want. . . . Even though I walk through the darkest valley, I fear no evil; for you are with me . . ." (Psalm 23:1, 4).

David was buried on Mount Zion, quite near the site he had selected for the temple. "Then David slept with his ancestors, and was buried in the City of David. The time that David reigned over Israel was forty years; he reigned seven years in Hebron, and thirty-three years in Jerusalem" (I Kings 2:10–11).

King Solomon and All His Glory: The Books of 1 and 2 Kings

David was succeeded by his son, Solomon. The reign of King Solomon is narrated in 1 Kings 1–10. Solomon was known for an incredible number of things. He made a peace treaty with Egypt. He had seven hundred wives (1 Kings 11:1). He was an astute politician, a competent diplomat, and excellent administrator. Solomon, however, was remembered primarily for two outstanding achievements: his wisdom was legendary and he built the temple in Jerusalem that became the focal point of Israel's religious life.

In the ancient Near Eastern world, wisdom was the quality of kingship par excellence. From his first days as king, Solomon was credited with special wisdom. God bestowed it on him as a gift after a dream in Gibeon (1 Kings 3). He soon showed his ability to make wise decisions in the famous story of how he discovered the true mother of a baby by threatening to split it in half and give a part to each

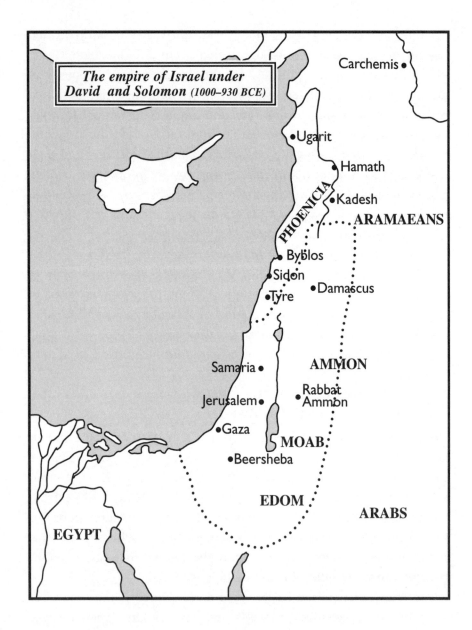

The empire of Israel under David and Solomon (1000–930 BCE)

woman who claimed to be the child's mother (1 Kings 3). Solomon's wisdom is affirmed again when he is said to be the author of thousands of proverbs and songs, and to have knowledge of all plants and animals (1 Kings 4).

King Solomon was also a builder. He constructed the wall around the city of Jerusalem, fortified the strategic centers of Megiddo, Gezer, and Hazon as military bases for his chariots, and created an enormous palace and temple complex in Jerusalem. He imported artisans and craftsmen from Tyre and Sidon who worked for over twenty years with forced labor gangs from throughout the kingdom. 1 Kings 6 and 7 give detailed descriptions of the buildings and their contents, and chapter 8 narrates a speech by Solomon at the dedication of the temple. Solomon was deemed great because he established God's house—the temple—which was the center of the nation's worship, faith, and hope in their God.

Solomon also developed extensive trade with foreign countries and had a fleet on the Red Sea that brought back the wealth of Arabia and East Africa. According to 1 Kings 10, Solomon traded in horses and chariots. Part of the legendary splendor of Solomon's reign can be seen in 1 Kings 10, the story of the queen of Sheba, who came all the way from Arabia to see the magnificence of his court and experience his wisdom.

THE REIGN OF KING SOLOMON	THE BIBLICAL TEXTS
Solomon Becomes King	1 Kings 1:1–2:46
Solomon the Sage (wise person)	1 Kings 3:1–22; 4:29–30; 5:9–14
Solomon the Builder	
Building the Temple	1 Kings 5:15–6:37
Building Solomon's Palace	1 Kings 7:1–12
Building the Temple Furnishings	1 Kings 7:13–51
Dedication of the Temple	1 Kings 8:1–66
Solomon the Ship-builder	1 Kings 9:26–28
Solomon and International Trade	1 Kings 10:1–29

Above all, Solomon's reign was marked by a long period of peace. But there is another side of Solomon which the Old Testament condenses, which may be closer to the real truth. In chapter 11 of

1 Kings, he becomes a tyrant who outdoes even pagan kings in the opulent luxury of his lifestyle with multiple wives and concubines. In this, he violated the law of Moses about intermarrying with foreign peoples. But even worse, he built temples for their foreign gods as they wished. At the same time, he required vast amounts of supplies to feed and support the large bureaucracy he created, and these had to be obtained by taxing the citizenry. He also developed forced labor gangs. But even worse, he transferred rights and privileges from the twelve tribes to the person of the king, and he even encouraged religious practices that opposed the worship of the sole God of Israel.

Near the end of his reign, troubles developed everywhere. The Edomites rebelled, and the Syrians under the leadership of a new king also won their freedom. The Israelites themselves were fed up with forced labor and a major revolt broke out under the former head of labor gangs, Jeroboam.

Solomon died at this moment, a king who had begun with great promise and brought Israel glory to an extent it had never known before nor would again, but who died out of touch with his people. He had become like the kings of other nations in every bad sense, just as Samuel had warned earlier (1 Samuel 8:10–18)—a total master of their lives. Ironically, Israel had received what it asked for when it asked to be like other nations.

Israel's Kings—Another View:
The Books of 1 and 2 Chronicles

While we have centered our attention in this chapter thus far entirely on the books of Samuel and Kings and their portrayal of the monarchy, there are yet two other books in the Old Testament that deal with the biblical kings. They are the books of First and Second Chronicles. They contain a compilation of data on Israel's history made by the "chronicler." These books may be divided into four sections.

DIVISION OF THE BOOKS OF CHRONICLES	
1 Chronicles 1–9	Genealogies and lists, the story from Adam to the period of restoration after the exile from Babylon
1 Chronicles 10–29	The reign of King David prefaced by a presentation of Saul's failure and culminating in Solomon's commission to build the temple
2 Chronicles 1–9	The reign of Solomon centered on building the temple
2 Chronicles 10–36	The monarchy of the Davidic line in the kingdom of Judah to its downfall in the exilic period

The books of Chronicles are examples of "revisionist history" in the Bible. In fact, the two books of Chronicles practically define the notion of "revisionism," as changing historical fact to suit a specific purpose. These books, when read objectively, present some of the best evidence for the multiple—and very human—authorship of the Bible. These are awkward books, difficult to explain away in their numerous contradictions of other biblical materials.

Put rather simply, Chronicles is the Bible's *Reader's Digest* condensed-book version of everything that has already taken place, from Genesis on. It is abridged, condensed, simplified, and a lot of the nasty parts are left out. That is why it is a perfect example of revisionism. Essentially, someone set out to tell the story of the kingdoms of Israel and Judah from the creation of Adam to the beginnings of the Persian empire, culminating with the decree of Persia's King Cyrus that the Jews exiled in Babylon could return to Jerusalem. But the "chronicler" wanted to tell a safer version with some considerable changes in details. These were not small details. For instance, David's adulterous relationship with Bathsheba, a central event in the Samuel version, is ignored, and David's role in planning the temple is greatly enhanced. Solomon's worst excesses are similarly glossed over, and Chronicles dwells on his more glorious achievements in constructing the temple.

The Division of the Monarchy

Solomon was succeeded by Rehoboam, his son. At the beginning of his reign, people were disillusioned with the monarchy. They resented the taxes, they disliked the conscription. They longed for more freedom. So they came to Rehoboam to ask him to relent. His reply was a pledge to be tougher than his father had ever been. The result was immediate division of his kingdom. The ten tribes of the north seceded in 922 B.C.E. to form the kingdom of Israel with its capital at Samaria. They chose Jeroboam, a general of Solomon who had fled to Egypt, to be their leader. The two remaining tribes formed the kingdom of Judah, with its capital in Jerusalem ruled by the Davidic dynasty.

THE KINGS OF NORTHERN ISRAEL AND JUDAH (922–568 B.C.E.)			
Northern Israel (Capital: Samaria)		**Southern Judah (Capital: Jerusalem)**	
Jeroboam I	922–901	Rehoboam	922–915
Nadab	901–900	Abijah	915–913
Baasha	900–877	Asa	913–873
Elah	988–876	Jehoshaphat	873–849
Zimri	876	Jehoram	849–842
Omri	876–869	Ahaziah	842
Ahab	869–850	(Athaliah)	842–837
Ahaziah	850–849	Joash	837–800
Jehoram	849–842	Amaziah	800–783
Jehu	842–815	Uzziah (Azariah)	783–742
Jehoahaz	815–801	Jotham	742–732
Jehoash	801–786	Ahaz	732–715
Jeroboam II	786–746	Hezekiah	715–686
Zechariah	746–745	Manasseh	686–642
Shallum	745	Amon	642–640
Menahem	745–738	Josiah	640–609
Pekah	744–732	Jehoahaz	609
Pekahiah	738–732	Jehoiakim	609–598
Hoshea	732–722	Jehoiachin	598–(?)
Zedekiah	597–586		

The Crisis of the Assyrians

For nearly two hundred years, each kingdom went its own way. There was trade between them, occasional alliances, and even intermarriage between the royal families. During the reign of Uzziah, in the south, and Jeroboam II, in the north, there was again prosperity. However, it was short lived. After the death of Jeroboam II, political unrest gripped the north. Five monarchs reigned during the five years following his death. When stability was achieved under King Pekah, the threat of an Assyrian invasion loomed over the northern kingdom of Israel. The Assyrian empire began to exercise its strength over neighboring nations around 740 B.C.E. Pekah sought strength through an alliance with his northern neighbor, Syria. This alliance was known as the Syro-Ephraimite Alliance. (The largest portion of the land in the northern kingdom originally belonged to the tribe of Ephraim. So many referred to the northern kingdom Israel as Ephraim; hence the term, Syro-Ephraimite.)

As the north lapsed into political unrest, the south—the kingdom of Judah—continued strongly under the Davidic rulers. There was anxiety over the Assyrian threat. Yet the great threat came from Israel and Syria. The members of the Syro-Ephraimite Alliance saw value in bringing Judah into their alliance. When Judah's king, Ahaz, refused, they decided to force Judah into the alliance. This precipitated the Syro-Ephraimite War (2 Kings 16; see Isaiah 7). As the northern armies marched south, King Ahaz inspected the fortifications of Jerusalem and the water supply. The prophet Isaiah met him and informed him not to worry about an attack from the north. Those two countries would surrender to Assyria. He reminded Ahaz that Judah had God's protection, which was promised to David. Isaiah exhorted Ahaz to remain strong in his faith and he would be strong (Isaiah 7:9). He gave Ahaz a sign. A child would be born. Before the child had the ability to distinguish right from wrong, those two countries would be no more. This child was a sign of God's abiding presence in Judah and so his name should be called Emmanuel, which is Hebrew for "God is with us."

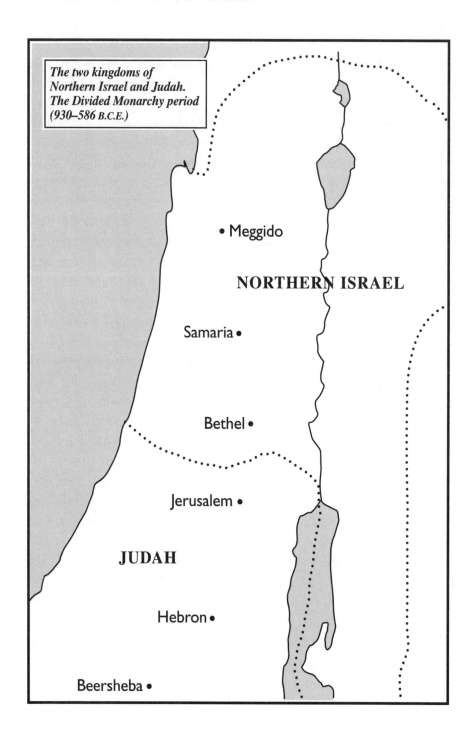

The two kingdoms of Northern Israel and Judah. The Divided Monarchy period (930–586 B.C.E.)

• Meggido

NORTHERN ISRAEL

Samaria •

Bethel •

Jerusalem •

JUDAH

Hebron •

Beersheba •

The Syro-Ephraimite War did not succeed in forcing the kingdom of Judah to join the alliance. Shortly afterward, Syria fell to Assyrian armies (732 B.C.E.). About ten years later, the northern kingdom of Israel fell (721 B.C.E.). Isaiah's prophecy had come true.

With the fall of the kingdoms of Israel and Syria, Assyria prepared to march into Judah. Hezekiah assumed the throne after his father's death. Since an Assyrian attack was imminent, he investigated the fortification of Jerusalem along with the water supply. He protected the water supply by enclosing all areas where water flowed into the city. He also had a tunnel dug underground for water that stretched from the spring of Gihon, outside the city walls, to the Pool of Siloam, inside.

Hezekiah's precautions seemed of little avail, for in the year 701 the armies of the Assyrian king, Sennacherib, swept through the region, destroying every city before them. Finally, the army was encamped around Jerusalem, ready to mount the final attack. Suddenly, in response to Hezekiah's prayer to God, a large portion of Sennacherib's army was slain. He retreated to his capital city, Nineveh. Jerusalem was delivered through the intercession of God.

Hezekiah, his court, and people thanked God for the mighty act of deliverance. The promises to David concerning the eternity of the dynasty, city, and temple were true. If there had been any time in the history of the monarchy when it was close to extinction, it was 701. People realized that God would protect his king, his temple, and his holy city—Jerusalem. A theological interpretation of the events of 701, known as "Royal Davidic Theology," began to emerge.

The unilateral nature of the covenantal promise to David (see 2 Samuel 7) was manifest here. The protection of the monarchy, the city, and the temple were not contingent on the people's conduct. Exemplary behavior did not characterize the people of Judah before the invasion of Sennacherib; yet the city was spared. This would have major consequences in the remaining years of the monarchy.

When Hezekiah died, Manasseh, his son, succeeded him. He was probably the most evil king to reign in Judah. Manasseh's son, Amon, was not much better. Bolstered by the belief that Jerusalem was impregnable, these kings allowed every possible infraction of the covenantal laws of Sinai that could be imagined. Altars to foreign gods were erected inside, outside, and on the roof of the temple. Cults to foreign gods thrived throughout Judah. The cult of the one true God of ancient Israel fell to the background. Festivals, such as Passover, were not celebrated.

No change seemed imminent until late in the sixth century. Amon's son, Josiah, at the age of eight took the throne in 640 B.C.E. and reigned for thirty-one years. He did not agree with his father's attitude toward the covenant. Josiah's policy found support when a scroll was discovered in 622 B.C.E., during the renovation of the temple.

This scroll contained legal commands and sanctions which had been codified centuries earlier and brought to Jerusalem by refugees of the northern kingdom. The document became the basis for the Deuteronomic Reform. When Josiah received this scroll, he rent his garments and said, "great is the wrath of the LORD that is kindled against us, because our ancestors did not obey the words of this book, to do according to all that is written concerning us" (2 Kings 22:13).

Immediately, Josiah began a far-reaching reform to return Judah to the original practice demanded by the Sinai covenant. The favor of God was contingent upon the people's acceptance of the commands and stipulations in the law.

While the reforms of Josiah were being carried out, another enemy appeared in the regions north and east of Judah, the Babylonian empire. As Babylon steadily made its move westward, prophets spoke of imminent destruction to Judah. They employed symbols of cauldrons boiling over from the north, almond trees being cut down, and other similarly graphic images. The people would not listen, recalling accounts of the Assyrian invasion of 701. They could not be persuaded to give up their evil ways. The prophets tried to enforce the stipulations of the covenant of Sinai discovered in the Book of Deuteronomy. They exhorted the people to reform and return to the practice of the law while there was still time. If the people continued to refuse, they would fall before the Babylonian armies. On the other hand, the people harkened to the unilateral promises to David to protect the city, temple, and monarchy. What God had done before, he would do again.

It was their conviction that God had made an "everlasting covenant" with David and his line (2 Samuel 7; Psalm 89) and set aside Jerusalem with its temple as the "city of God" (Psalms 46; 84). This theological view provided a guarantee, or so the people thought, to the invincibility of the city of Jerusalem, protecting it from a military takeover.

The Monarchy and the Babylonian Exile

The Babylonian armies marched toward Judah. In 597 B.C.E., the city walls were breached. All of the learned and wise men, including Jehoiachin, the reigning king, and his family were deported. Zedekiah, his brother, was set up as a puppet king to rule in Jerusalem. The temple was sacked for its gold and silver. Yet the city was spared, the temple remained standing, and the king was still alive. Even this action did not motivate the people to return to the covenantal law.

To show how obsessed the people were with royal Davidic theology, in 589 B.C.E., Zedekiah withheld the tribute money from Babylon and sought alliance with Egypt. These actions caused the Babylonians to destroy much of Judah. Finally, in 587 B.C.E., they marched on Jerusalem and burned the city and temple to the ground. All those who were able were deported to Babylon. Many others fled to Egypt. These actions devastated the populace. The city and the temple were destroyed. The fall of Jerusalem was thus a spiritual blackout, especially for those who identified God's purpose with its preservation.

In the ancient Near Eastern world, removing people from their homeland was common practice by conquering armies; deportation undoubtedly sought to make resistance and revolution less likely.

Exile detached people from their land and suppressed their national identity. The Babylonian exile is memorialized in Psalm 137:1–4:

>¹*By the rivers of Babylon—*
>>*there we sat down and there we wept*
>>*when we remembered Zion.*
>²*On the willows there*
>>*we hung up our harps.*
>³*For there our captors*
>>*asked us for songs,*
>*and our tormentors asked for mirth, saying,*
>>*"Sing us one of the songs of Zion!"*
>⁴*How could we sing the* LORD's *song*
>>*in a foreign land?*

Little is known about the condition of the Jewish exiles. The sparse conclusions that can be drawn from the scant information in the Bible show that the exiles were not prisoners or slaves. Babylonian texts show that they were landowners and businesspeople. They enjoyed some freedom. Jeremiah encouraged them to build houses, plant vineyards, and marry the people among whom they had settled (Jeremiah 29:4–6). They lived in their own communities and settlements (Ezekiel 8:1; 20:1; Ezra 8:15–17). Jeremiah urged them to accept the exile because it was the will of God that they should be punished and await his good pleasure for the redemption of Israel.

The period of the exile is important to the religious development of Judaism. It was a time when ancient Israel's religious traditions were collected and recorded. The codification of the law as it now exists in the Torah (Pentateuch) began during the exile. The works of the preexilic prophets were put into order at this time. Two of the finest prophetic texts, the Book of Ezekiel and Isaiah chapters 40 to 55, were written during the exile.

The symbol of Babylon and most especially the Babylonian exile serves a theological purpose. It is used as a reference to God's just judgments against Judah's wickedness. Despite the profound grief felt by the Jews at the destruction of Jerusalem, the prophet Jeremiah at times refers to Babylon as an instrument of God's will. The text of Jeremiah 25:1–11 refers to Judah's disobedience to God and describes the king of Babylon as "my [God's] servant" (25:9).

The Bible tries to explain the exile as the consequences of Israel's sins. Such an explanation was necessary since the usual explanation for the fall of Jerusalem would have been that the city's patron deity, Yahweh—the God of ancient Israel—was defeated in heavenly combat by Marduk, the patron deity of Babylon. The Bible refuses to accept such an explanation and instead says that the exile happened because of what the people of Judah did by failing to live up to their covenant with God.

To the people of Judah what was so terrible was not just the physical calamity that the fall of Jerusalem and the exile had occasioned, but the religious despair and disillusionment that went with it. Jerusalem was not an ordinary city to them. It was a center of historical meaning—meaning which had been disclosed when God delivered the Israelites from Egypt and providentially guided their history to its greatest fulfillment in the establishment of the dynasty of King David.

The crisis of the fall of Jerusalem was experienced intensely, for they shared in the covenant theology associated with King David (see 2 Samuel 7). According to this theology, the climax of Israel's sacred history was God's choice of David to be king and his choice of Jerusalem to be his "dwelling place" (Psalms 78; 132). It was the people's conviction that God made an "everlasting covenant" with David and his line (Psalm 89) and set aside Jerusalem with its temple as the "city of God" (Psalms 46; 84). This theological view provided a guarantee of social stability amid the disorders of history, when every change of administration was an opportunity for disruptive chaotic forces to break loose. Yet the poignant question inevitably arose: If God had made unbreakable promises of grace to David and had designated Jerusalem as the central place of worship, why did God allow a terrible calamity like this one to occur, which brought the Davidic line to an end and destroyed the temple? The anguish of this question is vividly expressed in Psalm 89, particularly in the lament with which it concludes (verses 38–51).

The Babylonian exile was a radical dismantling of any security in a Davidic dynasty or a God who dwelt *only* in one geographical place. Both the fall of Jerusalem and the exile widened the horizon of Jewish belief to realize that God went into the exile with the people of Israel and could dwell in Babylon as well as Judah. The exile also dismantled the notion that one did not have to remain faithful to God's covenant and raised the consciousness of the people to the fact that there were consequences to their unfaithfulness and sinfulness.

In a remarkable letter to those who had been deported to Babylon in 597, Jeremiah dismantled any hope for a return from exile (Jeremiah 29:4–7). Instead, he urged the people to settle down for the long haul. He even advised people to pray for Babylon—in its prosperity would be the prosperity of the exiles. This advice to pray indicated that worship was possible for the Israelites in the unclean land of Babylon. Jeremiah urging prayer for Israel's *enemy* dismantled the whole notion that one prayed for only oneself, one's family, and one's allies.

Jeremiah's advice suggests that he considered it possible to survive in a land that other people would have called "unclean" (Amos 7:17; Hosea 9:1ff). This survival, moreover, was a long-range proposition. In a sense, Jeremiah said exile should be home, that there would be no revising the collapse begun in 597. The very best "figs" were those who had already begun the exile (Jeremiah 24:4–5). This realistic but radical message had vigorous opponents among the exiles in Babylon.

To sum up, the Babylonian exile was a historical event that reshaped Israel's understanding of her God and her relationship to God. She discovered that as a people she had to dismantle any notion that she had captured God in a geographical place—the temple and Jerusalem—and embrace the idea that God also functioned in Babylon. Further, as a people she had to dismantle any thought that God could not act through her enemies for whom she was to pray.

The Monarchy in the Postexilic Period

The Babylonian empire began to decline after 587 B.C.E. In a matter of years, it fell to the Persians under Cyrus the Great. Cyrus immediately began to return those who had been deported by the Babylonians to their homelands. The Jews began to return to Jerusalem. The leader of the first returning exiles was Sheshbazzar, son of Jehoiachim, a legitimate heir to the throne. Soon after, his nephew Zerubbabel led a large number of exiles to Judea. The initial tasks involved rebuilding the walls and the temple. Most of the buildings in the city and the temple were completed by 515 B.C.E.

With the restoration of the city and the temple, and the presence of a legitimate heir to the throne, many wondered when the monarchy would be restored. Prophets of the postexilic period, particularly Haggai and Zechariah, saw the restoration of the monarchy as imminent (Zechariah 6:9–15; Haggai 1:12–15). However, the Persian government was not so optimistic. Cyrus and his successors were interested in allowing people to live on their own lands, exercise their own customs, and practice their own religion as long as they remained subject to the Persian empire. Establishing an independent monarchy was out of the question. To be certain that any messianic aspirations in Judah did not get too far out of hand, the Persian government quietly removed Zerubabbel and withdrew political power from the Davidic house. That action ensured that there would be no rebellion in Judah and no monarchy.

It was clear to all in Judah that the monarchy would not be restored. How did this action affect the promise of the eternity of the Davidic monarchy? The throne of David did not exist any longer. Local political authority fell into the hands of the priests, while the class of scribes arose as the chief interpreters of the law in Israel. The scribes saw the word of God as eternal and true. The promises of David still were valid. If there was no monarchy now, the promise must be reinterpreted to affirm that there would be a monarchy at some time in the future. The expectation arose that some day, at some time, a descendant of the royal line of David would reestablish the throne. The royal messiah would secure freedom from domination for the Jewish people. This expectation was strong when Jesus began his ministry.

From Kings to Prophets

While the kings never quite adequately lived up to their vocation of being God's anointed (messiah), there was a group of leaders in the Old Testament who were faithful spokespersons for God. These were the prophets, some of whom were avid vocal critics of their kings, such as Nathan, Elijah, and Isaiah. It is these faithful servants of the Lord—the prophets—champions of the poor and disenfranchised, faithful ministers of the covenant, and proclaimers of social justice that we will encounter in the next three chapters of this book.

For Discussion

1. What are the strengths and weaknesses of each of the kings of Israel?
2. What is the religious significance of the king as the "anointed one of God" or God's messiah?
3. How is the approach to kingship in the books of Chronicles different from the approach in the books of Samuel and Kings?
4. What is the significance of the destruction of Jerusalem and the Babylonian exile?
5. Explain how the Babylonian exile was both a spiritual blackout and a radical dismantling.

For Further Reading

Ackroyd, Peter R. *Exile and Restoration*. Philadelphia: Westminster, 1968.

Bright, John. *History of Israel*. (Fourth Edition) Louisville, KY: Westminster/John Knox Press, 2000.

Brueggemann, Walter. *David's Truth in Israel's Imagination and Memory.* Philadelphia: Fortress Press, 1985.

Conroy, Charles. *1–2 Samuel, 1–2 Kings.* Wilmington, DE: Michael Glazier, 1983.

Fretheim, Terence E. *First and Second Kings.* Louisville: Westminster/John Knox, 1999.

Gunn, D. M. *The Fate of King Saul.* Sheffield, England: Sheffield Academic Press, 1980.

Japhet, S. *I and II Chronicles.* Louisville, KY: Westminster/John Knox Press, 1993.

Provan, I. W. *1 and 2 Kings.* (New International Bible) Peabody, MA: Hendrickson Publishers, 1996.

5

"THUS SAYS THE LORD": INTRODUCING THE PROPHETS

A FEW YEARS AGO, WHILE VISITING CHICAGO, I happened to wander into a store that displayed a wonderful collection of posters. There was one hanging above the entrance which the artist had entitled "The Making of a Prophet." It was a humorous scene depicting a scrawny lad almost knocked flat by what was happening to him. With his knees sagging, his mouth agape, and his eyes nearly bulging out of his head, he was gazing up at a cloud suspended overhead out of which lightening was flashing. In the center of a cloud, one could make out an eye, and surmise a voice was radiating from the mist. Transfixing the newly made "prophet," the voice boomed out, "Well, then, my son, having said yes, how would you like to have your goose cooked now?"

While the poster and its quip do not represent a verbatim account of any specific making of a prophet, at least as the Bible records it, the poster does depict some of the aspects that surround the summoning of biblical prophets.

Another story may be helpful. This one is from the "Peanuts" cartoon strip.

In the first frame, we see Charlie Brown, and Charlie Brown says, "When I grow up, I will be a great prophet. I will speak profound truths, but nobody will listen to me."

In the second frame, Lucy says to Charlie Brown, "If you know ahead of time that no one is going to listen to you, why speak?"

Then, in the last frame, Charlie Brown says, "We prophets are very stubborn."

Once again, such a cartoon does not adequately describe a prophet, nonetheless it does reveal another aspect of biblical prophets, their tenacity for their vocation.

Finally, when reflecting on biblical prophets, a rabbinic story is in order. A rabbinic student came to a very holy rabbi and asked the rabbi, "How can I tell a true prophet from a false one?" The rabbi turned to the student with a look that would have killed seven choirs of archangels, and said in a bellowing voice, "A false prophet is one who makes you feel good about the way you practice your faith; a true prophet will make you feel very uncomfortable. Listen to him!"

The Meaning of the Term "Prophet"

The primary street meaning of the term "prophet" in English is "predictor," so we think of a prophet as one who predicts the future. This is tremendously *misleading* when applied to the Bible, especially the Old Testament.

In Hebrew, the word for "prophet" is *nabi*. The origin of the Hebrew word is uncertain; scholars agree that *nabi* is derived from an ancient Akkadian word meaning "one who is sent" or "one who is a spokesperson." The prophet as *nabi* is a person who is chosen and sent by another as their spokesperson. The prophet in Israel is, therefore, one who is chosen and sent by God to communicate his message.

A second Hebrew word *ro'eh*, meaning "seer," is used in the Hebrew Bible to describe prophets. This term does not occur as frequently as the term *nabi*. Yet some prophets were designated *ro'eh* (seer). As a result, emphasis on the prophet as one who could foretell the future developed. It should be emphasized that foretelling the future is *not* the essential component of prophecy. The prophet, *nabi*, essentially communicated God's message to the people in the present. The essential prophetic word is addressed to the present.

In the Septuagint, which is the Greek translation of the original Hebrew Old Testament, the Hebrew word *nabi* is always translated by the Greek word *prophetes*. The Greek noun *prophetes* comes from a Greek verb, *phemi*, meaning "to say" or "to speak" plus the prefix "pro." This prefix "pro" is *not* temporal—in the sense of foretell—but substantive, in the sense of "to speak in the place of" or "in the name of another." Thus, the Greek word *prophetes*, which we translate in English "prophet" means one who speaks in the place of another, or for another. The Old Testament prophet, then, is a spokesperson, or a herald, who speaks in the name of God; or he or she is one called by God to be God's spokesperson. A biblical prophet, then, technically speaking, is one who speaks for God. He or she is God's ambassador. Thus, biblically speaking, it is incorrect to understand a prophet as one who predicts or foretells the future. Prophets were religious leaders who spoke on behalf of God.

In the Old Testament, a prophet was a man or woman of faith who spoke for God. He or she passed on to the people a message which he or she had received from God. The prophet could speak of God in the first person. Thus, in the Hebrew language and in the Old Testament we have a formal phrase used by the prophets; the phrase is "thus says the Lord . . ." and sometimes "thus says God . . .". To see how often this phrase is used by a prophet, look at the following passages from the Book of Amos: 1:3; 1:6; 1:9; 1:11; 1:13; 2:1; 2:4; 2:6.

This phrase, "thus says the Lord," comes from the diplomatic language of the ancient Near Eastern world. It was the formula used by the ambassador of a king; he came to speak, not in his own name, but to deliver the message confided to him by his king. Thus, the prophets in the Old Testament, like ambassadors, spoke for the Lord, for God.

Prophet as Ambassador(s)

In the time of ancient Israel, the normal means of communicating over long distances was by means of a human messenger. We have a number of good examples of this in the pages of the Old Testament. One example involves Jacob and his clan, who are about to pass through a territory belonging to Jacob's brother, Esau. The two brothers had been at odds since Jacob cheated Esau out of his birthright (see Genesis 27:1–45), and now Jacob is a bit apprehensive about crossing over Esau's land, so he sends messengers:

> ³Jacob sent messengers before him to his brother Esau in the land of Seir, the country of Edom, ⁴instructing them, "Thus you shall say to my lord Esau: Thus says your servant Jacob, 'I have lived with Laban as an alien, and stayed until now; ⁵and I have oxen, donkeys, flocks, male and female slaves; and I have sent to tell my lord, in order that I may find favor in your sight' " (Genesis 32:3–5).

What is of interest is the way in which the messengers were told to introduce their message. When they arrived before Esau, they would begin, "Thus says your servant Jacob." They spoke on behalf of Jacob.

Another example shows us how messages were sent between nations. The ancient Israelites were being harassed by their Ammonite neighbors. They asked a seasoned warrior named Jephthah to be their leader, hoping he could bring an end to the Ammonite raids. There follows an account of the sending of messengers. When they arrived at the court of the king of Ammon, the messengers introduced their message with, "Thus says Jephthah. . . ."

The message concludes, "It is not I who have sinned against you . . ."—the "I" here being the "I" of the message sender, Jephthah himself (Judges 11:12–27).

Finally, during the reign of King Hezekiah and the ministry of the prophet Isaiah, when Jerusalem was under siege, Sennacherib (king of Assyria) sent three of his military officials to try to convince King Hezekiah to surrender Jerusalem without a fight. These three are met by members of Hezekiah's council. One of the king of Assyria's ambassadors (representatives) says to them:

> [19]Then the Rabshakeh said to them, *"Say to Hezekiah: Thus says the great king, the king of Assyria: On what do you base this confidence of yours? [20]Do you think that mere words are strategy and power for war? On whom do you now rely that you have rebelled against me?"* (2 Kings 18:19–20).

In a second speech, the king's ambassador (representative) says:

> [28]Then the Rabshakeh stood and called out in a loud voice in the language of Judah, *"Hear the word of the great king, the king of Assyria! [29]Thus says the king: 'Do not let Hezekiah deceive you, for he will not be able to deliver you out of my hand' "*
> (2 Kings 18:28–29).

Again, we hear the expression "thus says the great king," and we see that the "I" of the messenger's speech is really the "I" of the message sender—the great king.

In considering these biblical examples of message sending, we note the following:

1. The phrase "thus says X" is frequently used to begin the message, with X indicating the message sender.

2. The "I" of the messenger's speech is the "I" of the message sender. For example, "thus says your servant Jacob (Genesis 32:3–5), "thus says Jephthah" (Judges 11:15), "thus says the great king" (2 Kings 18:19–20).

155

3. It seems that the messenger apparently had a degree of freedom in the formulation of the message. We might imagine that the Asyrian representative was told by his king, "Get Hezekiah to stop rebelling and start acting like an obedient Assyrian vassal again!" That was the gist of the message. The actual formulation and delivery of the message was the task of the messenger himself. In other words, he was more an ambassador than a letter carrier or a United Parcel Service or a Federal Express delivery person, with his own personality playing a role in the formulation of the message.

4. The authority behind the message rested with the message sender. The messenger in the ancient world, like our modern-day ambassador, had credentials and was given a certain respect. He was also granted a certain protection because of the one whom he represented.

Possibly, a simple illustration at this point will help to clarify the position of the messenger. I remember many years ago, when I taught high school, trying to work in my office but being disturbed by a loud game of touch football that was being played on the high school lawn. I asked a young freshman to run out and tell them to keep the noise down. I heard the outside door to the school slam, but then it opened again, with no change in the noise. "They won't stop!" the student informed me. Then I said, "You go back out there and tell them that I said they should stop the noise, and right now!" Then the freshman, no longer appeared in the role of a harmless underclassman, but as a duly commissioned representative of a somewhat higher power. When he said my title (at that time the assistant principal) says, "stop the noise . . ." (thus says the teacher), the noise stopped because now the messenger spoke as one who had been given some authority.

But what, you might well ask, has this to do with the prophets? As we listen to their voices, we hear one expression repeated time and again. When King Ahab illegally annexed the vineyard of Naboth to his property, Elijah marched right in to criticize the king and said, "Thus says the LORD" (1 Kings 21:19). When Amos preached his sermon against Israel's neighbors and then against Israel, he began each section with "Thus says the LORD" (Amos 1:3, 6, 9, 11, 13; 2:1, 4, 6). When Elisha confronted the kings of Israel, Judah, and Edom, he said, "Thus says the LORD" (2 Kings 3:16). We hear the same formula in the preaching of Isaiah, "Thus says the LORD" (Isaiah 7:7; 10:24; 22:15), Jeremiah (2:2; 5:9, 15; 6:16), Ezekiel (2:4; 3:11; 5:5), and with some variations throughout the prophetic books. We recognize this, "Thus says the Lord," as the "thus says X" formula used by the messenger in the ancient world. The prophet appears in the role of a messenger, a messenger from God and for God. The "I" of his message is the "I" of the message sender, God.

As messengers from God, the prophets enjoyed certain respect and protection because they represented and were empowered by a person greater than themselves—God. Thus, a prophet like Nathan, for example, could walk into the court of King David and accuse him of murder and adultery. What gave Nathan this kind of authority? His only credentials were, "Thus says the LORD" (2 Samuel 7; 12). Or Amos could walk into the royal sanctuary at Bethel and confront the priest, Amaziah, with the eventual exile of Israel to Babylon by a simple quote, "Thus says the LORD" (Amos 7:17). Further, Jeremiah could stand in Jerusalem, accuse the citizenry of breaking God's commandments, and then announce that the temple was going to be destroyed (Jeremiah 7:1–15; 26). This sounded very much like heresy and treason to Jeremiah's contemporaries, and we might have expected a lynching. But the prophet Jeremiah was given a trial. His accusers said, "This man deserves the sentence of death because he has prophesied against this city, as you have heard with your own ears" (Jeremiah 26:11). His only defense was, "It is the LORD who sent me" (Jeremiah 26:12–15), and the political leaders recognized that the messenger of God had the right to deliver the message entrusted to him: "This man does not deserve the sentence of death, for he has spoken to us in the name of the LORD our God" (Jeremiah 26:16).

Thus, a prophet came to speak not in his own name, but to deliver the message confided to him by his Lord. The prophets in the Old Testament did not speak on their own authority, but on delegated authority—the authority given them by God.

The Vocation of the Prophets

All the biblical prophets felt called by God. One common characteristic was their absolute belief and assurance that God had called them personally into God's service.

Even a cursory reading of the prophetic books reveals that specific calls came to various prophets in widely diversified ways. Isaiah, for instance, heard God's call for a messenger during a temple service (Isaiah 6:1–8). Jeremiah understood himself to have been selected by God before his conception to be "a prophet to the nations" (Jeremiah 1:5). Amos was a rancher and tender of sycamore trees whom God ordered to prophesy (Amos 7:14–15). Samuel was a youth living in the temple sanctuary at Shiloh when he was called by God to be God's prophet (1 Samuel 3). Hosea's call came through his personal marital crisis (Hosea 1:1–3).

The pattern that emerges is that each prophet understood his or her vocation to have been a divine one. There seems to have been three essential elements in the call or vocation of a prophet. (1) The prophet seems to have had a vision or an audition with or from God; (2) God communicates his word or message to the prophet; and (3) The prophet was officially empowered by God to pass this word or message on to the people.

Generally, the prophets were laypersons. Also, women such as Miriam (Exodus 15:20), Deborah (Judges 4:4), and Huldah (II Kings 22:14) functioned as prophetesses. The prophetess Miriam danced and revealed the joy of the Exodus event (Exodus 15:20). Deborah the prophetess (Judges 4:1–5:31) was a valiant warrior, while Huldah the prophetess was consulted by King Josiah (2 Kings 22:14–20) about the importance and meaning of a book found in the temple.

Apparently, not many of the biblical prophets had easy lives. Elijah sat down under a broom tree and asked that he might die: ". . . Oh, Lord, take away my life . . ." (1 Kings 19:4). Similar sentiments are shared by Jonah, "And now, O Lord, please take my life from me, for it is better for me to die than to live" (Jonah 4:3). Hosea's marriage was torn by the adultery of his wife. Amos faced opposition from the priest, Amaziah, who charged the prophet with sedition before the king (Amos 7:10). Jeremiah was ostracized by his contemporaries, forcing him to lament his loneliness (Jeremiah 12:7–11). Later, he was publicly humiliated and branded as a traitor, being thrust into prison for his efforts at saving the nation. A prophet named Uriah fared even worse. He was put to death by King Jehoiakim (Jeremiah 26:20–24).

The lives of the prophets were probably difficult because the message God delivered through them placed them frequently in roles that were in opposition to those of their contemporaries. The prophets were the conscience of ancient Israel. Prophets were and are men and women of faith who read the signs of the times in light of faith and called or will call the believing community to a response in faith. It is a mistake, therefore, to depict the prophets as wild-eyed loners standing outside the fellowship of the believing community, addressing an "alien" group. Actually, the prophets saw themselves as belonging to the people to whom they were called to minister. While roaring like lions for change within society and in individual lives, their den was always the religious community they were challenging. For it was the religious community, despite its shortcomings, sins, warts, distortions, and failures, which in fact produced the very ones God called to be God's prophetic messengers!

What the Prophets Taught

No one can summarize adequately everything that the prophets taught. However, one can cull some basic attitudes or insights about the prophets' teachings. The prophets taught belief in and worship of one God; total loyalty to the covenant made between God and his people, and a real concern for social justice.

Belief in One God

If there is one passage that sums up the prophets' understanding of God, it is found in Deuteronomy 6:4–5:

> ⁴*Hear, O Israel: The* LORD *is our God, the Lord alone.* ⁵*You shall love the* LORD *your God with all your heart, and with all your soul, and with all your might.*

The prophets were concerned that the people never forget this. The prophets were strict monotheists. They inveighed heavily against all forms and practices of polytheism.

Loyalty to the Covenant

With regard to the covenant, prophets were its champions. Covenant is a sacred bond between two parties, either between human beings or between God and human beings, between the immortal and the mortal. Covenant is an intimate relationship between God and God's people, as intimate as the relationship between spouses.

Commitment to and belief in the covenant was one of the main thrusts of the message of the prophets. Amos proclaimed doom for those who transgressed the covenant by dishonesty, lust, hypocritical behavior, false worship, and other ethical deviance. Hosea bore the same message but presented it in poignant, passionate terms. He showed that the covenant bond between God and humankind was as intimate, as sacred, and as inviolable as wedlock between man and woman. Hosea vividly portrayed in his own life the story of God striving to reconcile the rebellious covenant partner (Israel) when, at God's command, he took back his wife, Gomer, who had been a prostitute. Prostitution was for Hosea a metaphor for worshiping the false gods of the Canaanite fertility cults.

Jeremiah talks about the need for an interiorization of the covenant.

> ³¹*The days are surely coming, says the* LORD*, when I will make a new covenant with the house of Israel and the house of Judah.* ³²*It*

will not be like the covenant that I made with their ancestors when I took them by the hand to bring them out of the land of Egypt—a covenant that they broke, though I was their husband, says the LORD. *[33]But this is the covenant that I will make with the house of Israel after those days, says the* LORD: *I will put my law within them, and I will write it on their hearts; and I will be their God, and they shall be my people. [34]No longer shall they teach one another, or say to each other, "Know the* LORD," *for they shall all know me, from the least of them to the greatest, says the* LORD; *for I will forgive their iniquity, and remember their sin no more* (Jeremiah 31:31–34).

Social Justice

With regard to social justice, the prophet Amos thunders, "But let justice roll down like waters, and righteousness like an ever-flowing stream" (Amos 5:24). Micah puts it this way:

He has told you, O mortal, what is good; and what does the LORD *require of you but to do justice, and to love kindness, and to walk humbly with your God?* (Micah 6:8).

An important response to social justice preached by the prophets is a special concern for the powerless, including the widow, the orphan, the poor, the stranger, and the aged. If these were forgotten, the prophets, the conscience of ancient Israel, trumpeted God's concern and love:

[6]Thus says the LORD . . . *[7]they who trample the head of the poor into the dust of the earth, and push the afflicted out of the way; . . . [13]So, I will press you down in your place, just as a cart presses down when it is full of sheaves* (Amos 2:6, 7, 13).

According to the prophets, one does justice when he or she acts on behalf of the powerless. In the Bible, "justice" is not just an intellectual affirmation of fairness and equality for all. It is a behavior! It is imitative of the behavior of God, who is justice personified. Doing justice, then, is the response of the people of God to what God has done for them.

What the prophets taught can be summed up as follows. Basically, they call for commitment to God, no matter what the demands. One had to forego the attractions of the sensuous fertility cults. One must never use the poor or defenseless or anyone for his or her own enrichment. Further, no one is beyond God's rebuke, whether he be king or layperson. Finally, one had to trust in God when all human prudence cried out that one should seek the opposite.

How the Prophets Taught

Although we discover the prophetic message in the prophetic books of the Bible, the message started with preaching. The prophets were also teachers. But they did not teach by word alone. They also taught by actions. These symbolic actions include, among others, the contest between Elijah and the prophets of Baal at Mount Carmel (1 Kings 18:20–40), Jeremiah's placing of an oxen's yoke around his neck, symbolizing the coming of the Babylonian exile (Jeremiah 27:2), and Isaiah's walking around Jerusalem naked and barefoot as a sign (Isaiah 20:3). In short, as teachers, the prophets believed in the old adage that actions speak louder than words.

The prophets also taught by criticizing the form that worship took, criticizing the nation, criticizing the king, and the people. The prophet Nathan criticized David; the prophet Samuel criticized King Saul. The prophet Elijah criticized King Ahab and Queen Jezebel. The prophets Isaiah and Zephaniah criticized the form that worship took and the priests. Amos criticized the rich who oppressed the poor.

We are challenged by the biblical prophets to discover as they did our vocation is from God and that, as such, we are God's spokespersons. Our lives may not be easy, but, like the prophets, we are called to witness in our lifestyle and through our teaching to this one true God, who has entered into covenant with us and, as God's covenant partners, to work for justice in the world. We are challenged to become God's voice speaking in the world today so as to prepare the way of the Lord.

The Books of the Literary Prophets

The message of the literary prophets—those who have books in the Bible named after them—are contained in fifteen books of the Old Testament. Three of the books, Isaiah, Jeremiah, and Ezekiel, are longer than the remaining twelve. Since these books were originally preserved as scrolls, such scrolls were of a particular length, not too long, not too short. Each of the longer books (Isaiah, Jeremiah, Ezekiel) represents approximately the amount of writing that could easily be contained in one of these scrolls. The shorter books too were originally written on scrolls, not individually, however, but together on a single scroll. Because this scroll contained the writings of twelve prophets, they were known as the Scroll of the Twelve. Initially, then, there were four prophetic scrolls: Isaiah, Jeremiah, Ezekiel (often referred to as the major prophets), and the Scroll of the Twelve (often referred to as the minor prophets). These are the prophetic books that we encounter in our Bibles.

Biblical scholars delineate the Old Testament prophets in relationship to the Babylonian exile (597/87–537 B.C.E.). The following illustrations provide a quick view of this approach.

THE PREEXILE PROPHETS

Prophet	Date (B.C.E.)	Place and Reigning Monarch(s)
Amos	c. 760-750	Israel under Jeroboam II
Hosea	c. 745	Israel under Jeroboam II
Isaiah	c. 742-701	Judah under Uzziah, Jotham, Ahaz, and Hezekiah
Micah	c. 750	Judah under Jotham, Ahaz, Hezekiah
Nahum	c. 625-710	Judah under Josiah
Zephaniah	c. 621	Judah under Josiah
Habakkuk	c. 615-598	Judah
Jeremiah	c. 627-587	Judah to the fall of Jerusalem

THE POSTEXILE PROPHETS

Prophet	Date (B.C.E.)	Place and Reigning Monarch(s)
Ezekiel	c. 597–563	Babylonian Exile
Haggai	c. 520	Jerusalem in the postexilic period
Zechariah	c. 520–518	Jerusalem in the postexilic period
Malachi	c. 460–450	Jerusalem after the empire is rebuilt
Obadiah	c. 460–400	Unknown
Joel	c. 350	Unknown
Jonah	c. 350	Uncertain
Daniel	c. 167–164	Uncertain

In the next two chapters we will explore in greater detail and at greater length the major and minor prophets. Emphasis will be placed on their ministry, the historical context in which they functioned, and their theological or religious message.

Prophets and the Kings

The prophets of the Old Testament who were closely associated with kings were Samuel (associated with Saul and David), Nathan (associated with David), Gad (associated with David), and Elijah (associated with King Ahab). Each of them was the divine spokesperson at court—the one who often called the king to examine his conscience on the way he lived out his faith life. The most colorful of these was Elijah.

Elijah, King Ahab, and Queen Jezebel

Elijah, whose ministry was around 860 B.C.E., was a colorful and charismatic spokesperson for God, of the same stature as Samuel and Nathan. He came from the town of Tishbe in Gilead in the northern kingdom of Israel. He prophesied during the reign of King Ahab (874–853 B.C.E.). There are a whole series of narratives for the Elijah cycle, and they are listed on the next page.

ELIJAH CYCLE OF STORIES

Story	Biblical Text
Elijah being fed by ravens	1 Kings 17:1–7
The widow, her son, and the oil and flour that never end	1 Kings 17:8–24
The contest between Elijah and the prophets of Baal on Mount Carmel	1 Kings 18:1–46
A theophany and Elijah	1 Kings 19:1–18
The call of the prophet Elisha	1 Kings 19:19–21
The story of Naboth's Vineyard	1 Kings 21:1–29
The reappearance of Elijah	2 Kings 1:1–18
Elijah's ascent to heaven and being succeeded by the prophet Elisha	2 Kings 2:1–25

Two themes dominate the cycle of narratives concerning Elijah's prophetic ministry. First, a drought, and second, his reprimand of King Ahab. The cycle begins with Elijah telling Ahab that for several years no rain will fall except at his word (1 Kings 17:1). The drought that follows provides the backdrop for the first narrative in the Elijah cycle.

The first story shows Elijah entering the town of Zarapheth, where he meets a widow who lives with her only son (1 Kings 17:8–16). The drought has caused a famine. The widow has resigned herself to the fact that she and her son will die when the little oil and flour she has is used up. Elijah requests some food. The woman shares what she has. As a result, Elijah speaks the word of God that the flour will never run out, nor the jug of oil go dry until rain comes upon the earth.

A second story tells of the miraculous resuscitation of the widow's son by Elijah. This prompts the widow to recognize Elijah as a "man of God" from whose mouth the word of the Lord truly comes forth. Both of these narratives are miracle stories.

The second theme in the Elijah cycle of stories concerns Ahab, king of Israel, who was married to a Phoenician princess, Jezebel, daughter of the Phoenician king, Ethbaal. This marriage was part of a political alliance between Israel and Phoenicia arranged by Ahab's father, Omri. When Jezebel came to live with her new husband, she brought much of her religious heritage with her. Consequently, several shrines to the god Baal appeared in Israel. Jezebel was so committed to and strong about her religion that she ordered prophets of Yahweh, the God of ancient Israel, executed. King Ahab, weak as he was (he was a "milquetoast"), cooperated with Jezebel. After these murders, which infuriated Elijah, Ahab met Elijah and addressed him as "you troubler of Israel" (1 Kings 18:17). Elijah responded to this with a stern rebuke of Ahab's cooperation with his wife. He pointed out that Ahab's actions opposed the commands of God (1 Kings 18:18). This is a greater troubling to Israel than any word or act of Elijah.

The narrative of Elijah's dramatic encounter with the 450 prophets of Baal on Mount Carmel (1 Kings 18:21–40) follows. This narrative combines the two themes of the cycle. Elijah graphically uses the drought to illustrate his rebuke of Ahab for setting aside the commands of God. The narrative depicts a contest between Elijah and Jezebel's prophets of Baal. The object is to prove whose god is really God. Each must pray to their god to send fire down to consume a sacrifice which has been prepared. The narrative is laced with irony and sarcasm. It is one of the sharpest satires on non-Hebraic religion ever penned. Elijah taunts the prophets to shout louder when they receive no answer. Their god might be asleep or away or on vacation. As they get lathered up to prophetic frenzy, they still receive no answer: ". . . they raved on until the time of the offering of the oblation, but there was no voice, no answer, and no response" (1 Kings 18:29).

Before Elijah begins his prayer to God, he rebuilds the altar to Yahweh the God of Israel which had been desecrated at Mount Carmel. Then he orders that the sacrifice be doused with water three times, until the water flows from the sacrifice onto the ground. He then prays to Yahweh, the God of Israel, to demonstrate that he is God. Yahweh answers, sending fire down to devour the sacrifice, even the water. The people proclaim, "The LORD is God." Elijah immediately orders the prophets of Baal to be seized and killed. (Since these prophets are not part of the covenantal people, Elijah is not bound by the covenant toward them.)

Elijah flees to Mount Horeb (Sinai), where he encounters God (1 Kings 19:1–18). There a magnificent theophany happens:

> *[11]He [God] said, "Go out and stand on the mountain before the LORD, for the LORD is about to pass by." Now there was a great wind, so strong that it was splitting mountains and breaking rocks in pieces before the LORD, but the LORD was not in the wind; and after the wind an earthquake, but the LORD was not in the earthquake; [12]and after the earthquake a fire, but the LORD was not in the fire; and after the fire a sound of sheer silence* (1 Kings 19:11–12).

In this experience the prophet Elijah realizes that God must be found in the quiet and silence of one's own inner being rather than in the hustle and bustle that goes on outside one's being.

The last story in the Elijah cycle presents a serious violation of the covenant. It is the story of Ahab's murder of Naboth (1 Kings 21:1–29). Naboth owned a vineyard adjacent to Ahab's palace, which Ahab wished to buy for a vegetable garden. When Naboth protested because the vineyard was his ancestral inheritance and he wanted to keep it, King Ahab went to his room and pouted and sulked. Jezebel vehemently upbraided him for his childish behavior. She had Naboth killed and laid claim to the property. When King Ahab went to take possession of the property, he encountered Elijah. Elijah declared that since Ahab and Jezebel had spilled the blood of Naboth, their blood would also be spilled. That prophesy was later fulfilled.

Elijah and his successor Elisha, along with Nathan, Gad, and Samuel, used their calling as prophets to reprimand, correct, and rebuke the monarchs when they did not follow the covenant. For in the eyes of the prophets, the kings were not above the covenant—above the law—but were called to be obedient to it. The other prophets in the Old Testament who followed them continued that tradition, calling the king to faithful obedience to the covenant. But, in addition, they also called the people to be obedient to the covenant.

For Discussion

1. Do prophets foretell the future or do they speak for God? Explain.
2. Why were the lives of the prophets so demanding?
3. What did the prophets teach and how did they teach it?
4. Do you think the prophets ever feared for their lives? If yes, then why; if no, then why?
5. Do you ever feel called to be a prophet?

For Further Reading

Brueggemann, Walter. *The Prophetic Imagination.* (Second Edition) Minneapolis: Fortress Press, 2001.

Buber, Martin. *The Prophetic Faith.* New York: Collier Books, 1949.

Heschel, Abraham J. *The Prophets: An Introduction.* Vols. 1 & 2. New York: Harper & Row, 1962.

Mays, James Luther & Paul J. Achtemeier, eds. *Interpreting the Prophets.* Philadelphia: Fortress Press, 1987.

McKenna, Megan. *Prophets: Words of Fire.* Maryknoll, New York: Orbis Books, 2001.

Zucker, David J. *Israel's Prophets: An Introduction for Christians and Jews.* New York: Paulist Press, 1994.

6

THE MAJOR PROPHETS— ISAIAH, JEREMIAH, EZEKIEL

In THIS CHAPTER WE WILL EXPLORE THE BOOKS OF THE three major prophets: Isaiah, Jeremiah, and Ezekiel. These prophets, who were God's spokespersons, were the conscience of ancient Israel. They read the signs of the times through the eyeglasses of faith and called the believing community of ancient Israel to respond in faith. Dogged in their commitment to God's covenant, Isaiah, Jeremiah, and Ezekiel led difficult and misunderstood lives. Isaiah gave his son an unusual name (Isaiah 7:3). Ezekiel saw visions (Ezekiel 1–2; 8; 10; 37; 40). Jeremiah was thrown into a cistern (Jeremiah 38:6) and placed in stocks (Jeremiah 20:2–3; see 29:26) because of his prophecies. Yet all three left a legacy in their books that adds to the richness of the Old Testament.

The Book of Isaiah

The Book of Isaiah is the product of three different authors. The first thirty-nine chapters belong to an author who goes by the name of

Isaiah of Jerusalem; chapters 40 through 55 are referred to as Deutero Isaiah, or Second Isaiah; and chapters 56 through 66 are referred to as Trito Isaiah, or Third Isaiah. The book is the composition of three different prophets and their disciples existing in three different contexts at three different times. We will treat them here as separate units in their historical context.

Isaiah of Jerusalem: The Man Behind the Book

Isaiah ben Amoz prophesied from 746–686 B.C.E. His work and ministry spanned the reigns of kings Uzziah, Jotham, Ahaz, and Hezekiah (Isaiah 1:1). The text of Isaiah gives us some insight into his personal life. He had access to the court, thus he could have been a royal advisor (Isaiah 7:3). He had at least two sons to whom he gave symbolic names, thus we can presume he was married. Like other prophets, he had a core of disciples who followed him, who hung on his words, and later recorded them for posterity (Isaiah 8:16).

The best insight we can gain about the prophet comes from his call to be a prophet, what is referred to as his inaugural vision, found in chapter 6.

> ¹In the year that King Uzziah died, I saw the Lord sitting on a throne, high and lofty; and the hem of his robe filled the temple. ²Seraphs were in attendance above him; each had six wings: with two they covered their faces, and with two they covered their feet, and with two they flew. ³And one called to another and said: "Holy, holy, holy is the LORD of hosts; the whole earth is full of his glory." ⁴The pivots on the thresholds shook at the voices of those who called, and the house filled with smoke. ⁵And I said: "Woe is me! I am lost, for I am a man of unclean lips, and I live among a people of unclean lips; yet my eyes have seen the King, the LORD of hosts!"
>
> ⁶Then one of the seraphs flew to me, holding a live coal that had been taken from the altar with a pair of tongs. ⁷The seraph touched my mouth with it and said, "Now that this has touched your lips, your guilt has departed and your sin is blotted out."

⁸Then I heard the voice of the Lord saying, "Whom shall I send, and who will go for us?" And I said, "Here am I; send me!" (Isaiah 6:1–8).

The above passage is what scholars refer to as a "call narrative." Such narratives describe the interior process that leads a person to a new life of service in God's name. There is a structure to such a narrative: a divine encounter followed by human objection, followed by reassurances and explanation from God, followed by God's commissioning of the person called with a sign being given and acceptance on the part of the person.

Isaiah's call occurs in no less place than the temple. The temple was built on the highest point in Jerusalem. Just south of it was the royal palace which also commanded a height. In this passage we have a glimpse of both buildings. The glory of the Holy of Holies, the dwelling of the glory of the living God, is contrasted to the royal throne room where death is present. The contrast accents the difference between God's holy Word and the passing glory of human kings. This is a theme that permeates the Old Testament: royal (earthly) glory confronting God's true and eternal glory; our frail human word confronted by the truth of God's Word. The triple holy is an introduction to Isaiah's insistence that God must have sovereignty over all, not just the king. To be "holy" is to be different, to be separated from the rest of things.

The earth is filled with God's glory. In biblical times, glory was the sum of what one owned. The more you had, the more important you were. For Isaiah, God owns the universe. God is glorious indeed! In contrast to the superlative holiness of God, Isaiah recognizes his own unworthiness. God, however, wipes away the objection with a burning coal. Isaiah has no more excuses.

The second part of Isaiah's inaugural vision (6:9–13) has a surprising twist in it. Isaiah, who was eager to initiate his new ministry after the spectacular vision, has God tell him his mission is impossible. Despite his finest efforts, he is doomed to failure. The prophet plaintively asks, "How long?" The answer from God is somewhat ambiguous. It seems the message will not be easy to absorb. Yet the words of the inaugural vision would come to pass. Recall that all around Judah, the Assyrians were laying waste to the countryside. In the face of this very real threat to Judah and Jerusalem, God speaks through Isaiah. Isaiah castigates the people for relying on empty ceremonies to trick God. Isaiah does not increase his popularity by comparing Judah's leaders to the people of Sodom and Gomorrah. This is harsh, uncompromising language. Even though the people are angered, Isaiah is not intimidated. He sees that in the power of Assyria, which is devastating everything in its path, God has an agent, or instrument, to use against those who are violating the covenant. This kind of thinking is taboo to many of Isaiah's Jerusalem contemporaries. Could God truly approve and use a pagan nation against the chosen nation? Can God, who is so committed to the people through the covenant, also be against them? The answer of the prophet is a resounding "Yes!" The prophet's "yes" is a qualified one: God will use Assyria to dramatically show the results of infidelity to the covenant, but God will not let Assyria dominate forever.

The Book of Immanuel

Chapters 7 through 11 of Isaiah are called the Book of Immanuel. To understand the content of these chapters some background is needed. The southern kingdom of Judah is afraid. Efforts to stave off the attacking Assyrians completely absorb the attention of the king and his advisors. King Ahaz (735–715 B.C.E.) was invited by his neighbors to enter into an alliance with them and the Assyrians. Aram (Damascus) and Israel (the northern kingdom) believed that together they could withstand Assyria. Ahaz wasn't so sure. He refused to get entangled in the alliance. In revenge, Israel and Damascus threatened to attack Ahaz and force compliance. Now Isaiah enters the scene:

²When the house of David heard that Aram had allied itself with Ephraim, the heart of Ahaz and the heart of his people shook as the trees of the forest shake before the wind. ³Then the LORD *said to Isaiah, Go out to meet Ahaz, you and your son Shearjashub . . . ⁴and say to him, Take heed, be quiet, do not fear, and do not let your heart be faint because of these two stumps of firebrands . . .* (Isaiah 7:2–4).

A confrontation between two ways of looking at the world is presented in this passage. One, the "way of the world," the way of political expediency; the other, the way of God. The geographical setting for the meeting between Ahaz and Isaiah is near the Gehon Spring. At the end of the rock escarpment upon which ancient Jerusalem is built, the valley of Hinnon cuts through the hills. Now Ahaz is going there to check out the water supply in anticipation of a siege of Jerusalem by its northern neighbors. On the road, he meets Isaiah, who informs the king he should have faith in God and the covenant and not in political alliances. Isaiah warns Ahaz: "If you do not stand firm in faith, you shall not stand at all" (Isaiah 7:9). Without faith there is no real strength, militarily or otherwise. Despite these words of Isaiah, Ahaz doesn't believe. In an attempt to bring this faithless king to a change of heart, God speaks:

¹⁰Again the LORD *spoke to Ahaz, saying, ¹¹"Ask a sign of the* LORD *your God; let it be deep as Sheol or high as heaven"* (Isaiah 7:10–11).

Yet this hard-headed king, feigning piety, still wouldn't do what God commanded. The response to this faithlessness is one of the most famous prophecies in the Bible, the sign of Immanuel.

¹⁴Therefore the Lord himself will give you a sign. Look, the young woman is with child and shall bear a son, and shall name him Immanuel (Isaiah 7:14).

The purpose of the sign is to make the power of God visible, to show that this covenant-making, covenant-keeping God is very much with us, on our side. God is not aloof from the travails of history. God is not uncaring. God is as present and as hidden as an unborn child in the womb. The promise includes the notion that a child is about to be born who will be faithful, unlike faithless Ahaz. This new leader will exercise the duties of kingship properly, will know good from evil. He will be named "Wonderful Counselor, Mighty God, Everlasting Father, Prince of Peace" (Isaiah 9:7). His rule would usher in "endless peace" (Isaiah 9:6). He would be possessed of ". . . the spirit of wisdom and understanding, the spirit of counsel and might, the spirit of knowledge and the fear of the LORD" (Isaiah 11:2).

The question everyone wants answered, of course, is: Whom did Isaiah foresee as this messiah, and when would he begin his reign? Perhaps Isaiah was looking forward to an ordinary political ruler—perhaps Hezekiah—who would institute a return to pure religion. This interpretation is not completely out of the question.

But there is a deeper dimension of Isaiah's prophecy. While Isaiah undoubtedly hoped for an ordinary political ruler who would come to the throne and quickly reestablish righteousness in Judah, he also had a vision of and a hope in a greater type of king who would somehow reign in perpetuity. The reign established by this ideal king would be universal and perfect. Isaiah himself undoubtedly lacked real understanding of how his prophecy might be fulfilled, but he had faith in its eventual fulfillment. It is this deep faith purveyed in these messianic passages of Isaiah which was accepted by the early Christian church when it applied these passages to Jesus of Nazareth, acclaimed as both "Immanuel" and "the Christ" (the "Anointed").

Hope in a Remnant

The message of hope found in Isaiah's messianic prophecies was mirrored in his teaching on the remnant. Isaiah believed that a day would come when Judah would be restored, a day when a faithful few would continue the mission of God's fallen people:

> [31]*The surviving remnant of the house of Judah shall again take root downward, and bear fruit upward;* [32]*for from Jerusalem a remnant*

shall go out, and from Mount Zion a band of survivors. The zeal of the Lord of hosts will do this" (Isaiah 37:31–32).

The establishment of a remnant would be solely God's doing. God's interest, both in preserving the remnant and in raising up the messiah, would be based on his continuing desire to make his people holy, as God's self was holy. Isaiah of Jerusalem constantly stressed the holiness of God, especially as it contrasted with the wickedness of the people. It was God's holiness which impelled God to purge his people of their guilt. Just as the prophet Isaiah himself was cleansed by a burning coal, so the entire people would have to be cleansed of their sins and remade into a holy people.

Second Isaiah: Prophet of the Exile

Among the Jews exiled in Babylon there rose up a great prophet who was also a poet. No one knows his true name, and scholars have given him the nickname "Second Isaiah," based on the fact that his works were included with the writings of Isaiah of Jerusalem. But the fifteen chapters of the Isaiah scroll (chapters 40–55) that are attributed to him are quite different from those of his predecessor, who functioned prior to the exile. While Isaiah of Jerusalem promised a purged remnant, Second Isaiah, writing 150 years after his namesake, prophesied to the exiles that they were God's chosen remnant, and that their deliverance from bondage was imminent. Second Isaiah's message is one of comfort, optimism, and hope. He begins his prophecy on this note: "Comfort, O comfort my people, says your God" (Isaiah 40:1).

Second Isaiah wanted to establish for his exiled audience both God as universal creator and having universal supremacy over all other deities and peoples. In majestic poetic language, the prophet wanted to show that the one true God of Israel was Savior-God to all people.

Contextually speaking, Second Isaiah was moved to write because of the world-changing events taking place in the Babylonian empire in the decade 549–539 B.C.E. of the exile. During this time, a new power arose to threaten Babylon's mastery of the ancient world. As the Babylonians had once supplanted the Assyrians, now the Persians superseded the Babylonians as the chief power among the nations. In 539 B.C.E., Cyrus the Great of Persia won a significant battle against the Babylonians, breaking the will of the Babylonian leadership to resist further the shifting tide of power. As a result, the city of Babylon surrendered to Cyrus.

Cyrus decided to pursue a policy of religious toleration. He encouraged conquered peoples to maintain their own religious traditions. Consistent with his policy, Cyrus issued a decree of liberation for the Jews living in exile, encouraging them to return to Judah and rebuild their temple.

It was against this background that the prophet Second Isaiah wrote. To the hopeless and gloomy exiles who had perhaps begun to think they would stay in Babylon forever, Second Isaiah exclaimed:

> Sing, O heavens, for the LORD has done it; shout, O depths of the earth; break forth into singing, O mountains, O forest, and every tree in it! For the LORD has redeemed Jacob, and will be glorified in Israel (Isaiah 44:23).

Second Isaiah compared God's liberation of his people from Babylon to the original exodus event, when God had led his people from Egypt to the promised land. Unlike the first exodus, which terminated eventually in the tragedy that was the exile, this new liberation would lead to the final and permanent establishment of God as universal sovereign and of his people as the dominant power on earth. Speaking through the prophet, God promised his discouraged people:

> ³I will make with you an everlasting covenant, my steadfast, sure love for David. ⁴See, I made him a witness to the peoples, a leader and commander for the peoples. ⁵See, you shall call nations that

you do not know, and nations that do not know you shall run to you, because of the LORD your God, the Holy One of Israel, for he has glorified you (Isaiah 55:3b–5).

As the above text shows, Second Isaiah reasserted the messianic prophecies begun by Isaiah of Jerusalem, but with a different twist. He interpreted the *entire people*, the chosen remnant, as fulfilling many of the messianic prophecies. He thus felt that the nation in some dramatic way would assert the prerogatives of the Davidic messiah presented by earlier prophets. The messianic era was about to begin, he believed, and the remnant returning to Judah would play a major role in ushering in this new age.

How would the people do this? Further, what were to be the characteristics of the remnant's mastery over nations? Were the people to dominate nations—as foreign empires like Assyria and Babylon had done—or were they to serve in some other capacity in God's plan?

Servant Songs of Second Isaiah

The answer to these questions is discovered in Second Isaiah's most famous poems—the Songs (poems) of the Suffering Servant. These

---

SERVANT POEM-SONGS IN SECOND ISAIAH

Text	Content
Isaiah 42:1–9	The servant will bring justice to the world. The speaker in the text is God.
Isaiah 49:1–6	The servant is called from his mother's womb before he was born. The speaker in the text is the servant.
Isaiah 50:4–11	The servant is portrayed as a student who daily learns his lessons. The speaker in the text is the servant.
Isaiah 52:13–53:12	The servant is portrayed as a "man of sorrows." It is not clear in the text just who the speaker is.

---

masterfully written poem-songs are listed in the visual on the previous page.

In the first song (Isaiah 42:1–9), we find that God speaks of "his servant" as one who is endowed with God's spirit: "I have put my spirit upon him" (Isaiah 42:1). The servant will be:

> *⁶. . . a light to the nations, ⁷to open the eyes that are blind, to bring out the prisoners from the dungeon, from the prison those who sit in darkness* (Isaiah 42:6–7).

The natural question to ask is, "Who is this servant?" In the second song we learn a bit more about the servant's identity. In 49:3, we are told specifically that the servant is "Israel." Paradoxically, in 49:5–6, we find out that the servant will ". . . bring Jacob back to him, and that Israel might be gathered to him . . . to restore the survivors of Israel." Is the servant just one person or a whole people?

In the third song, the servant speaks, revealing more about his identity.

> *⁴The Lord GOD has given me the tongue of a teacher, that I may know how to sustain the weary with a word. Morning by morning he wakens—wakens my ear to listen as those who are taught. ⁵The Lord GOD has opened my ear* (Isaiah 50:4–5).

This third song rather clearly affirms that the servant is thought of as an individual. He reveals that he will have to undergo great suffering on behalf of the people.

The full measure and depth of the servant's suffering is set forth in the final song. The servant will become:

> *. . . despised and rejected by others; a man of suffering and acquainted with infirmity; and as one from whom others hide their faces he was despised, and we held him of no account* (Isaiah 53:3).

The fourth song also reveals why it is that the servant will suffer:

But he was wounded for our transgressions, crushed for our iniquities; upon him was the punishment that made us whole, and by his bruises we are healed (Isaiah 53:5).

By the end of the fourth servant song we might conclude that Second Isaiah had entirely shifted his emphasis from the servant as people to the servant as one person. Yet this would be to look upon his prophecies from a twenty-first-century viewpoint, not his perspective.

Through the four servant songs, Second Isaiah was describing principally the Jewish mission to the nations. The Jews would be God's servant. They would be a light to the nations and would establish justice for all peoples. In doing this, they would have to suffer. Through suffering they would bring healing and liberation to others. Second Isaiah thus saw the servant primarily as a collective entity, representing the entire Jewish community.

Second Isaiah was primarily concerned with the redemptive suffering which the people as a whole would have to endure in bringing non-Jewish nations to salvation. He used the theme of the servant as individual in the same way that the word "Israel" itself was used in Genesis and later books to refer both to the man Israel (Jacob) and the people whom the man fathered. Second Isaiah was not, therefore, suggesting a dichotomy between an individual and the community when he described the servant. His main teaching was that God would lead the exiled remnant back to Judah and give them a mission to bring all peoples under God's leadership. In doing this, the Jews would have to endure much suffering. This deeper reflection on God's ways marks Second Isaiah as one of the Old Testament's most creative and original thinkers.

Third Isaiah (chapters 56–66)

Just as the themes and style of Second Isaiah could be isolated from the previous materials, so can the final chapters of this scroll. This prophet—Third Isaiah or Trito Isaiah, is also anonymous. He introduces himself with the customary call narrative.

> *¹The spirit of the Lord GOD is upon me, because the LORD has*
> *anointed me; he has sent me to bring good news to the oppressed,*
> *to bind up the brokenhearted, to proclaim liberty to the captives,*
> *and release to the prisoners; ²to proclaim the year of the LORD's favor,*
> *and the day of vengeance of our God; to comfort all who mourn;*
> *³to provide for those who mourn in Zion . . .* (Isaiah 61:1–3).

Third Isaiah sees himself as anointed by God as both kings and priests were in the Old Testament. He also sees himself as filled with God's breath (spirit) to be a spokesperson for God.

The God for whom Third Isaiah speaks is imaged by him as a potter.

> *Yet, O LORD, you are our Father; we are the clay, and you are our*
> *potter; we are all the work of your hand* (Isaiah 64:8).

The image of God as a potter and each of us as a clay pot reminds us of the second creation story, where God scoops up clay from the earth and forms the first human being and breathes life into the being (Genesis 2:7). The idea of God's hands shaping us like clay is intimate and comforting. No one but the potter knows how much time, energy, and love went into fashioning a particular vase or cup or pot. The potter gives each pot its own special design and markings. The potter also knows its flaws. The potter and the pot share a bond that seems much like the one between each of us and God. Third Isaiah gives us a vivid and beautiful image for God's relationship with each of us. It causes us to reflect on how God has molded us into the unique person we are with our own distinctive markings and flaws, as well as how God is still molding us.

Third Isaiah ends his prophecies with a vision of universalism and joy—people rising from their dark past into a new and glorious light. It is a vision of hope and energy. Likewise it ends with the vision of universalism, that all peoples will be gathered to Israel to Jerusalem, to its temple, and to the truth of the Torah.

"For as the new heavens and the new earth, which I will make, shall remain before me," says the LORD; so shall your descendants and your name remain" (Isaiah 66:22).

The Book of Jeremiah

Have you ever been at a party and been asked to introduce someone you know to the rest of the guests? This can be quite a challenge, for you hope that your introduction will be both thorough and brief. The same challenge exists when trying to introduce the Book of Jeremiah, for behind it are both the prophet himself and the historical context in which he lived.

Let us begin by being introduced to the prophet. Scholars date the call of Jeremiah by God to be a prophet at around 626 B.C.E.; Jeremiah lived until after the fall of Jerusalem at the hands of the Babylonians in 587 B.C.E. This means he ministered as a prophet before, during, and after the Babylonian exile. During his lifetime he had a collection made of his important prophecies, which he later expanded. It is likely that Jeremiah continually updated his collection of messages from God as he received them. The various messages were not written down in chronological order, so when additions were made, prophecies from later periods were inserted randomly among the prophecies from earlier times.

At some point, stories about Jeremiah were added to the collection either by one of his disciples or, most likely, by his secretary, Baruch. Unquestionably, the Book of Jeremiah grew after his lifetime, as people who treasured his messages added other bits and pieces to the collection—perhaps anecdotal or biographical incidents in the life of the prophet, or messages they thought he may have delivered. There is no way to reconstruct who added what when. What we can say is that it is very unlikely that the edition of Jeremiah that we read in the Bible today was put in final form by Jeremiah himself. Rather, it is the product of Jeremiah, his followers, his secretary Baruch, and others.

After all, the compilation of the Book of Jeremiah happened in very turbulent times. Some of his prophecies had probably been taken to Babylon by the people exiled there. Such disconcerting and unsettling conditions were ill-suited for calmly making the definitive collection of a lifetime of prophetic messages.

This may be the reason why two different versions of the Book of Jeremiah were in circulation right up until the time of Christ. Both were written in Hebrew, but one was shorter than the version we find in our modern English Bibles, and some of the prophecies are arranged in a different order. Fragments of this shorter Hebrew version were found among the Dead Sea Scrolls. It was this shorter version of the Book of Jeremiah that was translated into Greek (a translation known as the Septuagint) by Jews in Egypt around the third century B.C.E., and is found in the ancient Greek editions of Jeremiah. Jews and Christians accept the longer Hebrew version as Sacred Scripture and that is the version which is referred to here.

Historical Background

The Book of Jeremiah, like all biblical books, is best understood within its cultural and historical background. Jeremiah spoke God's Word within the context of specific situations. The Book of Kings narrates this context, particularly the religious reform under King Josiah and the ultimate fall of Jerusalem to the armies of Babylon (see 2 Kings chapters 22 through 25). Jeremiah lived and ministered in a time of crisis, in the waning years of the kingdom of Judah. The powerful and often strident tone of his prophecies must be understood against the eventual destruction of Jerusalem by the Babylonians.

Jeremiah's career as a prophet was challenging. He lived in changing times. He grew up during the reign of King Josiah (639–606 B.C.E.), when the nation of Judah was at peace, and when king, priests, and people were actively engaged in a renewal of their faith and worship. He died around 580, in exile in Egypt, when Judah was no longer a nation, Jerusalem lay in ruins, the temple had been burned to the ground, and the people had been deported into exile in Babylon. On the stage of world history, Jeremiah's life spanned the last twenty years of the Assyrian empire, which was destroyed by the Babylonians sometime between 612 and 605 B.C.E., and the first twenty years of the Neo-Babylonian empire (605–539 B.C.E.).

Jeremiah was born in the small village of Anathoth, a few miles north of Jerusalem, belonged to a priestly family, and was called by God to the office of prophet at an early age (around 626 B.C.E.). During the forty-plus years he ministered and served as God's prophet (626–580), the tiny kingdom of Judah went through one religious reformation (626–609); three wars: against Egypt in 609, Babylon in 597 and 587; three exiles: 597, 587, and 585; and five Davidic kings: Josiah, 639-609; Jehoahaz, who reigned for only three months in 609; Jehoiakim, 609–597; Jehoiachin, who reigned for only three months in 597; and Zedekiah, 597–587. During these years, the nation of Judah went from one of the brightest periods in its history under King Josiah (639–609) to the darkest (609–587). No other biblical prophet saw as many wars, exiles, and kings as did Jeremiah.

Further, no other prophet was involved so crucially in the fate of his nation as was Jeremiah. He passionately preached the renewal of the covenant under King Josiah in 621. He lived through the first and second siege of Jerusalem. He saw the temple destroyed, and watched his people marched off into exile in Babylon. At the end, he himself was marched off into exile in Egypt. There, according to Jewish legend, he was allegedly stoned to death by his own people.

As this historical background indicates, Jeremiah lived in wrenching times. This permeates the message that God gave Jeremiah to deliver and accounts for the extremely strong tone of many of Jeremiah's prophecies. The Book of Jeremiah presents the prophet as spending most of his time asking the people to listen to him and God's message and shouting "Watch out!" like the mother of a toddler to her young child, as Jeremiah saw the armies of Babylon bearing down on Jerusalem. Yet people laughed at Jeremiah and his words and continued in their ways that would bring their destruction. Further, Jeremiah knew as he preached that he was failing in his mission, and this doubled his pain. In brief, Jeremiah watched his nation and his people be dismantled by the Babylonians.

Jeremiah was not married (Jeremiah 16:2). He had a secretary named Baruch (Jeremiah 32:12–16; 36; 43:1–6; 45:1–2) who helped compile his prophecies in written form. Jeremiah lived until after the fall of Jerusalem to the Babylonians in 587 B.C.E. Our last view of Jeremiah takes place in Egypt, where he had been forcibly taken after the fall of Jerusalem, perhaps around 582 B.C.E. (see Jeremiah 43 and 44).

Jeremiah certainly won no popularity contest in his day. God, who called Jeremiah from before his birth to be a prophet, gave him a hard-nosed attitude that likened him to ". . . a fortified city, an iron pillar, and a bronze wall" (1:18). The people he ministered to did not listen to him—some twenty times in his book this refrain is heard: "They did not listen." In addition, the people wanted him sentenced to death (see Jeremiah 26:8–11). While Jeremiah was never killed he sure was abused. He was thrown into a cistern (38:6), publicly humiliated and placed in stocks (20:1–3), and had an entire scroll of his prophecies burned up piece by piece by King Jehoiakim (36:23). Undaunted by such abusive behavior of the king, Jeremiah composed another scroll (36:28–32).

OUTLINE OF THE BOOK OF JEREMIAH

I. Visions, prophecies of judgment, and personal laments (chapters 1–24)
II. Speeches of and stories about Jeremiah (chapters 25–45)
III. Prophecies against the nations (chapters 46–51)
IV. Historical appendix (chapter 52)

Jeremiah's Dramatic Prophecies

Biblical prophets often preached God's message to the people or delivered oracles. This is also true of Jeremiah. Yet he went a step further and often performed symbolic actions, or what we might call acted-out prophecies. For example, in chapter 13, at God's command he wears a linen loin cloth, the garment that clothed his genitals. Instructed by God to bury it at the river Euphrates, he later returned to retrieve it only to find it rotted to rags and useless. That is the way it was between God and God's people. God wanted to cling to them, as close as their underwear. "For as the loincloth clings to one's loins, so I made the whole house of Israel and the whole house of Judah cling to me, says the LORD, . . . But they would not listen" (Jeremiah 13:11).

A visit to a potter's studio (Jeremiah 18:1–12) provides the prophet with another dramatic utterance. Watching a potter throw a vessel and rework the clay when the first pot does not turn out right, Jeremiah sees another link with God's action. Just as the potter's first attempt at throwing the pot did not work but required that the clay be reworked and reshaped, so God the divine potter was reshaping his people. Taking the connection another step, Jeremiah buys a potter's earthenware flask and breaks it, symbolizing God's smashing of the people and the city (Jeremiah 19:1–11). Thus it will be with the citizens of Jerusalem—broken, smashed, tossed aside, when God permits Babylon to overtake them.

The neck yoke worn by oxen for harnessing is used by Jeremiah as a symbol of enslavement to proclaim his unpopular message of surrender to the king of Babylon: "Bring your necks under the yoke of the king of Babylon . . ." (Jeremiah 27:12). A rival prophet by the name of Hananiah tries to dismiss and downplay Jeremiah's prophecy by breaking the wooden yoke Jeremiah was wearing (Jeremiah 28:10). But Jeremiah is told by God that he (God) will substitute an unbreakable yoke of iron to show that the people will be taken off into exile in Babylon (Jeremiah 28:12–16).

Jeremiah and His Lamentations

Of all the prophets in the Bible, none express their inner feelings of anguish at being a prophet as does Jeremiah. He is the only prophet who reveals his profound struggles with his vocation as a prophet of God.

There are a series of texts scattered throughout chapters 11 through 20 in the Book of Jeremiah where he pours out the intimate feelings of a restless heart. These are referred to as the "confessions" or "lamentations" of Jeremiah. They are a series of lament prayers, similar in type to the laments in the Book of Psalms, and may reveal a spiritual crisis Jeremiah was having (see Jeremiah 11:18–12:6; 15:10–21; 17:14–18; 18:18–23; 20:7–13; 20:15–18).

These personal outcries are unparalleled in the writings of Israelite prophets. Not only does Jeremiah proclaim the "word of God" but, like the people to whom it is addressed, he struggled with it. He complains about his lot, cries out for vindication, and even hurls defiance at God. He undergoes the trials of faith—a faith that is shadowed by doubt, rebellion, self-pity, and despair. Indeed, Jeremiah has the courage to doubt. His doubt does not cause him to deny his faith but rather to dialog and rage with God.

These confessions or laments are honest outbursts toward God that arise from Jeremiah's prophetic office. Similar to the lament psalms, in which a supplicant cries out of distress, pleads for vindication, and expresses confidence in God, Jeremiah prays to God out of the depths of his distress. He sounds just like the Psalmist who prays: "Out of the depths I cry to you, O Lord" (Psalm 130:1). Jeremiah sees himself like "a gentle lamb led to the slaughter" (Jeremiah 11:18–12:6). He sees God as a deceitful brook, like waters that fail (Jeremiah 15:10–21) and prays to God for healing: "Heal me O Lord!" (Jeremiah 17:14–18). Jeremiah refers to his enemies as those who ". . . dug a pit for my life" (Jeremiah 18:18–23) and tells God that even though he would rather not speak on God's behalf, nonetheless God's message is like a "burning fire shut up in my bones" (Jeremiah 20:7–13). In his final lament, Jeremiah is so full of despair that we are told he cursed the day he was born and the man who brought the news of his birth to his father for not having aborted him instead (see Jeremiah 20:14–17).

What brought Jeremiah to such depths of despair? It was—among other things—the discovery that the people of his own village, Anathoth—yes, even of his own family—were plotting to kill him (Jeremiah 11:18–21; 12:6). Never in his wildest imagination had he anticipated such a thing happening, for it was, after all, the elders of Anathoth, together with his family, who had taught him to believe as he did, and who up to this point had undoubtedly been his most loyal supporters. More than any other biblical prophet, Jeremiah seemed to need the affection and acceptance of his family and friends. But his lot was to be that of a rejected man, ". . . a man of strife and contention to the whole land" (Jeremiah 15:10), constantly surrounded by enemies and "sitting alone" because God's hand had been laid upon him. The anguish of loneliness lay heavy upon his heart. Throughout his career, Jeremiah was torn on the one hand by his natural longing for peace and companionship, and on the other hand by the prophetic task that catapulted him into the arena of conflict. His confessions bear witness to the sufferings involved in being a prophet of God and the prophet's passionate plea for vindication. The prayers for vindication which Jeremiah uttered are not a plea for personal triumph but for the triumph of God's cause that the prophet represents.

Few individuals have suffered so deeply as Jeremiah, and we must be careful not to criticize too easily the passionate queries and protests that Jeremiah hurled at God. Yet his laments—like so many human utterances—express the self-pity and even the self-righteousness that often arise when a person's faith is put to the severest test. His question, "Why does this happen to me?" suggests that he had been badly treated after all the sacrifices he made for God's sake. He had not sat in the company of merrymakers, nor had he committed any injustice in borrowing or lending. He was innocent. Hence he pleads his case to God, hoping that his own righteousness would be vindicated and that the unrighteousness of his persecutors would be punished (see: Jeremiah 11:20; 12:1–3; 17:17–18; 18:19–23; 20:11–12).

What are we to make of these confessions as a whole? They are a collection of prophetic prayers and, if read in succession, they describe a road that leads step by step into greater despair and threatens to end in some abyss. Jeremiah's "cross," so to speak, is eclipsed with darkness—the unanswered questions of his own prophetic suffering. The final poem, in which he curses the day he was born, has the effect of a prayer of total abandonment, similar to the one of Jesus on the cross (Psalm 22:1; see Mark 15:34).

The confessions of Jeremiah provide us with vivid descriptions of suffering as part of the prophetic vocation. These were not private prayers. Rather, they serve as a public witness to the prophet's commission as one who, in a special way, was called to walk through "the darkest valley" (Psalm 23:4) with the divine assurance, "I am with you," and in the confidence that the vindication lay ahead. Indeed, God was personally involved in the suffering of the people that was typified by Jeremiah's own anguished experience. In a profound sense, Jeremiah's suffering was a participation in God's suffering, so much so that God's concerns became Jeremiah's concerns and God's emotions, whether anger, rage, or love, flowed through Jeremiah's whole life and thought. Jeremiah challenges all of us to consider whether God's concerns are ours; if our life is a participation in God's life; if our suffering is a participation in God's suffering.

The Book of Ezekiel

Of all biblical figures, Ezekiel the prophet is truly in a class by himself. It is alleged that some rabbis said that reading the Book of Ezekiel may be hazardous to your spiritual health. Some of them sought to withdraw Ezekiel from circulation because of his daring description of God in the first chapter. In the book, Ezekiel the prophet is remote and his behavior is bizarre, suggesting to some that he may have been mentally unbalanced. Despite all these criticisms, the Bible would be much less appealing without the unique personality and message of the prophet Ezekiel.

Ezekiel: The Man Behind the Book

The man Ezekiel and his message are so intricately bound together that it is almost impossible to separate one from the other. It is fair to say that Ezekiel was himself the medium of his message. Scattered about in forty-eight chapters of his book is a priest, as well as a criticizing and energizing prophet of rare stature.

OUTLINE OF THE CONTENTS OF THE BOOK OF EZEKIEL

I. Oracles of judgment against Judah and Jerusalem (1:1–24:27)
   A. Vision of God's glory and the call of Ezekiel (1:1–3:21)
   B. Symbolic actions: The coming siege of Jerusalem (3:22–5:17)
   C. Oracles of judgment and announcement of its immediacy (6:1–7:27)
   D. Abominations in the temple: the glory of God departs (8:1–11:25)
   E. Symbolic actions describing the exile and sayings against the people and false prophets (12:1–14:23)
   F. Historical allegories and sermons against people and their kings (15:1–23:49)

II. Oracles against the foreign nations of Ammon, Moab, Edom, Philistine, Tyre, and Egypt (25:1–32:32)

III. Prophecies of destruction and restoration (33:1–39:29)
   A. Announcement of Jerusalem's fall: Ezekiel's role as watchman (33:1–33)
   B. Promises of deliverance from exile and restoration of the land (34:1–37:28)
   C. God and Magog: the enemy's ultimate defeat (38:1–39:29)

IV. Program for reorganization of the restored community after the Babylonian exile (40:1–48:35)
   A. Plans for a new temple: God's glory returns (40:1–43:12)
   B. Temple regulations and personnel (43:13–46:24)
   C. The healing waters of the temple spring (47:1–12)
   D. Division of the land (47:13–48:35)

The Priest

The opening chapter of the book informs us that Ezekiel is a priest (Ezekiel 1:3). However, this is something we might suspect even without being told. Ezekiel has a deep loathing for cultic defilement. According to chapters 8 through 11, it is cultic sins, the worship of loathsome beasts and weeping for the Babylonian god Tamuz, that force the Lord to abandon the city and its temple. Other passages announce how the people have profaned the Sabbath (20:12), worshiped on high places (6:13), and defiled the sanctuary (23:37–38). While these are serious offenses, they are especially heinous in the eyes of priests, whose role includes preserving cultic purity.

Hand in hand with this priestly sensitivity to defilement goes Ezekiel's insistence on God's holiness, especially the holiness of his name. "I will sanctify my great name . . . and the nations shall know that I am the LORD when through you I display my holiness" (Ezekiel 36:23). Since Israel bear's God's name, it must show proper respect by avoiding idol worship (20:39). Ultimately, it is the divine sense of holiness that can adequately explain the reason for the destruction of the land and the people.

The Committed Prophet

Ezekiel demonstrates his willingness to become God's spokesperson by his openness to God's spirit. He allows this divine power or energy to raise him up after being prostrate in the presence of God (Ezekiel 2:2). He also permits the spirit to move him about during his visionary experiences (8:3; 11:1). His submission to God's power is a clear sign of his acceptance of the prophetic office.

Ezekiel is willing to surrender (though not totally) his own identity as a priest in the temple and acquire a new status as prophet, especially a prophet of judgment. His binding (3:25) and confinement to his house (3:24) are symbolic expressions of his new status. Likewise, eating the scroll is most telling. He eats not simply words that he must speak; rather, he takes into his very being the fate of his people (3:1–2). To that extent, Ezekiel is the very embodiment of the message.

The prophetic office is never a flight from reality. Having received his new commission, Ezekiel sits distraught among the exiles for seven days (3:15). To be sure, God's hand lies heavily upon the prophet. He is now compelled to share a message with his community that will be nothing less than "lamentation and mourning and woe" (2:10). The heavenly realm of his inaugural vision has given way to the earthly arena of human reality. The priest-turned-prophet must

190

now confront his own people, assuring them that the fate of Jerusalem and its temple is inexorably sealed.

The Criticizing Prophet

In criticizing, a prophet must tell the way it really is. A prophet must point out the evils festering in the community and preach a message that the community adamantly refuses to hear—the hollowness of purely human plans and programs, and the sovereignty of God's holiness. The challenge for Ezekiel is formidable.

While Ezekiel points out individual abuses, he goes beyond other prophets in announcing something resembling a corporate understanding of sin. Right from the very beginning of its existence, Israel sinned enormously. In speaking of the origins of Jerusalem, Ezekiel points out her pagan roots: "Your father was an Amorite, and your mother a Hittite" (Ezekiel 16:3). For the prophet, it is not surprising that Jerusalem was so hardened in sin. In speaking of the background of the kingdoms of Judah and Israel, Ezekiel is very blunt. These two kingdoms, personified as women, committed acts of infidelity when they were only young girls in Egypt (23:2–3). Finally, the prophet focuses on Israel's most sacred tradition, the one that set it apart from other people—the exodus. However, this tradition offers no consolation for Ezekiel's audience. He proclaims that the original Israelite community in Egypt and the two generations involved in the wilderness wanderings rebelled against the Lord. Thus, from the very beginning, Israel's history was tarnished.

Ezekiel's audience is one that loves to pass the buck. They insist that they have done nothing wrong and are unfairly suffering for the sins of their ancestors (Ezekiel 18:2). Ezekiel simply responds that a generation that obeys God's laws will not suffer for the sins of its ancestors. Similarly, future generations will not escape punishment for their sins because of the mortal integrity of a past age (14:12–23; 18:1–32; 33:10–20). Each age in each generation must take its moral obligation seriously and not pass the buck. The ethically genuine community is the responsible community.

Ezekiel captures this teaching on individual responsibility in his image of the sentry, sentinel, or watchman (Ezekiel 3:17–21; 33:1–20). If the sentry or sentinel warns the wicked and urges them to repent, and they still refuse, then they shall die for their sins. If, however, the wicked heed the words of the sentry or sentinel and truly repent, they shall surely live—they shall not die. It is not without significance that Ezekiel sees himself in the role of a sentry or sentinel (Ezekiel 3:17–21). His responsibility is enormous since the fate of the people is linked to the performance of his office.

The Energizing Prophet

Ezekiel also performs symbolic actions that may strike one as being impossible, or at the very least bizarre. In Ezekiel 4:45, he is instructed to lie on his side for a period of 390 days. In Ezekiel 12:5, he is directed to dig a hole through a wall with his hands. In Ezekiel 3:3, he is commanded to eat a scroll. Some authors describe such symbolic actions as a type of street theater that is designed to provoke the audience to listen. As the book shows, the people find Ezekiel's actions amusing, but they do not let his message radically change their lives.

In bringing hope to others, the prophet must tell the way it can be. A prophet must make the community aware of the hopes and dreams that have been denied or suppressed. In this capacity, the prophet preaches a god of surprises. The God of Israel cannot be defeated by Israel's sinfulness. God has the ability to change evil into good.

In the vision of the dried bones, the people have concluded that they are all dried up and their hope is gone. In response to this despair, Ezekiel underlines the role of God's spirit. It is this spirit that gives life to Israel: "The breath came into them and they lived, came and stood on their feet, a vast multitude" (Ezekiel 37:10). The Lord proceeds to open the graves and have the people rise from them. This resurrection scene will come to fruition when Israel is settled on its land (37:14). Life, not death, will be God's final word.

Ezekiel uses the symbol of the shepherd to corroborate God's resolve to renew his people. In Ezekiel 34:11–31, God overcomes the evil perpetrated by evil human shepherds (Israel's kings) by assuming that role himself. To be sure, he will provide for the flock, but he will also provide justice and uphold the weak. "I will feed them with good pasture, and the mountain heights of Israel shall be their pasture . . . I will seek the lost, and I will bring back the strayed, . . ." (34:14, 16). Ezekiel's God is indeed a God of compassion! Ezekiel insists that the restoration of Israel is not due to the people's repentance or willingness to change. It is God who will effect a profound change and reorientation among the people. To that end, he speaks to the promise of a new heart and a new spirit (11:17–20; 36:26–28). Because of this divine gift-giving, Israel will desire, and be enabled, to walk in the Lord's ways. "A new heart I will give you and a new spirit I will put within you; . . . I will put my spirit within you, and make you follow my statutes and be careful to observe my ordinances" (36:26–27).

A final image of restoration is God's return to the city of Jerusalem in Ezekiel 43:1–12. That return marks the end of the exile. From the interior of the temple, one hears the voice of God himself, who solemnly proclaims: ". . . I will reside among the people of Israel forever" (43:7). This new building will function as the place of God's throne and the footstool of his feet. God and Israel are thus reunited. Death and destruction have given way to life and reconstruction.

In the final analysis, Ezekiel's God is one who provokes amazement and bewilderment. God's gift-giving is sheer grace, not the result of our human efforts. Ezekiel's God is indeed a God of surprises, who urges us to marvel at his manifold gifts. Evil cannot defeat this God. Rather, God uses human failures to bring about a new creation.

Ezekiel and the Babylonian Exile

Ezekiel was undoubtedly among the eight thousand exiled by Nebuchadnezzar to Babylon in 597 B.C.E. In 593 B.C.E., he began his ministry among the exiles, and continued at least until 585 B.C.E., during the days of total devastation. Like his contemporary, Jeremiah, Ezekiel was adamantly opposed to the plan of Zedekiah and his advisors to rebel against Babylon (see Ezekiel 12:1–15; 17:1–22; 21:18–32).

In exile, the elders or leaders of the people who represented the governing body of the community consulted Ezekiel (see Ezekiel 8:1; 14:1–3; 20:1; 33:30–31). These consultations probably afforded Ezekiel a kind of political platform. It should be noted that the exilic community anticipated remaining only a short time in Babylon and a quick return to Jerusalem. It was the task of Ezekiel, however, to counteract such enthusiasm and announce the inexorable fate of Jerusalem and its citizens. The correspondence between Jerusalem and Babylon shows that there were many prophets of peace who proclaimed the defeat of Babylon. For Ezekiel, however, the fate of the city was sealed.

During the time prior to the fall of Jerusalem, Ezekiel had to preach a message of doom. The sinfulness of the people had reached such a point that God had no choice but to destroy the great city. As one might imagine, such a message was not well received. However, once news of the city's fall arrived and plunged the exiles into even greater despair, Ezekiel embarked on a new dimension of his ministry, i.e., one of hope. In the face of such disaster, God would restore the people and bring them back home. The vision of the valley of dry bones (Ezekiel 37:1–14) epitomized this vision of hope.

Ezekiel and the Character of God

Ezekiel emphasizes the character of God. A constant phrase is: "And they [or you] shall know that I am the LORD" (Ezekiel 6:10). God's involvement in history reveals that only he can punish and restore. This form of activity shows that God takes Israel's sinfulness seriously, and also that the Lord never ceases to be concerned about and provide for his people. In the face of death, the Lord confers life.

Ezekiel and Holiness

The God of Ezekiel is concerned about holiness. While God is involved with Israel, this God is also transcendent. For example, when describing God's appearance in the first chapter, Ezekiel uses terms such as God's "likeness" or "appearance" (Ezekiel 1:26–28). For Ezekiel, God's name is holy (Ezekiel 36:20; 43:7). The implication is that the people are not to profane that name by any form of disobedience.

Like his prophetic predecessors, Ezekiel inveighs against sins of injustice and false worship. Unlike those prophets, however, Ezekiel underlines cultic offenses, such as not keeping the Sabbath holy (Ezekiel 20:12), worshiping on high places (areas associated with pagan religious practices of the Canaanites—see Ezekiel 20:28), and defiling the sanctuary (Ezekiel 23:37–38). The prophet must candidly acknowledge that although God gave his laws to help Israel serve him, they were clearly not enough. From the very time of the exodus, Israel has displayed an uncanny spirit of rebellion.

Ezekiel and Individual Responsibility

Individual responsibility is one of the hallmarks of Ezekiel's message. While his audience blames an earlier generation for its problems, the prophet constantly insists each individual must take responsibility for his or her actions. If Israel hopes for a new and different future, then it must reject its evil past and present, and live a faithful and persevering life. On several occasions, Ezekiel focuses on his vocation as sentinel or watchman (Ezekiel 3:17; 33:7). As such, he must warn his people about their failings with a view to their conversion. Hence, both prophet and people must carry out their responsibility.

While Ezekiel proclaims God's judgment over Israel, he also stresses the possibility of repentance and God's willingness to forgive. There is thus a tension between human efforts and divine grace. To enable Israel to repent, God will provide a new heart and a new spirit (Ezekiel 11:19; 18:31; 36:26). Human response comes in the wake of God's will to save.

For Discussion

1. The prophet Isaiah presents God as holy. What does that mean to you?
2. How do you react to the suffering servant songs of Second Isaiah? What role does suffering play in your life?
3. Jeremiah laments and rages with God. Do you ever do the same? Would Jeremiah's lamentations help you to wrestle with God?
4. The prophet Ezekiel emphasizes individual responsibility for one's behavior. Does this teaching challenge you?
5. What do you think of Ezekiel's image of God?

For Further Reading

Blenkinsopp, Joseph. *Ezekiel*. Louisville: John Knox Press, 1990.

Boadt, Lawrence. *Jeremiah 1-25*. Wilmington, DE: Glazier, 1982.

Boadt, Lawrence. *Jeremiah 26–52, Habbakuk, Zephaniah, Nahum*. Wilmington, DE: Glazier, 1982.

Hals, Ronald M. *Ezekiel*. Grand Rapids, MI: Wm. B. Eerdmans, 1989.

Scullin, John. *Isaiah 40–66*. Wilmington, DE: Glazier, 1982.

Sweeney, Marvin A. *Isaiah 1–39, With an Introduction to the Prophetic Literature*. Grand Rapids, MI: Eerdmans, 1996.

7

THE MINOR PROPHETS AND THE BOOKS OF LAMENTATIONS, BARUCH, EZRA, AND NEHEMIAH

In ENGLISH, ONE DEFINITION OF THE WORD "MINOR" means a child or youth who has not reached adulthood. A minor cannot legally consume alcohol or purchase tobacco products in public businesses. Further, the term "minor" is often interpreted as someone who is less than an adult, possibly implying lack of maturity and life experience. This is not how the word "minor" is being used when applied to twelve of the Old Testament prophets. These twelve books are called "minor" only because of the brevity of their written size, in comparison to the books of the major prophets Isaiah, Jeremiah, and Ezekiel. Several of these so-called "minor" prophets were major figures of their own time, for example, Hosea, Amos, Haggai, and Zechariah.

The minor prophets will be treated in this chapter in the order of their appearance in the Hebrew (Jewish) Canon (the order of most

English translations of the Bible), which is not chronological. Because history is important in the study of the biblical prophets, every attempt will be made to situate them within the proper historical context. One of the books of the minor prophets, the Book of Jonah, will not be discussed in this chapter, for it appears in chapter 11.

The Book of Hosea

Both Hosea's name and that of his father are mentioned in verse 1 of Hosea. Other than that, we do not know a great deal about the personal origin of the prophet. We do know that he was a contemporary of Amos, preaching in the northern kingdom of Israel slightly later than Amos (ca. 750–724 B.C.E.) and just before it was eventually conquered by the Assyrians in 721 B.C.E. Hosea was from the northern kingdom—these people were his people. Over a quarter of a century, Hosea saw seven kings come and go, most of them corrupt. He took the kings and people's sins personally and passionately ached with God over this.

Even more powerful than his oracles was the living symbol of his marriage. His life is a parable. His marriage became a metaphor of the relationship between God and Israel. In the book, Hosea deals with Gomer, his wife, as the Lord deals with Israel; the prophet's marital life is an embodiment of God's relationship with his people.

In the middle of a violent dispute, the prophet Hosea cries out an utterance about his God: "Therefore I have hewn them by the prophets, I have killed them by the words of my mouth" (Hosea 6:5). These words are fulfilled in chapters 1 and 3 of this prophetic book where we learn how God hewed Hosea by his words. In these chapters we are told about three unprecedented impositions or challenges from God to the prophet.

The first challenge from God to Hosea is that he is to take a whore as his wife: "Go, take for yourself a wife of whoredom and have children of whoredom, for the land commits great whoredom by forsaking the LORD" (Hosea 1:2). There is hardly any other sphere in which humans are so supersensitive as when they are choosing a companion for life. Anyone who dares interfere has to watch his or her step. But here the unthinkable is demanded: to marry a prostitute. But it is important to realize that Hosea is not being asked to enter into marriage with some random tart or streetwalker. Hosea is referring to Canaanite fertility cults (rites). Israel's worship of them is, in Hosea's mind, an act of prostitution. In the metaphor it is Israel who is the whore, symbolized by Hosea's wife Gomer, for she has gone whoring away from God, who in the story is symbolized by Hosea. Hosea has to consummate and demonstrate his God's utter disappointment. God's beloved, his wife Israel, runs away from him in order to give herself to an untold number of false foreign gods. Hosea the prophet is to put into living terms, in his own existence, God's ache and Israel's guilt.

The second challenge is no less upsetting. It too intervenes in one of the most sensitive events of marriage; it involves the naming of children.

> *³So he went and took Gomer daughter of Diblaim, and she conceived and bore him a son.*
>
> *⁴And the LORD said to him, "Name him Jezreel, for in a little while I will punish the house of Jehu for the blood of Jezreel, and I will put an end to the kingdom of the house of Israel. ⁵On that day I will break the bow of Israel in the valley of Jezreel."*
>
> *⁶She conceived again and bore a daughter. Then the LORD said to him, "Name her Lo-ruhamah, for I will no longer have pity on the house of Israel or forgive them. ⁷But I will have pity on the house of Judah, and I will save them by the Lord their God; I will not save them by bow, or by sword, or by war, or by horses, or by horsemen."*
>
> *⁸When she had weaned Lo-ruhamah, she conceived and bore a son. Then the LORD said, "Name him Lo-ammi, for you are not my people and I am not your God"* (Hosea 1:3–8).

Hosea is expected to give his three children names that are not normally personal names at all, names that are indeed gruesomely repellent because of their meaning. The eldest son is to be called Jezreel—that is the name of a city and a district (the broad, fertile valley). In this context the name of the city is clearly reminiscent of a bloodbath perpetuated by the ruling dynasty of Jehu. Jezreel was a town of mass genocide in ancient Israel. As the name for a child, Jezreel is a monstrous name, as if a Jew in modern Germany were to burden a son of his with the name Auschwitz, or an American were to name a son Hiroshima. Through his name, Hosea's first child is to be a reminder that God will requite the blood guiltiness of Jezreel.

The second child, a little girl, is to be given the name Lo-ruhamah, which means "not pitied." That sounds as shocking as if one were to name a female child "Hopeless" instead of Hope. The name of the third child, a boy, is evidence of the complete breach between the people of Israel and God, for this child is to be called Lo-ammi, which means "not my people." It is as if one were to choose "I hate you" for a little boy instead of Matthew; or "Devil" instead of Daniel. Notice how all three names shock the hearer into listening to what is being said. The prophet Hosea is to intertwine his prophetic ministry with his family life. Hosea enters into the pathos of God by naming his children this way. Later on in the Book of Hosea, when the people do return to God, two of the childrens' names are reversed: Lo-ruhamah ("not pitied") becomes Ruhama ("pitied") and Lo-ammi ("not my people") becomes Ammi ("my people") (Hosea 1:10–2:1).

The third challenge God presents to Hosea is to buy his wife back, presumably from her lover.

> ¹The LORD said to me again, "Go, love a woman who has a lover and is an adulteress, just as the LORD loves the people of Israel, though they turn to other gods and love raisin cakes." ²So I bought her for fifteen shekels of silver and a homer of barley and a measure of wine. ³And I said to her, "You must remain as mine for many days; you shall not play the whore, you shall not have intercourse with a man, nor I with you" (Hosea 3:1–3).

It should be mentioned at once to the modern reader that "raisin cakes" were used in pagan Canaanite festivals (see Isaiah 16:7; Jeremiah 7:18) and here they are a synonym for the people worshiping false gods. Hosea, who represents God in the story, is to purchase the people of Israel back, even though the law strictly forbids anyone to take back a divorced person (Deuteronomy 24). God is to take back Israel from her "lover," the god(s) of the Canaanites. The point being, of course, that in his love God never stops loving the Israelites, although in their self-deception they promise themselves a pleasanter existence with other gods. So in his actions Hosea represents God's solicitous, compassionate wooing love as well. Nowhere is this brought out more beautifully than in the following passage:

> *[14]Therefore, I will now allure her, and bring her into the wilderness, and speak tenderly to her. [15]From there I will give her her vineyards, and make the Valley of Achor a door of hope. There she shall respond as in the days of her youth, as at the time when she came out of the land of Egypt. [16]On that day, said the* Lord, *you will call me, "My husband," and no longer will you call me "My Baal." [17]For I will remove the names of the Baals from her mouth, and they shall be mentioned by name no more* (Hosea 2:14–17).

These are whisperings of a faithful God to his beloved. God will allure Israel to the wilderness, the place where they first encountered one another, where there are no longer the enticing voices of the surrounding culture, the place where the heart is open for the wooing of love and the beloved follows her lover once more.

Hosea never tired of proclaiming the indestructibility of God's love. Divine love, which is the basis of human hope, does not die; humanity can never cause God to stop loving.

The deeply sensitive and emotional Hosea experienced the reality of God's love through the intimate relationship of marriage with his spouse and children, a relationship not without its own tragedy. Anyone who could speak so eloquently about the unqualified love of

God in the midst of extraordinary domestic and national disaster has a message of hope that is timeless.

The Book of Joel

Concerning the prophet Joel himself, nothing is known except that he was the son of Pethuel (1:1). His name means "the Lord is God" and it is not unique, for it is shared by many other Old Testament figures. Evidence in the book suggests that he lived in Judah during the Persian period of Jewish history (539–331 B.C.E.). We know only some general conditions about Jerusalem under Persian rule. It is a rule of political stability. Jews are free to worship their God, even if they do not have political independence. There is no immediate prospect of a restoration of the throne of David. Leadership of the Jewish people is in the hands of the priests.

As a prophet, Joel was not only well acquainted with the temple at Jerusalem, but was considered a cultic prophet, that is, a prophet who could exercise his ministry within the life of the temple, even using liturgical forms—such as asking for a fast or a solemn assembly (see 1:14). Joel's message may have been transmitted through priestly circles. He is also the prophet of penance, and his exhortations to fasting and prayer later found a natural place in the Ash Wednesday liturgy of the church.

During Joel's ministry, a national disaster occurred. A plague of locusts swept across the land, the worst attack of locusts in memory. Every crop was destroyed. For an agrarian people it was a devastating blow. Joel uses this tragedy to call Israel's attention toward God and renew its faith. He compares the plague of locusts to an invading army that brings devastation to a city.

The prophet Joel called the people to national mourning and repentance. He saw the plagues of locusts as not merely a natural disaster but a portent of God shaking the earth. Eventually, prayer and penance end the plague and bring rain for new crops. More important, the gift of the spirit renews the people of God. "I will pour out my spirit on all flesh; your sons and your daughters shall prophesy, your old men shall dream dreams, and your young men shall see visions" (Joel 2:28–29). This text is read at Pentecost, the church feast day that celebrates both the coming of the Holy Spirit and the birth of the church (see Acts of the Apostles 2:17–21).

A major element of the Book of Joel is a warrior-type song in which Joel speaks of the coming day of the Lord (2:1–17). He describes this as the day when judgment will be delivered against the nations that have destroyed Israel. The day of the Lord is a theme that runs throughout the Bible. It is sometimes described as a joyful time of celebration (Isaiah 9:3), and at other times as a day of punishment and destruction (Amos 5:19–25). Initially, writers of the Sacred Scriptures applied the term "day of the Lord" only to Israel; Joel applied it to all nations. Gradually, it became connected to the final judgment.

The Book of Joel ends by affirming that the Lord dwells in Zion (Jerusalem) and the land will be fruitful once more. This is Joel's central message: despite plagues and even war, God is present in Judah, and there is a reason for hope.

The Book of Amos

Amos lived and functioned as a prophet when there were two separate kingdoms of Israelites: the northern kingdom, named Israel, and the southern kingdom, named Judah. Amos lived during the reigns of King Uzziah of Judah (783–742 B.C.E.) and Jeroboam II of Israel (786–746 B.C.E.). He was born in the small village of Tekoa in the southern kingdom, where he functioned originally as a herdsman and a tree trimmer (Amos 7:14). Amos tells us that he did not start out to be a prophet, but that God called him to preach to the northern kingdom. Amos was not an official court prophet, like Nathan had been to King David, so he was free to speak against the king and the court and to be unabashedly honest in delivering God's message. Amos is not welcomed by everybody in the northern kingdom of Israel. Amaziah, the priest in the sanctuary at Bethel, orders him out of the country, telling him to go preach in his own country of Judah

(7:12–13). But Amos is undeterred by this clerical rejection and continues unflinchingly in his prophetic ministry.

It is fair to say that among all the Old Testament prophecies, Amos's are the least hopeful. He stresses Israel's destruction, complete and total. There are three reasons for this.

First, Amos focused on a point of pride for Israel: being God's chosen people. Amos agrees wholeheartedly that this is important, but says that being most favored by God means being held most responsible to keep God's law (3:2). Speaking for God, Amos tells the people: "Hear this word that the LORD has spoken against you. . . . You only have I known of all the families of the earth; therefore I will punish you for all your iniquities. . . . Prepare to meet your God, O Israel!" (Amos 3:1–2; 4:12).

Second, Amos sees the leadership not practicing social justice. Amos is the prophet of social justice; his clarion call is: "Let justice roll down like waters, and righteousness like an ever-flowing stream" (5:24). In Amos's worldview, God has a special love for the poor and will judge all nations by the way they treat those who are helpless or in need (see chapters 1–2). The rich who are getting richer at the expense of the poor will themselves be left destitute. The herdsman from Tekoa compares the wealthy and greedy women of Samaria (it was the capital city of the northern kingdom of Israel) to fat cows whom God will judge.

> ¹Hear this word, you cows of Bashan who are on Mount Samaria, who oppress the poor, who crush the needy, who say to their husbands, "Bring something to drink!'"²The Lord GOD has sworn by his holiness: The time is surely coming upon you, when they shall take you away with hooks, even the last of you with fishhooks (Amos 4:1–2; see 6:1–7; 8:4–7).

Third, Amos attacks complacency. Those who think that the day of the Lord, the day of God's judgment, will be a day of great victory for them should think again. Because of their sinful ways, the day of the Lord will be instead a day of great distress (Amos 5:18–20).

Because they have not been faithful to God they should expect to be exiled from their land (Amos 5:27; 6:7).

In sum, it is fair to say that Amos knows the traditions of his people well. He speaks clearly and without ambiguity that marks the speech of priests and kings. When people abuse the poor, Amos inveighs against them. When people place their hope with enemies in military power, rather than God, Amos turns the hope against them. When they place their hope in beautiful but phony worship, he turns their prayer against them. There is no escaping the will or word of God. In the words of Amos, the voice of God is like a lion roaring in the forest (Amos 3:4). God walks with Amos (Amos 3:3). God's words in the mouth of the prophet wither the lush green heights of Mount Carmel (Amos 1:2). In truth, Amos personifies the words: "The lion has roared; who will not fear? The Lord GOD has spoken; who can but prophesy?" (Amos 3:8).

The Book of Obadiah

The Old Testament gives us no clues about the identity or life of the prophet Obadiah. What we do know for sure is that he wrote the shortest book in the Old Testament—just one chapter long. Scholars are convinced that the book was written toward the end of the fifth century B.C.E. after the Babylonian exile.

To understand the Book of Obadiah some background needs to be shared. In the Book of Genesis, some conflict is recorded between Jacob (the father of the nation of Israel) and his brother Esau (the father of the nation of Edom, later called Idumea). Subsequent generations and hundreds of years later, the Israelites still fought with the Edomites. In the Book of Obadiah, this bitterness is ever present and deepens.

In 587 B.C.E., Jerusalem was destroyed by the Babylonians. Evidently, the Edomites not only did not aid their "brother" (Obadiah 1:10), but took advantage of Israel's situation by gloating (1:12), looting (1:13), and raiding its territory (1:14). Because of the Edomites' severe cruelty, the prophet Obadiah declared the destruction of Edom by another country (1:15).

Like many of the Old Testament prophets, Obadiah ultimately saw a hopeful future for Israel. All Israel's armies would perish before the strong arm of the Lord. And there would come a day—"the day of the LORD" (Obadiah 1:15)—when all Jews would unite and return to Mount Zion (the place where the temple stood in Jerusalem). Mount Zion would "rule Mount Esau" and that new ". . . kingdom shall be the LORD's" (1:21).

The Book of Micah

Micah, whose name means "who is like Yahweh," was an eighth-century B.C.E. prophet from the obscure village of Moresheth in the southern kingdom of Judah. The book gives no further direct information about the prophet. According to Micah 1:1, he was active as a prophet during the reigns of kings Jothan (ca. 750–735 B.C.E.), Ahaz (ca. 735–715 B.C.E.), and Hezekiah (ca. 715–687 B.C.E.), and thus a contemporary of Isaiah of Jerusalem, Amos, and Hosea. The seven chapters of the Book of Micah consist of three parts.

DIVISION OF THE BOOK OF MICAH

I. Judgment against leaders and people (chapters 1–3)
II. Hope for God's Messiah and the gathering in God's holy city (chapters 4–5)
III. From judgment to hope (chapters 6–7)

Micah warns the people that because of their sinfulness disaster is certain to come. God is angry because of their greed. The rich exploit the poor by taking their land (Micah 2:2) and merchants cheat with false scales and inflated prices (6:11). Judges accept bribes to render false judgments (3:11; 7:3). Priests and prophets preach and teach for money (3:11). Micah's harshest criticism falls on the leaders of the people (chapter 3). But he also announces a lawsuit in which the Lord accuses the whole people of turning away (6:1–8).

Not all of the passages in the Book of Micah are bad news, however. Micah recalls the traditions of Judah: the hope for a messianic king like David (Micah 5:1–5) and for the gathering of all people in Zion to hear God's word (4:1–5). The final passage in the Book of Micah is a beautiful testimony to the power of God's forgiveness. God will trample our sins underfoot and throw them into the depths of the sea (7:18–20).

There are passages in the Book of Micah that merit some further comment. The first deals with treatment of the poor. Micah seems to have been a poor person himself, who suffered with the poor. The plight of the poor was central to his ministry and this is why he speaks so passionately about their abuse: ". . . you who hate the good and love the evil, who tear the skin off my people, and the flesh off their bones; who eat the flesh of my people, flay their skin off them, break their bones in pieces, and chop them up like meat in a kettle, like flesh in a caldron" (Micah 3:2–3). This statement is uttered by the prophet to the religious leaders who are the abusers of the poor. Micah did not mince words when it came to confronting those who abused the disenfranchised of society.

While railing against the abuses of power on behalf of the royal establishment, he offers a word of hope. There will come a leader who will shepherd God's people rightly.

> *2But you, O Bethlehem of Ephrathah, who are one of the little clans of Judah, from you shall come forth for me one who is to rule in Israel, . . . 4[H]e shall stand and feed his flock in the strength of the LORD, in the majesty of the name of the LORD, his God* (Micah 5:2–4).

These verses announce the arrival of a new "David," a ruler from the traditional house of David, who will do right for the people according to God's own desires.

Micah also has to contend with false prophets, whose interpretations of realities around them are more pleasing in the ears of the people. He soundly scolds them (Micah 3:5–7). Micah is not afraid to speak the words people might not want to hear. That is the personality of a true prophet.

A final passage from Micah is set in the context of a covenant lawsuit (Micah 6:1–8). God places all the people on trial for failing to live up to the prescriptions of the covenant. In it God rejects the people's empty worship, in favor of justice and goodness. God delivers his request through the marvelous oracle of Micah, who proclaims: "He has told you, O mortal, what is good; and what does the LORD require of you but to do justice, and to love kindness, and to walk humbly with your God?" (Micah 6:8). Here the prophet Micah offers a classical definition of biblical religion.

Themes Common to the Prophets
Hosea, Amos, and Micah

The themes of "covenant" and the "passion of God" are common to all three eighth-century B.C.E. prophets. Each prophet stressed the themes a little differently and provided a plurality of vivid images.

Covenants

The covenant transforms the identity of both parties: "I will be your God, and you shall be my people" (Leviticus 26:12; Jeremiah 7:23; 31:33; Ezekiel 37:27). God is now named the "God of Abraham" or the "God of Jacob" or the "God of Israel" (Exodus 3:6; 5:1). The people are now forever known as God's people (Psalms 28:8–9). So when Hosea is told to name one of his children "not my people," it is a shattering statement that both God and the people have lost their identity. God says, ". . . for you are not my people and I am not your God." (Literally, "I will not be your I AM"; Hosea 1:9.) As covenant people we are either God's people or we are no one. Even more amazing, God is either our God or not God!

This identity that the people have in the relationship known as covenant, the prophets begin to describe as a life-sharing bond between them. Of the two most intimate relationships we know (husband and wife, parent and child), Hosea uses both in his book. In the first three chapters of his book, God is described as the husband of Israel. In chapter 11, the parent-child metaphor appears. God says,

"When Israel was a child, I loved him, and out of Egypt I called my son" (Hosea 11:1). What can this mean? We are God's beloved, as close to God as a husband is to a wife, a parent to a child. We are called, in turn, to love God with our whole heart and soul and mind and strength (see Deuteronomy 6:5).

Through the covenant, we are also called to be what we were created to be: images of God, like God as a child is like a parent (see Genesis 1:27). We share life with God, and therefore we must live like God, loving one another and all creation as God loves (Leviticus 19:1, 18, 34). The prophets insist on this. Almost every time they accuse the people of sin, the sin is a failure to love one another: ". . . they who trample the head of the poor into the dust of the earth, and push the afflicted out of the way" (Amos 2:7). They say they are ". . . buying the poor for silver and the needy for a pair of sandals, and selling the sweepings of the wheat" (Amos 8:6). ". . . they all lie in wait for blood, and they hunt each other with nets" (Micah 7:2). Thus they break the covenant bond.

When God renews the covenant with Israel, God says, "And I will take you for my wife forever; I will take you for my wife in righteousness and in justice, in steadfast love and in mercy" (Hosea 2:19). God insists: "For I desire steadfast love, and not sacrifice" (Hosea 6:6). Hosea exhorts us: "Sow for yourselves righteousness; reap steadfast love; break up your fallow ground; for it is time to seek the LORD, that he may come and rain righteousness upon you" (Hosea 10:12). Amos says that we must "Hate evil and love good, and establish justice in the gate; . . . But let justice roll down like waters, and righteousness like an ever-flowing stream" (Amos 5:15, 24). But perhaps Micah sums it up best: "He has told you, O mortal, what is good; and what does the LORD require of you but to do justice, and to love kindness, and to walk humbly with your God?" (Micah 6:8).

The Passion of God as Portrayed in the Prophets Hosea, Amos, and Micah

God cares so much for his people that when they turn away he becomes passionately angry. The language of the prophets reveals the intensity of this divine anger. The first words of the prophecy of Amos strike us with terror: "The Lord roars from Zion" (Amos 1:2). God roars in judgment against all the nations who have used violence to increase their wealth and power. But most of all, God roars against the beloved people of Israel (Amos 2:6–16). They have worshiped other gods. They have trampled the poor in their greed. They have failed to recognize that everything is God's gift. Yet they are the people God loves most, "You only have I known of all the families of the earth" (Amos 3:2). So God will punish them.

In Hosea, God is an angry husband who denies his children and drives away his wife (Hosea 1:6–2:7). God is a lion who tears the people apart (5:14). God will tear out their hearts like a bear robbed of her young cubs (13:8). Why? Because "they were satisfied, and their heart was proud" (13:6). God complains that they strayed and sinned: "I would redeem them, but they speak lies against me" (7:13). So God ". . . will remember their iniquity, and punish their sins" (8:13).

Micah describes the coming of the Lord in judgment (Micah 1:2–4). As God advances, ". . . the mountains will melt under him and the valleys will burst open, like wax near the fire, like waters poured down a steep place" (Micah 1:4). His condemnation falls particularly upon the leaders who have failed to shepherd the people and lead them toward God. Instead these wicked leaders are like cannibals, devouring God's beloved people. So when ". . . they will cry out to the Lord, . . . he will not answer them; he will hide his face from them at that time" (Micah 3:4).

The prophet Micah also gives us a glimpse into the wounded heart of God. God brings the people to trial (Micah 6:2). But when it comes time to accuse them of their crimes, God cries out instead: "O my people, what have I done to you? In what have I wearied you? Answer me!" (Micah 6:3). God longs for his people passionately. God has given them everything and yet they ignore him. When they plead guilty, God does not impose a harsh sentence. God still has not given up. Their sentence reveals God's hope, care, and compassion for them: ". . . do justice, . . . love kindness, and . . . walk humbly with your God" (Micah 6:8).

Thus, it is not surprising that Micah does not fear God's anger. He knows God does not persist in anger forever and so he is determined to wait. "I must bear the indignation of the LORD, because I have sinned against him, until he takes my side and executes judgment for me. He will bring me out to the light; I shall see his vindication" (Micah 7:9). God's anger is not the last word.

God's Passionate Mercy As Portrayed in the Prophets Hosea, Amos, and Micah

The three prophets—Amos, Hosea, and Micah—were compelled to deliver painful messages to God's people. Yet all three of them knew, beyond the shadow of a doubt, that God's mercy would always overcome God's anger! In two visions of disaster, the prophet Amos pleads with God to relent. "O Lord GOD, forgive, I beg you! How can Jacob stand? He is so small!" (Amos 7:2; see verse 5). Twice God holds back the disaster. How could God resist? But in the other two visions (Amos 7:7–9; 8:1–3), God announces judgment before Amos can speak. The end will indeed come. Still there is a niche for hope. Perhaps the Lord will again have mercy (see Amos 5:15). This little fissure in the wall of God's judgment makes room for the announcement of mercy at the end of the Book of Amos: "I will not utterly destroy the house of Jacob" (Amos 9:8). "I will restore the fortunes of my people Israel" (Amos 9:14).

The longing of God to have mercy on his beloved people is even more evident in Hosea. In the midst of God's attempt to divorce himself from his people, he announces: "I will now allure her, and bring her into the wilderness, and speak tenderly to her" (Hosea 2:14). The thought of punishing the people wrings this cry from God's heart: "How can I give you up, Ephraim? How can I hand you over, O Israel? . . . My heart recoils within me; my compassion grows warm and tender. I will not execute my fierce anger" (Hosea 11:8-9).

It is Micah who most eloquently describes God's mercy:

> [18]"Who is a God like you, pardoning iniquity and passing over the transgression of the remnant of your possession? He does not retain his anger forever, because he delights in showing clemency. [19]He will again have compassion upon us; he will tread our iniquities under foot. You will cast all our sins into the depths of the sea" (Micah 7:18–19).

God's passionate desire for this people will not allow him to have anger have its way. God's love is always stronger than God's wrath.

The Endurance of God's Passionate Love

The prophets teach us over and over that there is no end to God's love (see Psalm 136). The whole prophecy of Amos depends on God's declaration of love, "You only have I known of all the families of the earth . . ." (Amos 3:2). The repeated cry of God in chapter 4, "Yet you did not return to me," is the cry of a lover who longs for the beloved to come back (Amos 4:6, 8, 9, 10, 11). Even though this Book of Amos is so full of harsh words, they all spring from the yearning of God's heart for reunion.

God's longing is made clear in Hosea. Nothing else will do except a return of love for love: "For I desire steadfast love and not sacrifice . . ." (Hosea 6:6). God tells the story of his passionate love: "When Israel was a child, I loved him, and out of Egypt I called my son. . . . I taught Ephraim to walk, I took them up in my arms; . . . I led them with cords of human kindness, with bands of love. I was to them like those who lift infants to their cheeks" (Hosea 11:1, 3–4). So God's final word must be healing. God says: "I will be like the dew to Israel; he shall blossom like the lily, he shall strike root like the forest of Lebanon" (Hosea 14:5).

It is because of enduring love that God brought his people out of the land of Egypt and gave them wise leaders to guide them through the wilderness. It is because of enduring love that God brought them into the promised land, so that they might realize what God has done for them (Micah 6:4–6). In the last analysis, everything comes from love.

The Book of Nahum

Nothing is known about the prophet Nahum other than his name and his place of birth, Elkosh, a town in southwest Judah. More is known, however, about the time contemporaneous with and just prior to when the Book of Nahum was written. During this time period, the Assyrian empire had been the terror of the ancient Middle East for several centuries. In 721 B.C.E., it destroyed the northern part of Israel, called at that time the Kingdom of Israel, leveling its capital city, Samaria. In 701 B.C.E., it invaded the southern part of Israel, called the Kingdom of Judah, and laid siege to its capital, Jerusalem. The siege broke off and Jerusalem did not fall, but the people of the city received a gruesome taste of Assyria's savage cruelty. This historical background has led scholars to date the writing of the Book of Nahum sometime during the half century between 663 and 612 B.C.E. These dates are fixed by the reference in Nahum 3:8 to the fall of Thebes (663 B.C.E.) and the fact that Nineveh (the capital of the Assyrian empire) was destroyed in 612.

The sole concern of the ministry of the prophet Nahum and the central message of his book is the destruction of the Assyrian empire, which is seen as evil. In the first chapter of his book, Nahum declares the coming wrath of God upon Assyria and the good news that this is for the kingdom of Judah and the inhabitants of Jerusalem. In chapters 2 and 3, Nahum describes in violent and graphic detail the destruction of Nineveh. Nahum does not want his readers to be too surprised when Assyria falls in 612 B.C.E., for he sees the justice of God being worked out. In Nahum's mind, the Assyrians are finally getting a taste of their own medicine. Nahum seems almost to be gloating over Assyria's demise:

> *[18]Your shepherds are asleep,*
> *O king of Assyria;*
> *your nobles slumber.*
> *Your people are scattered on the mountains*
> *with no one to gather them.*

> ¹⁹*There is no assuaging your hurt,*
> *your wound is mortal.*
> *All who hear the news about you*
> *clap their hands over you.*
> *For who has ever escaped*
> *your endless cruelty?* (Nahum 3:18–19).

We could come away from the Book of Nahum with an image of God as violent and angry. However, interspersed among the threats and violence against Assyria, Nahum also proclaims words of comfort to God's chosen people: good news and peace are coming for Judah (Nahum 1:15); the Lord will restore Israel to its original majesty (2:2). We even discover some profoundly wonderful reminders of God's love and protection, which counterbalance the image of the God of vengeance and destruction: ". . . the LORD is slow to anger but great in power" (1:3); "The LORD is good, a stronghold in a day of trouble; he protects those who take refuge in him . . ." (1:7). The Book of Nahum reminds us that there are many images for God, and that God has many sides and a multitude of portrayals and is always more than we can ever imagine.

The Book of Habakkuk

Practically nothing is known about the prophet Habakkuk, except that he was a prophet in the southern kingdom of Judah in the late seventh century B.C.E., most probably during the reign of Jehoiakim (609–597 B.C.E.). The prophet Habakkuk was ready to despair because the Chaldeans (another name for the Babylonians) and the corrupt king of Judah, Jehoiakim, were causing so much trouble. So the prophet decided to cry out to God about this trouble. God answered him in a very surprising way, informing him that the Chaldeans—as bad as they were—were chosen as God's vehicle to punish the wicked all over the earth. Unimpressed and not satisfied with this answer, Habakkuk asked God why God was silent while the wicked destroyed the righteous. Habakkuk was the first prophet who dared to ask God about God's own behavior. God then spoke to

214

Habakkuk in a vision (Habakkuk 2:2), saying that justice would come to the wicked in its own time, but ". . . the righteous live by their faith" (2:4).

The prophet closes his book with a powerful prayer of confidence to God: "O LORD, I have heard of your renown, and I stand in awe, O LORD, of your work" (Habakkuk 3:2).

The Book of Zephaniah

Zephaniah is a prophet of the southern kingdom of Judah, whose prophecies span the reign of King Josiah of Judah (640–609 B.C.E.). King Josiah's reign is described in detail in 2 Chronicles 34–35 and 2 Kings 22:1–23:30. Zephaniah followed First Isaiah and Micah and functioned a little before Habakkuk and during the time of Nahum.

The central message of Zephaniah is that the fire of God's wrath is about to burn up a creation gone wrong (Zephaniah 1:1–2; 3:9), but this announcement is directed principally to Judah and Jerusalem in an effort to call forth their repentance. According to Zephaniah, there are four sins of the covenant people: their idolatry, represented by worship of such foreign deities as the Canaanite Baals (1:4), the Assyrian astral deities (1:5, 9), and the god Milcom of Ammon (1:5); their accommodation to foreign ways (1:8); unethical actions within their own society (1:9); and, above all, their indifference toward and unbelief in the God of Israel (1:12). The Judeans have become ruined, proclaims the prophet, because they no longer believe that God does anything in their world (1:12).

The Judeans and foreign peoples who share their unbelief will, therefore, be laid to waste on the coming day of the Lord. The coming of this awful day is described in Zephaniah 1:14–16, a passage whose initial words were translated into Latin as *Dies irae* (day of wrath), later developed into poetry, and then used in various Latin masses and numerous literary and musical works. The day will open with a sacrifice, when God will consecrate his warriors (Zephaniah 1:7), followed by the war cry of God as he wades into the fray (1:14). The battle will begin in Jerusalem's commercial center (1:10–11) and from there spread throughout the earth.

Only repentance and casting oneself on the mercy of God can save Judah on that day. The prophet Zephaniah, therefore, calls his compatriots to hold an assembly of fasting and repentance (Zephaniah 2:1–3) that will evidence Judah's humility, obedience, and trust in the Lord (2:3). If Judah so repents it may be saved (2:3). However, Judah and Jerusalem, symbolized by their corrupt leaders (Zephaniah 3:3–4), refuse Zephaniah's call, as they have always refused God's correction through the prophets (3:2), through military defeat (3:6), and through the evidence of God's work in the natural world (3:5). The judgment upon God's people is therefore inevitable. But according to Zephaniah, a remnant of faithful will be preserved in Judah (2:7, 9) and will spread out over foreign lands. Within Jerusalem there will be left a humble, trusting, and righteous folk (3:9–13) who do no wrong. God will establish his kingdom over all the earth (3:14–17). Jerusalem will rejoice (3:14) and God will exult in the midst of it (3:17).

The Book of Haggai

While there is no biographical information given in the Old Testament on the prophet Haggai, he along with the prophet Zechariah are mentioned in Ezra 5:1 and 6:14. Haggai's prophetic ministry was to the former exiles newly returned from Babylon to Judah and Jerusalem. He launched an active campaign to rebuild the destroyed temple. Evidently, he helped oversee reconstruction of the temple during a time of blight, drought, and general dissatisfaction on the part of the newly returned exiles. Haggai attributed all of these misfortunes to the failure to complete the new temple. Haggai says that God is punishing the people for concentrating on the decoration of their own houses before completing the house of the Lord. Haggai urges Zerubbabel, the governor of Judah and Joshua (Jeshua), the high priest, to rally the people to the crucial task of completing the temple.

The temple still lay in ruins when Haggai began to prophesy in 520 B.C.E. (Haggai 1:1). "Thus says the LORD of hosts: . . . Go up to the hills and bring wood and build the house, so that I may take pleasure in it and be honored, says the LORD. . . . Because my house lies in ruins, while all of you hurry off to your own houses" (Haggai 1:7–9). By the time Haggai ended his ministry, some three and a half months later, on 18 December 520, enormous progress had been made on rebuilding the temple.

The actual decision to rebuild the temple dates back to the first return of the exiles in 538 B.C.E. (Ezra 1:8–16; 3:6–4:4). This decision was evidently reactivated as the result of Haggai's eloquent exhortations. While Haggai lacks the great poetic visions or sweeping dramatic voice of the other prophets, the book is valuable because it documents the history of the period of the return from Babylon. Besides the books of Ezra and Nehemiah, only Haggai and the book of the prophet Zechariah cast any light on this significant period.

The Book of Zechariah

The Book of Zechariah has two parts. The first is chapters 1 through 8, made up of visions and oracles for the most part attributed to Zechariah, son of Berechiah, who was active as a prophet from 520 to 518 B.C.E. He will be referred to here as First Zechariah. The second part of the book is chapters 9 through 14, sometimes called Deutero-Zechariah (Second Zechariah). It is made up of anonymous oracles that, though difficult to date, derive from a period later than that of the first section, most probably the fifth and fourth centuries B.C.E.

The setting of the first part of the book (chapters 1 through 8) is rather clear. Zechariah lived around the same time as Haggai, after the exiled Israelites returned from Babylon to Jerusalem. Second Zechariah, who may have been one or more prophets, wrote about two hundred years later.

The optimistic message of the first prophet, in chapters 1 through 8, revolves around two concerns: the rebuilding of the temple and the end of time. That Zechariah, and his contemporary, Haggai, were sent by God to rebuild the temple is boldly stated in the Book of Ezra. "Now the prophets, Haggai and Zechariah son of Iddo, prophesied to the Jews who were in Judah and Jerusalem, in the name of the God of Israel who was over them" (Ezra 5:1). Haggai speaks directly about rebuilding the temple (Haggai 1:8). Meanwhile, Zechariah addressed a more basic issue: "Therefore say to them, Thus says the LORD of Hosts: Return to me, says the LORD of Hosts, and I will return to you, says the LORD of Hosts" (Zechariah 1:3).

Zechariah saw that a rebuilt temple was needed to restore the people's unity, identity, and relationship with God. Through a series of visions, he announced his message. Earlier prophets had seen visions, such as those given to inaugurate their prophetic ministries (see Isaiah 6 and Ezekiel 1, for example). But in Zechariah, visions are the chief vehicle used to convey God's message. The central message of the prophet's visions was that Israel would be restored. It would become a nation of justice, faith, love, mercy, and truth, where the Lord would dwell. Even the Gentiles (non-Jews) would come from faraway lands to worship God.

THEOLOGICAL THEMES IN THE BOOK OF ZECHARIAH

The Transcendence of God

God is considered beyond human experience, supreme. God was dramatically present and intimate with earlier prophets. He spoke to them directly. But while God is intensely present in the Book of Zechariah, he rarely speaks directly to Zechariah. He usually communicates in visions. Angels assume more importance as messengers and interpreters (see Zechariah 1:12–14).

Social Justice

Like other prophets, Zechariah emphasized the importance of love and action for the poor. Chapter 7 contains a powerful summary of the prophetic teaching on social justice: ". . . render true judgments, show kindness and mercy to one another; do not oppress the widow, the orphan, the alien, or the poor; and do not devise evil in your hearts against one another" (Zechariah 7:9–10).

Liturgy/Worship

Central to Zechariah is the restoration of the temple and the preparation of the high priest to lead the people in worship. The book is concerned with the revival of the temple liturgy, which is seen as the heart of the life of God's people. Worship is to bubble over into holy behavior. Zechariah promises that even horses will bear signs of holiness and ordinary pots and pans will be holy! (Zechariah 14:20–21)

> **The Coming of the Messianic Age**
> Zechariah concludes with an oracle that highlights Israel's final victory over her enemies (see chapters 12 to 14). In that messianic time, the Lord will rescue Jerusalem after much suffering and will give the people their great blessings.

Second Zechariah wrote later, when Israel was under Greek domination. Various bits of evidence point to an origin in the years following 333 B.C.E. It seems that Second Zechariah preached not through visions, but through oracles (prophetic speeches) of warning, violence, and also promise. He talked about a great battle that was about to take place between the forces of God and the forces of evil. This was the final war, which would bring an end to the present-day evil and corrupt world. But Second Zechariah also proclaimed the coming of a humble king, who would bring peace to all the nations. Jerusalem would be purified and would become victorious as the city where God reigns as the highest power for good.

The Book of Malachi

Nothing is known about Malachi, a name that may be a pseudonym, as it means "my messenger." Although Malachi stands as the last Book of the Christian Old Testament, and the last of the twelve minor prophetic books in the Hebrew Bible, it was not the last composed. The historical evidence suggests it was written some fifty years after Haggai and Zechariah and the reconstructed temple, but prior to the reforms carried out by Ezra and Nehemiah starting around 458 B.C.E.

A very brief book, consisting of only four chapters, Malachi is mostly concerned with laxity in relationship to keeping the covenant: "Why then are we faithless to one another, profaning the covenant of our ancestors?" (Malachi 2:10). In addition, Malachi is deeply concerned by the failure of Israel's priests to provide leadership. Through a rapid-fire series of questions and answers, the prophet Malachi utters biting and harsh words against the priests of the Temple for failing to live up to their calling to honor God, comparing them to Levi, who was a good and honest priest who kept God's covenant.

A second issue Malachi had to deal with was marriage and divorce (see Malachi 2:10–16). Evidently, many Jewish men were marrying non-Jewish women and divorcing their Jewish wives. The reason for this is not clear. Nonetheless, the prophet challenges the Jewish spouses to be faithful to one another, because their marriages are a reminder of God's covenant with the people.

In addition, like many of the prophets, Malachi decries crimes and sins in terms that remain as timely today as they were over twenty-five hundred years ago:

> Then I will draw near to you for judgment; I will be swift to bear witness against the sorcerers, against the adulterers, against those who swear falsely, against those who oppress the hired workers in their wages, the widow and the orphan, against those who thrust aside the alien, and do not fear me, says the LORD of hosts (Malachi 3:5).

The book ends with a prophecy that forms a bridge to the New Testament and the coming of Jesus. Malachi proclaims: "See, I am sending my messenger to prepare the way before me, and the Lord whom you seek will suddenly come to his temple. The messenger of the covenant in whom you delight—indeed, he is coming, says the LORD of hosts" (Malachi 3:1). This messenger is understood to be the prophet Elijah, who will come before the day of Judgment. His job will be to prepare the way for God. New Testament writers associate this prophecy with John the Baptist, who prepared the way for the coming of the Messiah, Jesus of Nazareth.

Other Prophetic Literature

The two books discussed in this section, while not part of the scroll of the twelve prophets, are both anonymous and yet have been connected to prophetic figures. (In Catholic Bibles, the books of Lamentations and Baruch follow right after the Book of Jeremiah.) They are being examined here because they were not composed at the time of Jeremiah, but later.

The Book of Lamentations

No modern person can quite grasp the feelings of the people of Judah over the destruction of Jerusalem by the Babylonians. For the people of the day it was beyond words. Written by an anonymous author during the Babylonian exile, the Book of Lamentations poetically and powerfully expresses the overwhelming shock and grief the Israelites felt over the loss of their homes, their freedom, their capital, and the temple.

In some Bibles, the book is entitled "The Lamentations of Jeremiah," after the trend set by the Greek translators of the Old Testament in 200 B.C.E. We know now that Jeremiah was not the author because of discrepancies in thought, terminology, and style when compared to Jeremiah's authentic writings. But it is easy to see why the book was attributed to him.

It was written in Jerusalem soon after the city's destruction by the Babylonians (587 B.C.E.), as foretold by Jeremiah, and the interpretation of the tragedy as punishment for the sins of the people echoes the utterances of the prophet. Further, the Book of Jeremiah itself contains a series of personal lamentations (see Jeremiah 11:18–12:6; 15:10–21; 17:14–18; 18:18–23; 20:7–13; 20:14–18).

Structure of the Book of Lamentations

While the Book of Lamentations is a collection of five psalm songs, each a separate chapter in the book, its structure is quite interesting. If you take a careful look, you will notice that each poem has twenty-two verses, except the third one, which has sixty-six. This is not an accident, it is deliberate. In the original Hebrew language, each verse of the first, second, fourth, and fifth poems begins with a different letter of the Hebrew alphabet, which has twenty-two letters. In the third poem—the one with sixty-six verses—every set of three verses begins with a different letter of the Hebrew alphabet. This poetic structure, called acrostic, cannot be conveyed or successfully seen in English translations of the Bible. (Interestingly, both the *Jerusalem*

Bible and the *New Jerusalem Bible* attempt to convey this by printing the names of the Hebrew letter in the left-hand margin next to the English translation.) Scholars are convinced that the alphabetical structure of the poems made them easier to memorize.

Moods in The Book of Lamentations

In the five lamentations there is a progression of moods rather than thought. In the first lamentation, a visitor to the ruined city ponders the tragic reversal from beauty to misery: "The roads to Zion mourn, for no one comes to her festivals; all her gates are desolate, her priests groan; her young girls grieve, and her lot is bitter" (Lamentations 1:4). Then Jerusalem speaks in her own name for her desolation (Lamentations 1:7–22). The second lamentation is by a citizen of Jerusalem who declares of the city that ". . . vast as the sea is your ruin; who can heal you?" (Lamentations 2:13). The third lamentation, the centerpiece of the book, expresses the profound pain of an average citizen of Jerusalem, a person who ". . . has seen affliction" (Lamentations 3:1). The fourth lamentation returns to a mood similar to that of chapter 1, with a "reporter" giving a more balanced picture of the devastation of the city. In the fifth lamentation, the inhabitants of Jerusalem address God directly: "Remember, O LORD what has befallen us; look, and see our disgrace! . . . Restore us to yourself, O LORD, that we may be restored" (Lamentations 5:1, 21).

It seems that one purpose of the poems in the Book of Lamentations is to help the ancient Israelites heal from the horrible tragedy of their loss. The poems may be seen as accomplishing this in three ways. First, in describing Israel's present loss and tragedy, they acknowledge that both grief and mourning are needed. Second, they challenge Israel to look at its past, to both accept responsibility for its sin—failure to live the covenant—and to remember its great blessings from God. Finally, they encourage Israel to have hope for the future. In image after image, Israel is assured that the door to God's mercy is still open, in spite of great pain and loss. "The steadfast love of the

Lord never ceases, his mercies never come to an end; they are new every morning . . ." (Lamentations 3:22–23).

The Book of Baruch

The author of this book claims to be a follower of the prophet Jeremiah, who was writing from Babylon with the exiles after 587 B.C.E. Jeremiah and Baruch were both supposedly taken to Egypt in 582 B.C.E. (Jeremiah 43:6–7). However, this is not the case at all. In the ancient Near Eastern world it was not at all uncommon for people to write books and letters in the name of famous ancestors or figures. This is known as authorship by attribution. Several Old and New Testament books were written in this manner, including the Book of Baruch. An anonymous person collected a variety of oral traditions and independent writings and named them for Baruch, the secretary of the prophet Jeremiah, most likely in order to emphasize their link with Jeremiah's tradition of prophecy.

The Book of Baruch is a reflection on the destruction of Jerusalem. The author freely borrowed from the imagery of Jeremiah. The book is composed of four distinct parts.

Part one is a narrative introduction (Baruch 1:1–14) which sets the writing in Babylonia during the exile. Baruch returns the temple vessels to Jehoiakim, the high priest in Jerusalem, along with funds for burnt and sin offerings and a request that the accompanying prayers of confession be read in the temple on feast days.

Part two is a prayer of confession (Baruch 1:15–3:8). It is a penitential prose prayer on behalf of the inhabitants of Judah as well as the exiles.

Part three is a hymn to Wisdom personified echoing both Job 28, in speaking of a search for Wisdom, and Ecclesiastes 24, in identifying her as the Torah, the law of God.

The concluding part of Baruch is a psalm of comfort (Baruch 4:5–5:9). It is composed primarily as a lament over Zion and over her lost children, somewhat similar in content to the Book of Lamentations.

Since both the author of and date for the Book of Baruch are unknown, it is not clear how its writer, who lived long after the sixth century B.C.E., chose to appropriate the memory of the exile. Possibly he wants to point out the painful lessons learned from the past, implying that unless we learn from history, we will repeat its mistakes.

The Postexilic Books of Ezra and Nehemiah

The books of Ezra and Nehemiah deal with the history of Judah after the return from exile in Babylon. The books not only describe the reconstruction of the temple, but the restoration of a "godly remnant," whose mission was to restore and uphold the true faith. Considered a single book until around the year 300 C.E., when the material was divided into two parts, the books were thought to have been written by the same person who wrote the books of Chronicles. Although there are some discrepancies regarding the precise dates when Ezra and Nehemiah made their trips to Jerusalem, the time frame of the return to Jerusalem, often called the postexile, is well within the bounds of documented "history," unlike many other earlier periods in the Bible.

The Book of Ezra: A Summary

The Book of Ezra opens with the decree of Cyrus, the king of Persia, following his capture of Babylon in 539 B.C.E., that those who want to may leave Babylon and return to Jerusalem to rebuild the temple. Unlike other "foreign" kings and pharaohs of the Bible, who were usually viewed as scoundrels, sinners, and murderers, Cyrus gets pretty good reviews from the Bible's composers. Founder of an extensive empire that lasted more than two hundred years, Cyrus was an extraordinary leader. Under Cyrus and his successors, much of the ancient Near East, from India to Egypt and the borders of Greece, were brought under one ruler, a feat neither the Egyptians nor earlier Babylonian empire builders had accomplished. Even the later Greek writers, who had no great love of the Persians—classical Greece's archrival—considered Cyrus a model ruler. Unlike other ancient conquerors who attempted to force their own religions and practices on conquered peoples, Cyrus and his successors permitted the "captive nations" to preserve and restore their own institutions. In light of this background, we can now turn our attention to a summary of the Book of Ezra.

The return of exiled Jews to Jerusalem was not a mass, sudden movement, but took place gradually, in waves. In the year after Cyrus captured Babylon, the initial group of Jews came back to Jerusalem starting in 538 B.C.E. They were led by Sheshbazzar, a "prince of Judah," despite his Persian name, who served as territorial governor. Under his leadership, reconstruction of the temple commenced almost immediately. But a conflict soon arose between those Judeans who had been left behind and the returning Jews. Over the nearly fifty years of exile, the mostly poor Judeans who had been allowed to remain behind had staked claims to some of the land left behind by the exiles, the elite of Judean society, mostly aristocrats or members of the priestly class. Animosity was natural between those who had stayed and the returnees, who expected to return to their previous status. The conflict between the two groups brought work on rebuilding the temple to a halt.

About seventeen years later, a second wave of returnees were permitted to return during the reign of Darius I, a twenty-eight-year-old soldier and relative of Cyrus, who took the Persian throne in 522 B.C.E. following a series of intrigues and plots. Now led by Zerubbabel, the grandson of King Jehoiachin and a descendent of King David and the high priest Jeshua, work commenced on the temple in 520 B.C.E. Encouraged by the prophets Haggai and Zechariah, the returnees completed the second temple in 516 B.C.E.

The Judah to which they returned was a far cry from Solomon's empire, and the second temple, completed in roughly March/April of 516 B.C.E., was a modest affair, reflecting these changed circumstances. Judah was a fraction of the size of Solomon's Israel, and territory once controlled by the Jews was now in the hands of neighboring Edom and the Samaritans. Despite the fact that Cyrus provided funding for rebuilding the temple, the new center of Jewish worship was not as grand as Solomon's in all its glory had been. There is very little description of the rebuilt temple in the Book of Ezra, except that it was to be sixty cubits (approximately one hundred feet or thirty meters) high and sixty cubits wide, with walls constructed of three courses of stone and one of timber. All of the gold and silver vessels salvaged from the original temple and taken to Babylon were also returned to Jerusalem. But unmentioned here or elsewhere in the Old Testament is the fate of the Ark of the Covenant, Judaism's most sacred object. Whether it was destroyed in 586 B.C.E., when Jerusalem was sacked and the temple burned by Nebuchadnezzar's army, or salvaged and taken by Babylon by the captives remains a biblical mystery to this day.

In 458 B.C.E., more than fifty years after the temple was dedicated, a third wave of returning exiles came back during the reign of Darius's successor, Artaxerxes. Ezra, a Jewish official of the Persian government, along with seventeen hundred Babylonian Jews, was sent to ensure that Jewish law was being strictly observed. To his great dismay, Ezra discovered that many of the former exiles, as well as those who had remained in Judah, had been intermarrying with non-Jews.

¹After these things had been done, the officials approached me and said, "The people of Israel, the priests, and the Levites have not separated themselves from the peoples of the lands with their abominations, from the Canaanites, the Hittites, the Perizzites, the Jebusites, the Ammonites, the Moabites, the Egyptians, and Amorites. ²For they have taken some of their daughters as wives for themselves and for their sons. Thus the holy seed has mixed itself with the peoples of the lands, and in this faithlessness the officials and leaders have led the way." ³When I heard this, I tore my garment and my mantle, and pulled hair from my head and beard, and sat appalled. ⁴Then all who trembled at the words of the God of Israel, because of the faithlessness of the returned exiles, gathered around me while I sat appalled until the evening sacrifice (Ezra 9:1–4).

In Jewish history, law, and theology, Ezra is a character of great significance. Some scholars rank him second only to Moses as a law-giver and prophet. Ezra was responsible for the extensive codification of the laws, including those governing temple worship and the scriptural canon (official list of books in the Old Testament). He also contributed to the eventual replacement of priests by rabbis or learned teachers.

The Issue of Mixed Marriages

One of Ezra's first decisions was none too popular, and from a modern perspective, cruel. He decided that all Jewish men had to get rid of their foreign wives and children. Over a period of a few months, the men reluctantly agreed, and Ezra ends poignantly with the words, "All these had married foreign women, and they sent them away with their children" (Ezra 10:44). The implication is that these women and their children were abandoned. Ezra apparently didn't consider the possibility of conversion.

Seemingly overlooked by the Book of Ezra are the many "foreign" women who were crucial heroines in Israelite history. Among these is Tamar (see Genesis), the Canaanite woman who tricked Judah but bore Perez, an ancestor of King David; and Rahab, the prostitute in Jericho. Interestingly, some scholars have suggested that Ruth, the story of a model foreign wife who converts, was specifically written to counter Ezra's decree.

The Book of Nehemiah: A Summary

Approximately eighty years after the initial return from exile, things were still not going well in Jerusalem. Ezra may have been great at the law, and a true genius if he is the man who crafted the Torah, but his divorce ruling hadn't made him popular among the locals. When Ezra also proved ineffective as a civil administrator, the Persian king Artaxerxes dispatched a Jewish "cup bearer"—an official presumably charged with testing the king's drinks for poison—named Nehemiah, living in Susa (the modern country of Iran), to Jerusalem in 445 B.C.E.

In the geopolitics of the period, Artaxerxes was interested in establishing a strong, loyal ally in Jerusalem to counter any potential threat from Egypt. The king commissioned Nehemiah to supervise repairs to the walls of Jerusalem, which had been breached and damaged in the Babylonian invasion in 587 B.C.E., and had crumbled from neglect during the intervening years of the exile. Nehemiah quickly began a repair program, endearing himself to the locals in the meantime by canceling all debts, since Jews were not supposed to charge fellow Jews interest. This move proved far more popular with the citizens of Jerusalem than Ezra's decision to make them give up their non-Jewish wives had been.

Much of the Book of Nehemiah is concerned with the reconstruction of Jerusalem's walls and watchtowers. When these public works were completed, Ezra was invited to rededicate the city by reading from the Book of Moses. Nehemiah returned to Persia, but in his absence laxity set in and he had to return to Jerusalem once more, possibly in 433 B.C.E., to lay down a new set of local laws. Gates were closed to merchants on the Sabbath and the issue of intermarriage was pushed to center stage once more.

In the historical sense, the Ezra-Nehemiah period also reflected a change in political realities for the Jewish people. Reorganizing the power of Persia, Nehemiah made no attempt to reestablish the Davidic line of kings. Without a viable monarchy in the postexile period, authority over Jewish internal affairs rested with temple officials. The new Judah was a "theocracy" in which the priesthood held power over local religious and social life; all political and military power remained with the Persian kings.

Under Ezra and Nehemiah, the second temple became the focal point of Jewish religion, customs, and power. The one God manifested himself in this place, the only place where sacrifices could be offered to God. The temple's central role was made even stronger by obligating Jews to make a pilgrimage to Jerusalem for three major religious festivals.

A Language Change

According to Nehemiah 8:8, most Jews no longer understood Hebrew. When Ezra read the law to them (Nehemiah 8:1–8), it was interpreted to the people in the more familiar Aramaic. By the time of the return from exile, Aramaic, a related Semitic language that originated in Aram (modern-day Syria), had replaced Hebrew as the common language of the ancient Near East, used for both trade and diplomacy, and the Law of Moses had to be translated into Aramaic for the Jews who gathered in Jerusalem to hear Ezra read. Later books of the Bible, including some late additions to Isaiah, parts of Ezra, and other books were composed in Aramaic.

For Discussion

1. Why were the prophets champions of social justice?
2. How do you react to both the various images for God and the theme of the passion of God found in the books of the prophets Hosea, Amos, and Micah?
3. How were the prophets proclaimers of fidelity to the covenant?
4. Do people still lament? How are laments an important part of life?
5. Some of the prophets had visions; how did these help them convey their message?

For Further Reading

Anderson, Bernhard W. *The Eighth Century Prophets.* Philadelphia: Fortress Press, 1978.

Doorly, William J. *Prophet of Love: Understanding the Book of Hosea.* New York: Paulist Press, 1991.

Peterson, Daniel L. *The Roles of Israel's Prophets.* Sheffield: JSOT Press, 1988.

Rosenbaum, S. *Amos of Israel.* Macon: Mercer Press, 1990.

Tucker, Gene. "Prophecy and Prophetic Literature" in *The Hebrew Bible and Its Modern Interpreters*. Philadelphia: Chico Press, 1985.

Wolff, Hans W. Haggai: *A Commentary*. Minneapolis: Augsburg-Fortress, 1988.

8

THE PSALMS: THE PRAYER BOOK OF THE BIBLE

My FIRST INTRODUCTION TO THE STUDY OF THE PSALMS took place long ago, in a Catholic grade school. The teacher was a small, petite nun. She handed out a stack of old worn *Confraternity of Christian Doctrine Bibles*. "Now take your Bible," she said, "and open it right to the middle. There you will find the Psalms."

Since that time, I often have quoted her instructions, as I have taught the Psalms in settings ranging from mountain retreats and lakeshores to classrooms, convents, and even the basement of a city hall, where a group of policemen were working on a college degree.

I think it fitting that the Psalms are located in the *middle* of the Bible, between accounts of the holy wars and conquests on the one side, and the Good News on the other. That is because, in the years since first being introduced to them, I have encountered the Psalms in the middle of life, giving expression to both the sorrows and the joys that mark our days.

One December morning, for instance, many years ago, a half-dozen of us walked through the mist and fog at Dachau, the concentration camp where thousands of Jews and political prisoners died. As we made our way to the crematorium, I remembered author Elie Wiesel telling about the gentle Hasidic Jews of Eastern Europe, old people, and children walking toward the gas chambers and saying the Hebrew psalms as they went. I stepped into a memorial church and saw in German the words of Psalm 130 on the wall, "Out of the depths I cry to thee, O Lord . . . ," and I could imagine hundreds, thousands, millions of prayers ascending to heaven.

The Psalms reflect the good times too. An aged widow, living alone in a small Midwestern town, was telling me about her children. "Then there was Lambert," she said, "but of course he is gone now. He always said the horses plowed best for him because he sang the Psalms to them in Dutch." Think of the ingredients in that scene: Psalms that originated in Hebrew in ancient Israel, sung in Dutch by the grandson of an immigrant from the Netherlands, as he plowed with horses on a prairie in America.

These Psalms, these prayers and hymns found in the middle of the Bible, have a way of turning up in the middle of our lives. Psalms show up at times of sickness and gratitude, at childbirth and stillbirth, loneliness, and the blessing of a dwelling. That the Psalms should be invited to such occasions is not surprising, since they originated in similar situations. They come from the depths of sorrow, "Out of the depths I cry to you, O LORD" (Psalm 130). Or the heights of celebration: "Praise the LORD! Praise God in his sanctuary" (Psalm 150). They reflect the pain of loneliness: "As a deer longs for flowing streams, so my soul longs for you, O God" (Psalm 42). Or they reflect the joy of community: "How very good and pleasant it is when kindred live together in unity!" (Psalm 133). The Psalms allow us to hear the prayer of an old person, worried about what lies ahead: "In you, O Lord, I take refuge" (Psalm 71); or look in on the everyday life of a young family, happily gathered around their table (Psalm 128).

The Book of Psalms: A Prayer Book

The Book of Psalms is the prayer book of both Jews and Christians. For centuries, these 150 prayer-poems have been read, prayed, and sung both in communal worship and by individuals. They form part of the very ritual of life. Prayed equally by expectant mothers and people as they die, the Psalms are also sung at the celebration of the Eucharist, the daily liturgy of the hours, baptisms, weddings, and funerals.

Recited daily by monks and contemplative women in the church universal, the Psalms are the tapestry and treasury of prayers considered to be both the inspired Word of God and the deepest expression of human emotion. Being immersed in the Psalms is like going to a school of prayer. The Psalms transcend time, history, and culture, and appeal to the emotion and intuition that is in all of us. Their ultimate meaning does not come from how well they are sung but from how their words tug at our hearts, souls, and minds. Fraught with images, the Psalms minister to our imagination, allowing inner creativity and consciousness to blossom like a rose whose beauty is beheld by both sight and scent. The fragrance of the Psalms is the aroma of life, with its joys, sadness, rages, and depressions.

The Psalmists are not stone-faced wordsmiths, but rather expressive actors, whose feelings and expressions are immediately obvious to the audience. When feeling abandoned or forsaken by God, the Psalmist exclaims, "My God, my God, why have you forsaken me?" (Psalm 22:1). While depressed he intones, "Out of the depths I cry to you, O LORD; LORD, hear my voice!" (Psalm 130:1). With a sudden change of mood, the Psalmist is concerned about ecology, "The earth is the LORD's and all that is in it; the world, and those who dwell in it" (Psalm 24:1) or is praising God: "Sing to the LORD a new song; sing to the LORD all the earth. Sing to the LORD, bless his name; tell of his salvation from day to day. Declare his glory among the nations, his marvelous works among all the peoples" (Psalm 96:1–3). In brief, the Psalms are a majestic expression of a people's faith in their God, a perfect union of poetry and religion.

The Psalms are the language of intimacy—the creature in dialogue with the Creator, the lover in dialogue with the beloved. They are also the language of community, God's special people—at times blessed, at times sinful, sometimes faithful, sometimes grateful—but always natural, honest, open, and trusting, in dialogue with their God, who is Creator, Liberator, and Savior.

The uniqueness of the Israelite people's relationship with God, known as covenant, allowed them to face God no matter what their emotion or need. Sung for eons, the Psalms have distilled the spiritual insights of one generation after another. They sing of praise, fear, faith, and final victory. They sing all the human emotions to God. They scour the world for answers to the unanswerable. They resound across time with the human memory of the fidelity of God, with the soul-searching of humanity, with the highest aspiration and deepest pain of the human soul. They sing of an approach to human life that transcends national boundaries, personal privatism, and private profiteering. The Psalms sing of the whole human race united in the God who is life. They sing of a people who sin as a people, are saved as a people, sigh for God as a people, and see God everywhere.

Naming the Book

The word "psalms" comes from the Greek word *psalmos*, which is a translation of the Hebrew word *mizmor*, which means "a song accompanied by instrumental music." The Hebrew title for the Book of Psalms, however, is *tehillim*, which means "praises." In one of the Psalms, God is described as, ". . . enthroned on the praises [*tehillim*] of Israel" (Psalm 22:3).

The title "Book of Psalms" comes from the New Testament (Luke 20:42; Acts 1:20). The early Christian community read the Hebrew Scriptures (Old Testament) in Greek translation (Septuagint), where the prevailing title was *psalmoi*, referring to "songs sung to the accompaniment of stringed instruments." Another title for the book found in an ancient manuscript is *psalterion*, referring primarily to a zither-like instrument, and secondarily to songs sung to stringed

234

accompaniment. From this title comes the often-used term "Psalter." While the Greek titles emphasized the musical dimension of the Psalms, the title in the Hebrew Bible, *tehillim* ("praises"), stresses their content.

Authorship of the Book of Psalms

Both Jewish and Christian tradition attribute the Psalms to King David. This is because many of the Psalms in the first part of the book have the superscription "according to David." However, modern contemporary biblical scholarship, sees this as an example of authorship by attribution; that some later redactor or editor attributed them back to King David. Historically, it is highly unlikely that King David wrote all 150 Psalms. Rather, the Psalms were composed by a guild of writers attached to either the Temple of Solomon, which existed from 922 to approximately 597 or 587(6) B.C.E. and was destroyed by the Babylonians, or to the second temple rebuilt by Ezra and Nehemiah, which dates roughly from about 519 B.C.E. In light of this, it is very hard to date the Book of Psalms. See illustration on the next page.

Coupled with the question of authorship is the issue of whether the Psalms were primarily private prayers or instead public prayers of the temple. Of course, the temple had something to do with the origin and preservation of the Psalter.

There is some clear evidence in the Book of Psalms of their liturgical/temple origin. According to Exodus 23:17, pilgrimage feasts which require males to go up for three major feasts each year are required. The title, "Song of Ascents," ascribed to Psalms 120–134, has often been associated with groups coming to the temple for major feasts/festivals. These Psalms contain themes of looking forward to the city or to what God has done, or remembering the processions of the Ark of the Covenant. In addition, entrance liturgies found in Psalms 15 and 24, in particular, seem to be sung at the gate of the temple by alternate choirs.

HISTORY OF THE TEMPLE IN JERUSALEM

It can be difficult to follow the history of the temple in Jerusalem. There were three temples.

The first temple was built by Solomon (see 1 Kings 6–8 and 2 Chronicles 2–4)	Built on Mount Zion, the easternmost hill of Jerusalem, about 962 B.C.E. It stood for about 400 years. It was destroyed by the invading Babylonians in 586 B.C.E. The Ark of the Covenant was lost during that invasion and never found again.
The second temple was built at the urging of the postexilic prophets and was expedited by the Persian governor Zerubbabel, and the high priest Joshua (see Ezra 3, Haggai 2, Book of Zechariah).	Built and dedicated in 519 B.C.E., after the return from the Babylonian exile. It was desecrated, appointed and despoiled by the Greeks in about 167 B.C.E., and the Maccabean war (revolt) followed.
The third temple was built by Herod the Great (37 B.C.E. to 4 C.E.).	Reconstruction began in 19 B.C.E. It was completed in 64 C.E., long after Herod the Great's death, and destroyed by the Romans in 70 C.E., when Jerusalem was destroyed. Part of the Western Wall from this temple still stands today and is revered by Jews; it is sometimes known as the "Wailing Wall."

Other signs that the Psalms were used primarily in the temple for public worship can be found in the directions for musical accompaniment that appear as superscriptions of many of the Psalms. Psalm 4, for example, begins with the note, "With stringed instruments." Psalm 8 is to be played upon "the gittith," while Psalm 5 is "for the flutes." Psalm 45 is to be sung according to the tune of "the lilies." Musical instruments were part of temple service. 1 Chronicles 16 lists the temple singers who joined Asaph in singing while the ark was carried to Jerusalem. 1 Chronicles 25 gives a detailed list of temple musical personnel. Further, many of the Psalms mention aspects of worship that are to be performed while the words are being sung. Processions are mentioned in Psalms 42, 68, and 132, and praying in the temple itself in Psalm 5:7 and 26:6–7. All of this clearly indicates that the primary contextual origin of the Psalms was in public worship.

Titles or Superscriptions in the Book of Psalms

Of the 150 Psalms, 116 have superscriptions or titles that appear above them.

There are three types of titles or superscriptions: (1) technical musical terms and instructions for performance, usually addressed to the leader or choirmaster; (2) personal names with which the Psalm is associated, for example, Solomon (Psalms 72 and 127), Moses

---

DIVISION OF THE BOOK OF PSALMS

The Book of Psalms is divided into five books.

Book One, Psalms 1–41	(Closing Doxology, Psalm 41:13) This book is made up almost entirely of psalms associated with David in the titles. In this first book, the name for God is *YHWH*.
Book Two, Psalms 42–72	(Closing Doxology, Psalm 72:18–20) A group identified with the "Sons of Korah" (see Psalms 42–49). The name for God in this book is *Elohim*.
Book Three, Psalms 73–89	(Closing Doxology, Psalm 89:52) This book is made up mostly of community laments. A majority of these psalms are associated with Asaph, most likely a musician. The name for God in this book is *Elohim*.
Book Four, Psalms 90–106	(Closing Doxology, Psalm 106:48) This book is made up of psalms which declare God's kingship (93, 95–99). A series of hymns (103–106). This book uses the name *YHWH* for God.
Book Five, Psalms 107–150	(Closing Doxology for the entire Book of Psalms, Psalm 150) This is the largest of the five books with forty-four psalms. It is a mixed group. This book uses the names *YHWH* and *Elohim* for God.

(Psalm 90), Jeremiah (Psalm 136), Asaph (Psalms 80–83 and others), Sons of Korah (Psalms 84–85 and others), Psalm of Hemam (Psalm 88), Psalm of Ethan (Psalm 89); and (3) there are superscriptions that are historical headings—these describe a particular historical context in which the Psalms were put together (see Psalms 30; 38; 51; 52; 54; 56; 57; 59; 60; 63, et al.).

From this division of the Book of Psalms, we learn two things. First of all, that there are different nouns used for God, which gives rise to a belief that there were different authors involved in putting the Book of Psalms together. Secondly, since it's a fivefold division, most scholars believe that it relates somehow to the Torah, the Pentateuch, the books of Genesis, Exodus, Leviticus, Numbers, and Deuteronomy. It is conjectured that book one of the Psalms would have been read in relationship to those readings coming from Genesis; books two through five to those coming from the remaining four books of the Pentateuch. While this is conjecture, it is a reasonable one because of the fact that we know there was a cycle of readings, at least at the time of the synagogue, from the Torah, and it could be that these particular books of Psalms were used in conjunction with those particular assigned readings.

Poetry of the Psalms

All of the Psalms are poems. In Hebrew they are written in poetry. This is easily demonstrated in any translation of the Bible—the Psalms are always printed in stanzas. The purpose of poetry is to inspire and engage the imagination and heart, not just to provide information. In order to appreciate poetry, it needs to be read with the utmost mental alertness, out loud, and more than once. The purpose of poetry varies from relaxing or soothing a person to arousing, awakening, and shocking the reader/listener into life. The same is true of the Psalms. These poem/prayers never became dated but live on in all generations of readers/listeners/prayers.

Hebrew poetry is characterized by the rhythm of sense. The technical term for this rhythm is "a sense of parallelism." Poetic parallelism is the main feature of Hebrew poetry. This means there is a balance, usually between one line of a poem and the second line. And then parallel between the third and fourth lines and on down. So parallelism is a balancing of thoughts, a balancing of ideas, a balancing of sense. Now this balancing can be done in several ways. For example, we can have what is called complete parallelism, sometimes called synonymous parallelism. The term in the first line is matched by a corresponding term in the second line. As an example, Psalm 146:1:

> *"Praise the Lord!*
> *Praise the Lord, O my soul."*

This synonymous parallelism is also described as the second line simply echoing or repeating the same idea as the first line. For example:

> *The earth is the Lord's and all that is in it,*
> *the world and those who live in it* (Psalm 24:1).

> *The mouths of the righteous utter wisdom,*
> *and their tongues speak justice* (Psalm 37:30)

> *Keep your tongue from evil,*
> *and your lips from speaking deceit* (Psalm 34:13).

Then there is the type of parallelism called "antithetic parallelism." The second line contrasts with the first line. Examples include:

> *[F]or the LORD watches over the way of the righteous,*
> *but the way of the wicked will perish* (Psalm 1:6).

> *The wicked borrow, and do not pay back,*
> *but the righteous are generous and keep giving* (Psalm 37:21).

Another type is called "continuous parallelism." The second line continues the thought of the first line. As an example:

> *"Ascribe to the LORD, O heavenly beings,*
> *ascribe to the LORD glory and strength"* (Psalm 29:1).

The purpose of parallelism is to clarify and expand on an image, to provide a more contemplative approach. It is based on the premise that repetition reinforces meaning and increases reflection.

The Various Literary Forms in the Book of Psalms

The following chart shows the various types of literary forms found in the Book of Psalms.

THE PSALMS CLASSIFIED ACCORDING TO THEIR FORM

Hymns of Praise

Motivation from nature	8; 19:1–7; 29; 33; 89:1–19; 93; 96; 104; 148; 150
Motivation from history or Torah	19:8–14; 24; 33; 35; 47; 48; 68; 76; 78; 91; 100; 105; 107; 113; 114; 117; 134; 135; 136; 145; 146; 147; 149; 150
Canticles of Zion	46; 48; 76; 84; 87; 122
Entrance or processional hymns	15; 24; 68; 95:1–7a; 100; 132
Yahweh-King	24; 29; 47; 93; 95:1–7a; 96; 97; 98; 99; 149

Royal Davidic Psalms

Coronation or anniversaries	2; 72; 89:2–38; 101; 110; 132
Supplication	20; 21; 61; 89; 144:1–11
Thanksgiving	18
Marriage	45

Prophetic Psalms   50; 81; 82; 95:7b–11

Psalms of Supplication (Laments)

Laments for the assembly	12; 36; 44; 58; 60; 74; 77; 79; 80; 83; 85; 90; 94; 106; 108:7–14; 137; 144:1–11
Laments for the individual	3; 4; 5; 6; 7; 9–10; 13; 14; 17; 22; 25; 26; 27; 28; 35; 38; 39; 40:14–18; 41; 42–43; 51; 53; 54; 55; 56; 57; 59; 61; 63; 64; 69; 70; 71; 86; 88; 102; 108:2-6; 109; 120; 123; 130; 139; 140; 141; 142; 143

Psalms for the sick	6; 16; 30; 31; 38; 41; 61; 69; 88; 91; 103
Seven penitential Psalms	6; 32; 38; 51; 102; 130; 143
Curses	10:15; 31:18–19; 40:15–16; 55:16; 58:7–12; 59:11–14; 68:22–24; 69:23–29; 83:10–19; 109:6–20; 137:9; 139:19–22; 140:9–11

Thanksgiving Psalms

For the assembly	22:23–43; 34; 65; 66; 67; 68; 75; 76; 92; 107; 118; 122; 124; 135; 136
For the individual	18; 23; 30; 31; 40:2–12; 63; 66; 103; 116; 118:5–21; 138; 144:1-11

Prayers of Confidence   11; 16; 20; 23; 27; 41; 52; 62; 63; 84; 91; 115; 121; 125; 126; 129; 131; 133

Zion Hymns   46; 48; 76; 84; 87; 122

Wisdom Psalms   1; 25; 32; 34; 36; 37; 49; 62; 73; 75; 78; 111; 112; 119; 127; 128

Acrostic (Alphabetical) Psalms   9–10; 25; 34; 37; 111; 112; 119; 146

Some Psalms are listed more than once since they can be classified in more than one of these categories.

The primary types of psalms are hymns, laments, and thanksgiving psalms. Each of these types fits a particular situation in human life. The hymns convey the joy and peace of experiencing God's greatness and goodness. The laments express the grief and pain that accompany all types of alienation from God and fellow humans, as well as the accompanying suffering. The thanksgiving psalms speak the gratitude of people who have experienced God's care, compassion, and mercy.

The feelings of these hymn psalms carry a corresponding attitude about God's presence or absence. When all is well, God's presence is a profound experience, a state of balance—homeostasis. When there is suffering, God's presence diminishes in the face of overwhelming loss and pain. Simply put, life experiences influence our awareness of God and the way we pray. In reflecting on the Book of Psalms, we will talk about the experience of God in the categories of (1) orientation to God, the profound sense of God's presence; (2) disorientation, the diminishment of feeling or the loss of God's presence; (3) reorientation to God, the restoration of God's presence—a return to balance. (This threefold categorization of the Psalms is based on the work of Walter Brueggemann in his book *Praying the Psalms*, Winona, MN: St. Mary's Press, 1993.)

The form and content of the hymns express one's orientation to God; the laments express disorientation; the thanksgiving psalms express reorientation to God. Utilizing this threefold approach, we will look at the Book of Psalms.

Hymns

If the Psalms are poetic expressions of religious experience, then the hymn articulates the feeling of wonder and the overwhelming sense of God's power and presence. A psalm hymn may be described as a poem/song that simply exalts the glory and the greatness of God, as that greatness and glory are revealed in nature, in people, and in history—especially the history of ancient Israel—God's people. The hymns of praise were probably composed for specific liturgical ceremonies and for the great religious feasts of Israel. That they were meant to be sung by the community is indicated by refrains ("his [God's] steadfast love endures forever" in Psalms 118 and 136) and responses ("Amen" in Psalms 72:19; 89:52; 106:48; and "Hallelulia" in Psalms 111–113; 115–117; and 146–150). The hymns also tend to follow certain general themes: praise of the Creator, praise of God as the one who reigns, longing for God, praise of God's presence at the liturgy, and praise of God's activity in history and in the Torah.

The hymns have a definite structure. They often begin with an imperative call to worship; then comes a section which gives the basis for praise, often introduced by "for"; and sometimes they conclude with a renewed summons to praise, thus echoing the note sounded first. Psalm 117 provides a good example of the structure of a hymn:

Introduction: Call to worship
> ¹*Praise the* LORD, *all you nations!*
> *Extol him, all you peoples!*

Main Section: Motive for praise
> ²*For great is his steadfast love toward us,*
> *and the faithfulness of the* LORD *endures forever.*

Conclusion: A renewed summons or recapitulation
> ²⁶*Praise the* LORD!

This structure is found with some modifications in a number of hymnic Psalms such as 33, 95, 100, 145, 148, 149, and 150.

When the presence of God is experienced, when an individual or community has the consoling grace of union with God, joy finds spontaneous expression. One's orientation is solely toward God. A song rises readily from the lips of the person at prayer, for example: "I will sing of loyalty and justice; to you, O LORD, I will sing" (Psalm 101:1). Peace prevails; the world is in harmony. The whole universe has a call to join in the expression of praise: "Let the heavens be glad, and let the earth rejoice; let the sea roar, and all that fills it" (Psalm 96:11).

The believer knows the presence of God so profoundly that this individual or community sings continuously of God "in our midst" or "with us" (Psalm 46:5, 7, 11). God's reign is established: The kingdom of God is present with all of life at peace:

> ⁷*For God is king of all the earth;*
> *sing praises with a psalm.*
> ⁸*God is king over the nations;*
> *God sits on his holy throne"* (Psalm 47:7–8).

God's reign guarantees that the evil forces will remain in check. No force holds power over the Lord of all, for example:

¹O God, do not keep silence; . . .
²Even now your enemies are in a tumult;
*   those who hate you have raised their heads . . .*
¹⁷Let them be put to shame and dismayed forever;
*   let them perish in disgrace.*
¹⁸Let them know that you alone,
*   whose name is the LORD,*
*   are the Most High over all the earth*
(Psalm 83:1–2, 17–18).

In these psalms of orientation, there is no situation or event that can separate one from the experience and presence of God. Peace and order prevail. Whatever troubles might be diminishing the joy of the moment are quieted. The "enemies" of God have been scattered. There is no one who can upset the peace, the happiness, the sense of security in God's love.

The hymnic psalms provide a continuous hymn of praise motivated by the goodness and greatness of God. The reason for the experience of the presence of God is not some specific deed which the Psalmist reveals, but rather simply because God is God. For example: "Praise the LORD, all you nations! Extol him, all you peoples! For great is his steadfast love toward us, and the faithfulness of the LORD endures forever" (Psalm 117:1–2).

The community praises because of God's greatness and goodness. Independent statements refer to these reasons for praise. In Psalm 113, the community is called to prayer: "Praise, O servants of the LORD" (verse 1). First because God is great, ". . . high above all nations, and his glory above the heavens" (verse 4). Then because God is good, "He raises the poor from the dust, and lifts the needy from the ash heap, to make them sit with princes . . ." (verses 7–9). In Psalm 95, the invitation, "O come, let us sing to the LORD" (verse 1) precedes the reasons for giving praise:

*³For the L*ORD *is a great God,*
    and a great King above all gods.
⁴In his hand are the depths of the earth;
    the heights of the mountains are his also.
⁵The sea is his, for he made it,
    and the dry land, which his hands have formed"
(Psalm 95:3–5).

Another invitation to praise, "O come, let us worship and bow down" (95:6) precedes the statement about God's goodness: "For he is our God, and we are the people of his pasture, and, the sheep of his hand" (95:7).

The pattern in the Psalms that are hymns is simple and obvious. One praises the Creator, Liberator, Savior, King, Lord of all, on account of God's goodness and greatness. Praise is given because God is experienced as great and good.

When the person or community praying experiences God's presence, the hymns from the Psalter offer a vast collection for us. Or, if the occasion prompts personal expression, these psalms offer the form to fit the occasion: a call to praise followed by a statement or series of statements on why praise is given, namely, the greatness and goodness of God.

Laments: Disorientation

If the hymns express the experience of God's power and presence, then the laments express those moments of pain, sorrow, suffering, and disorder—moments when God seems absent or distant. Laments acknowledge that the individual or the community is not in control but that God can change the situation, for the laments call on God to bring order out of chaos and to restore wholeness in times of disorientation and trouble.

The experience of God's absence corresponds to those times in life when a person or a community suffers from illness, abuse, rejection, loss, persecution, affliction. The situation is painful; the usual harmonious condition becomes unbalanced. The sufferer or the one being abused, rejected, or persecuted experiences life-threatening forces. In the Psalms, these are usually called the "enemy" or "evildoers" (e.g., Psalms 17:10; 22:17; 25:1–19; 42:11).

In the midst of anguish, it appears that God has abandoned the suffering creature: "My God, My God, why have you forsaken me?" (Psalm 22:1). With anguished cry, the seemingly forsaken individual laments God's absence: "How long, O LORD? Will you forget me forever? How long will you hide your face from me?" (Psalm 13:1). "Why are you so far from helping me, from the words of my groaning? O my God, I cry by day, but you do not answer; and by night, but find no rest" (Psalm 22:1b–2).

Yet the one who is hurting knows that only in God is there hope, wholeness, relief. The attitude of the lamenter's heart is that of trust. For example: "But I trust in you, O LORD; I say, 'You are my God.' My times are in your hand" (Psalm 31:14–15a). "You are indeed my rock and my fortress; . . . into your hand I commit my spirit" (Psalm 31:3, 5).

In complete trust, the sufferer petitions God to hear, to intervene, to save. With deep emotion, the one praying exclaims: "Be gracious to me, O LORD, for I am languishing; O LORD, heal me, for my bones are shaking with terror. . . . Turn, O LORD, save my life; deliver me for the sake of your steadfast love" (Psalm 6:2, 4). With confidence, the person praying demands: "Consider and answer me, O LORD my God! Give light to my eyes, or I will sleep the sleep of death" (Psalm 13:3). With boldness, the person praying requests some movement or action from God, saying: "Rise up, O LORD; O God, lift up your hand; do not forget the oppressed" (Psalm 10:12).

In the end, the turmoil ceases because the sufferer perceives that God is present even in the sickness, abuse, death, and affliction. A sense of quiet and trust moves over the one praying so that there is deep peace and trust in God's goodness. There is no longer fear, but only praise, as we hear the psalmist say:

> [8]Depart from me, all you workers of evil,
>   for the LORD has heard the sound of my weeping.

⁹The LORD has heard my supplication;
    the LORD accepts my prayer" (Psalm 6:8–9).

Characteristically, the lament psalms conclude on the note of peaceful quiet, trusting in the goodness and kindness of God.

The pattern of the lament described here—complaint, petition, trust, and praise—seems also to correspond to the human emotions persons experience in the face of life-threatening experiences and suffering. There is generally a movement from anger and complaint to peaceful acceptance. The person of faith, evident in the Psalms, cries out in pain during the time of darkness and pleads for God's help, but this person does so with trust in God's mercy and with the conviction that God does not forsake those who seek and believe.

Laments usually describe some crisis situation, plead for relief, and express confidence that God will help. A transition from complaint to confidence that God will help is the normal pattern. The Psalter contains both individual and communal laments. Communal laments are concerned with national issues, and most likely were offered on public days of fasting and prayer. Individual laments often deal with serious illness, old age, sinfulness, or personal distress and persecution.

Laments have a characteristic structure, and with some exception both communal and individual laments follow the same structure:

Invocation: Address to God, which may be a brief cry.

Complaint: In community laments, the distress may be some great crisis as an attack from an enemy, plague, or famine. Individual laments may be occasioned by such crises as sickness, persecution, or acute awareness of guilt.

Profession of Trust: In spite of the problematic situation, the supplicant relies on God's faithfulness.

Petition: The supplicant appeals to God to intervene and change the situation.

Vow of Thanksgiving: In the hope of confidence that God hears and answers prayer, the supplicant vows to witness to the community about what God has done. (This element is often lacking in community laments.)

To help us appreciate this structure, Psalm 44, which is a community lament, can be used as an example. In the *invocation*, the community, in a time of crisis, recalls the faith of ancestors who had told about the marvelous acts of God performed in the past (verses 1–8). The community raised its *complaint* as it contrasts former days with the present, when God has "cast us off" and "made us like sheep for the slaughter" (verses 9–16). Then comes the community's *profession* of its steadfast *trust* in God, conveyed in poignant language:

¹⁷All this has come upon us,
   yet we have not forgotten you,
   or been false to your covenant.
¹⁸Our heart has not turned back,
   nor have our steps departed from your way,
¹⁹yet you have broken us in the haunt of jackals,
   and covered us with deep darkness (Psalm 44:17–19).

The lament concludes with the community's fervent petition to God to act once again and to bring an end to the eclipse of God's presence (see Psalm 44:23–26).

Many of the individual laments are cries of people in deep distress. In these cases, the petitioner's suffering is veiled in imagery, so that it is next to impossible to determine the concrete life situation from which the lament originates. The heart of the complaint is that the person feels completely abandoned by God and about to be overwhelmed either by an enemy or death. Psalm 22 is an excellent example, for it begins with the gut-wrenching emotional cry:

¹My God, my God, why have you forsaken me?
   Why are you so far from helping me, from the words
      of my groaning?

²O my God, I cry by day, but you do not answer;
and by night, but find no rest (Psalm 22:1–2).

As a member of the covenanting worship community, the person falls back on the faith of the ancestors, which lives in spite of distress.

³Yet you are holy,
enthroned on the praises of Israel.
⁴In you our ancestors trusted;
they trusted, and you delivered them.
⁵To you they cried, and were saved;
in you they trusted, and were not put to shame
(Psalm 22:3–5; see also verses 9–10).

However, the recollection of the past, when God's mighty acts were made known to the ancestors, is only small comfort in the midst of suffering. In constantly shifting figures of speech, the lamentor complains to God:

¹²Many bulls encircle me,
strong bulls of Bashan surround me;
¹³they open wide their mouths at me,
like a ravening and roaring lion.
¹⁴I am poured out like water,
and all my bones are out of joint;
my heart is like wax;
it is melted within my breast;
¹⁵my mouth is dried up like a potsherd,
and my tongue sticks to my jaws;
you lay me in the dust of death (Psalm 22:12–15).

In the remaining verses, the crisis is described in different imagery: the person (lamentor) is being attacked by a pack of dogs, or by thieves who take away everything, including garments, and divide the spoils (verses 16–18). The supplicant's complaint reaches a climax in a cry for help out of the depths of distress:

> *[19]But you, O LORD, do not be far away!*
> *O my help, come quickly to my aid!*
> *[20]Deliver my soul from the sword,*
> *my life from the power of the dog!*
> *[21]Save me from the mouth of the lion!*
> *From the horns of the wild oxen*
> *you have rescued me* (Psalm 22:19–21).

The supplicant's prayer has been heard in verse 24. No longer is God's "face" (presence) hidden. "For he did not despise or abhor the affliction of the afflicted; he did not hide his face from me, but heard when I cried to him." The Psalm ends with a jubilant testimony before the congregation to God's demonstration of grace, which opens up a new possibility of life (verses 25–31).

Cursing Psalms

In a number of laments, the person at prayer cries out to God for vindication and even prays for divine vengeance against enemies: unidentified persons or powers that threaten him. These are sometimes referred to as the cursing or "imprecatory psalms" (Psalms 35, 59, 69, 70, 109, 137, 140). These psalms may embarrass us for they express anger, rage, and even the human propensity toward violence: "Break the arm of the wicked and evildoers; seek out their wickedness until you find none" (Psalm 10:15). "O LORD, you God of vengeance, you God of vengeance, shine forth! Rise up, O judge of the earth; give to the proud what they deserve!" (Psalm 94:1–2). "Happy shall they be who take your little ones and dash them against the rock!" (Psalm 137:9). "O that you would kill the wicked, O God, and that the bloodthirsty would depart from me" (Psalm 139:19). Such statements challenge the way things are, for enemies are cursed and vengeance is demanded. Disorder was seen as dangerous and contrary to the divine plan, so God was asked to do something about it. These "cursing psalms," like the rest of the laments, presuppose the view that God has entered into covenant relationship with the people of Israel and, therefore, can be appealed to as the one who defends the weak and upholds justice. "Vengeance," that is, vindication, is the prerogative of God, not the right of those who take justice into their own hands: "Vengeance is mine . . ." (Deuteronomy 32:35).

For modern readers of these so-called "cursing psalms," the words and images almost choke us. Images from Psalm 137:9 about smashing Babylonian babies against the rocks are simply not the way we pray. But words like these, or the revenge articulated in Psalm 109, echo the theology of the times: There was not much belief in or talk about afterlife then. The value of these prayers rests in the ability of the person praying to rage with God. He or she receives a hearing. However, such a hearing does not ensure God's acting the way the person at prayer might want God to act. Nowhere in the Book of Psalms do we find a sentence where God actually smashes babies against rocks. Rather, we have a person praying for God to do it.

Penitential Psalms

At the opposite extreme to the "cursing psalms" are a number of Psalms which are referred to as the "penitential psalms" (Psalms 6; 32; 38; 51; 102; 130; 143). Of these seven, six are laments and one, Psalm 32, is a psalm of thanksgiving. Christian church tradition gave these Psalms the title "penitential," and they are named as such as early as the time of Saint Augustine. Praying these psalms has long been considered an excellent path to repentance and forgiveness of sin.

In these "penitential psalms," profound cries "from the depths" (see Psalm 130:1), the human problem or situation is not located "out there" in the "enemies" or powers and structure of society, but rather within the heart. Conscious of human frailty, sin, and failure, people cast themselves upon the mercy and forgiveness of God. Psalm 51, composed in the typical fashion of a lament, is a good example. The person at prayer begins with an appeal to God:

¹Have mercy on me, O God,
    according to your steadfast love;
according to your abundant mercy
    blot out my transgressions.

> ²*Wash me thoroughly from my iniquity,*
>> *and cleanse me from my sin* (Psalm 51:1–2).

Then comes the expression of distress: an inner sense of being wrong (verses 3–5):

> ³*For I know my transgressions,*
>> *and my sin is ever before me.*
> ⁴*Against you, you alone, have I sinned,*
>> *and done what is evil in your sight* (Psalm 51:3–4).

The person praying petitions for purification, forgiveness, and inner renewal (verses 6–12):

> ¹⁰*Create in me a clean heart O God,*
>> *and put a new and right spirit within me.*
> ¹¹*Do not cast me away from your presence,*
>> *and do not take your holy spirit from me* (Psalm 51:10–11).

Reorientation: The Thanksgiving Psalms

The renewed experience of the presence of God occurs after prayer is either responded to or answered. Life is reoriented to God after the restoration of health, the cease of abuse, after the relief of suffering, after the establishment of peace. Life returns to wholeness and peace; anxieties cease because God has acted in the life of the individual. These dispositions gain expression in what is known as a thanksgiving psalm, whose basic description is a psalm that praises God in response to God's having delivered or rescued or helped someone or some group in particular need or crisis. With relief and joy, a prayer of thanksgiving is uttered, exclaiming:

> ²*O LORD, my God, I cried to you for help,*
>> *and you have healed me . . .*
> ⁴*Sing praises to the LORD, O you his faithful ones,*
>> *and give thanks to his holy name* (Psalm 30:2, 4)

¹I will give thanks to the LORD, with my whole heart;
I will tell of all your wonderful deeds.
²I will be glad and exult in you . . .
³When my enemies turned back . . . (Psalm 9:1–3)

Having acknowledged that God has indeed acted in an individual's life, the person praying continues by recounting for the community the reasons for thanksgiving. The individual gives an account of God's deeds, almost always divided into a review of the crisis and an account of the liberation. The death experience has been changed to an experience of life. The description of the crisis:

²He [God] drew me up from the desolate pit,
out of the miry bog; (Psalm 40:2)

Is followed by a description of the liberation:

²ᵇand set my feet upon a rock,
making my steps secure.
³He put a new song in my mouth,
a song of praise to our God (Psalm 40:2b–3a).

In Psalm 107, one description of a crisis is:

⁴Some wandered in desert wastes,
finding no way to an inhabited town;
⁵hungry and thirsty,
their soul fainted within them (Psalm 107:4–5).

The situation is changed:

⁷[h]e led them by a straight way,
until they reached an inhabited town (Psalm 107:7).

The life of the person who receives healing, the cessation of abuse, deliverance, thereupon takes on new meaning as a continual expression of praise. God turns the mourning into dancing so that one's soul might sing praise to God and not be silent (Psalm 30:11, 13).

The prayer of thanksgiving usually ends with the promise of continuing praise. Some examples are: "I shall not die, but I shall live, and recount the deeds of the Lord" (Psalm 118:17). "I will offer to you a thanksgiving sacrifice and call on the name of the Lord" (Psalm 116:17). "You are my God, and I will give thanks to you; You are my God, I will extol you. O give thanks to the Lord for he is good, for his steadfast love endures forever" (Psalm 118:28–29; see Psalm 116:1–2). A prayer of thanksgiving will usually contain the elements presented above: acknowledgment that God has acted in a specific situation; a description of the crisis and liberation; and, finally, promise of continual praises.

Royal Psalms

The royal psalms or divine enthronement psalms reflect the conviction of the southern kingdom of Judah that the promise made to the house of David (2 Samuel 7:13) would continue forever (see listings on page 242). They commemorate major events in the life of the king. The role of the king was to be a source of unity for the nation (see Deuteronomy 17), to protect the people (especially the poor), and to guarantee national security. The king was both the chief military officer and the supreme court official. The king also shared a cultic (liturgical) role. He was subject to the prescriptions of the Torah, not above them (see Deuteronomy 17:14–20). The king was to represent God to the people and the people to God.

All of this was possible if the king's life was firmly rooted in God and in keeping with God's covenant. Unlike some of Israel's neighbors, there was a clear distinction between the human king and God. In Egypt, for example, Pharaoh was god. Not so in Israel. For Israel the king was God's adopted son. Often the royal psalms indicate this relationship.

Even after the destruction of the temple in 587 b.c.e., the end of the Davidic lineage of kingship, these psalms were still used. They held out hope that some day there would once again be a messiah/leader like David of old. In postexilic times they became messianic in interpretation, idealizing the leader-king of Israel, primarily because no earthly king ever became all that he should have been.

> *¹Why do the nations conspire,*
>   *and the peoples plot in vain?*
> *²The kings of the earth set themselves,*
>   *and the rulers take counsel together,*
>   *against the LORD and his anointed, saying,*
> *³"Let us burst their bonds asunder,*
>   *and cast their cords from us."*
> *⁴He who sits in the heavens laughs;*
>   *the LORD has them in derision.*
> *⁵Then he will speak to them in his wrath,*
>   *and terrify them in his fury, saying,*
> *⁶"I have set my king on Zion, my holy hill."*
> *⁷I will tell of the decree of the LORD:*
> *He said to me, "You are my son;*
>   *today I have begotten you.*
> *⁸Ask of me, and I will make the nations your heritage,*
>   *and the ends of the earth your possession.*
> *⁹You shall break them with a rod of iron,*
>   *and dash them in pieces like a potter's vessel."*
>
> *¹⁰Now therefore, O kings, be wise;*
>   *be warned, O rulers of the earth.*
> *¹¹Serve the LORD with fear,*
>   *with trembling ¹²kiss his feet,*
>   *or he will be angry, and you will perish in the way;*
>   *for his wrath is quickly kindled.*
> *Happy are all who take refuge in him* (Psalm 2:1–12).

The Psalm is made up of three parts: (1) an introduction; (2) the adoption of the human king by God; (3) a warning to the foreign nations to leave the anointed of Israel alone.

This Psalm would have been used for the accession ceremony of a king or to celebrate his anniversary of enthronement. It gives confidence to both the king and the people that the promise made to David is being fulfilled.

The first verses (1–3) describe the commotion that would take place at the death of a king: panic over the loss of leadership and local enemies plotting against Israel in a moment of weakness. Then the scene shifts to the heavenly courtroom. In verses 1–3, the nations spoke. Now in verses 4–6, it is God who speaks. Verses 7 through 9 announce the legitimacy of the new king. In verse 1 we see the confidence that God has in his anointed. The nations are foolish to think that they can vanquish the chosen one of God.

The Psalter also preserves the texts from ceremonial liturgies for the king. Psalm 20 represents a prayer uttered by the people for the king before going out to battle: "Give victory to the king, O LORD; answer us when we call" (Psalm 20:9). Psalm 45 is a marriage song for a royal wedding.

Wisdom Psalms

Wisdom Psalms extol the virtues of the Torah and were composed after the Torah existed in written form (see listings on page 243). Most of them are postexilic. These Psalms speak of the value of the Torah and delight in this gift which God has so graciously given. According to the Psalmist(s) who composed these psalms, it is in the Torah that we can find the source of holiness and salvation, thus the praise for the Torah. The wise are those who are able not only to know the Torah and its spirit but to put that knowledge into action in everyday life.

These psalms are often acrostic (alphabetical). They invite the person at prayer to gain a sense of equilibrium, of perspective of balancing trust in God with everyday human experience. They tend to focus on the individual's response to God's initiatives in their lives. The wisdom psalms are down-to-earth and practical. One interesting characteristic of the wisdom Psalms is the use of a special word. It is usually rendered in English as "blessed" or "happy." The Hebrew is *ashre.* The idea of blessing in this word is not so much something that falls out of heaven upon us as it is something we come to realize through life experience, much like the expression used by married couples at their fiftieth wedding anniversary when they say their lives together have been a real blessing.

> *¹Happy are those*
>   *who do not follow the advice of the wicked,*
> *or take the path that sinners tread,*
>   *or sit in the seat of scoffers;*
> *²but their delight is in the law of the LORD,*
>   *and on his law they meditate day and night.*
> *³They are like trees*
>   *planted by streams of water,*
> *which yield their fruit in its season,*
>   *and their leaves do not wither.*
> *In all that they do, they prosper.*
> *⁴The wicked are not so,*
>   *but are like chaff that the wind drives away.*
> *⁵Therefore the wicked will not stand in the judgment,*
>   *nor sinners in the congregation of the righteous;*
> *⁶for the LORD watches over the way of the righteous,*
>   *but the way of the wicked will perish.* (Psalm 1:1–6).

This is the first psalm. What a wonderful way to begin the Book of Psalms—with a blessing. In Hebrew, this psalm begins with the first letter of the Hebrew alphabet, *aleph.* In simple, direct speech, the Psalm speaks about how delightful it is to study Torah (usually translated by the English word "law") and to live by its injunctions. This is the ambition of a truly wise person. Someone who learns that way of life is indeed happy/blessed (*ashre*). Another wisdom psalm, 119, is an acrostic, much longer, and expresses the same idea. Torah is a source of holiness, wisdom, and salvation.

Verses 1 through 3 of Psalm 1 describe the virtues of a godly life, while verses 4 through 6 are the exact opposite of verses 1 through 3, showing the result of ignoring Torah. Nothing works for the fool. Disaster follows upon disaster. Without Torah there is no grounding in life. In the biblical mind, Torah is like water. Both are necessary for life. Note the parallelism between water, which gives growth to plants, and Torah, which gives growth to the spirit. By contrast, in antithetical parallelism, chaff is dry and good for nothing but to be blown away. It is useless.

Finally, it is important to note that just as the Psalm begins with the first letter of the Hebrew alphabet (aleph), the last word of the Hebrew text of the Psalm begins with the final letter of the Hebrew alphabet (tav). This inclusion is a sagelike signal that like day and night, all wisdom can be found between these words of the Torah.

Reflecting on Praying the Psalms

No chapter on the Psalms would be complete without addressing the issue of praying with, in, and from the Psalms. As Christians, we are called to pray the Psalms. After all, Jesus died with psalms on his lips (Psalm 22 in Mark 15:34 and Matthew 27:46, and Psalm 31 in Luke 23:46).

Prayer is both conversation with God and reflection on life. The Psalms can help us do both—converse with God and reflect on life. This does not require us to step out of our ordinary world. We do not step outside of the world when we pray, we merely see the world through different lenses. That is what the Psalms do, they allow us to see the world through God's lenses, which are different. Prayer allows us to think the thoughts of God, not of humans. The purpose of prayer is to partake in the activity of God in our own lives, in the lives of our faith community, and in the world we live in. Prayer is at the very center of the life of any believer and prayer is always emotionally charged, as the Psalms are.

Some suggestions for praying the Psalms would include obtaining a good English translation of the Bible and reading the Psalms and the notes at the bottom of the page. Further, it would help if you read the Psalm(s) out loud, and read them more than once. In addition, find psalms or lines in psalms that resonate with where you are, in what you are feeling in your relationship with God and others. Stay with these psalms, these lines. Avoid feeling you have to move on to a new one each day.

Another suggestion is to concentrate on the images found in the Psalms. These images are countless; for example, animal images—sheep, lions, dogs, bulls; nature images—trees, plants, air, water, light; human images—mother, father, shepherd, king. Images matter because they engage the imagination, and the imagination is important in the spiritual quest. Growth often depends on stretching the imagination. We cannot achieve what we cannot imagine.

The images in the Psalms are training ground for stretching the imagination. Light is an image that appeals to me. When I read in Psalm 27 that "the Lord is my light" and reflect on natural light's effect on me—such as sunshine makes me a more balanced and alert person—it becomes a wonderful analogy for divine light.

Water is another wonderful image. There is a waterfall near my home. I find it a place of healing, of centering; seeing and hearing the water is cleansing. So, when the Psalms talk of God as water or as living water, I make connections with what happens to me at the waterfalls, and through my imagination, I have a sense of God as cooling, refreshing, healing.

When the bottom seems to drop out of life and you have that sinking feeling that all is lost, Psalm 130, "Out of the depths I cry to you, O LORD" helps one wrestle with apparent hopelessness. All the supports are gone. The only hope of not slipping into the abyss is a cry to God.

At the same time, God is more than all of us can imagine. But all of these images in the Psalms can be helpful in providing hints of God. If we have only one or two images of God, we tend to get in a rut and make these images into definitions of God. With all their images, the Psalms challenge us to break out of our limited notions of God. Further, all these images allow God to relate to us in many ways, in different experiences.

The Psalms do have negative as well as positive images of God. The Psalms say some terrible things. They speak of people having God "break the teeth of the wicked" (Psalm 3:7). While that sounds terrible, this kind of imagery can be helpful in prayer. Let's say we are angry, really angry. If we bring our anger to images like these in the Psalms, it can help us deal with it. This can help us let go of our anger and turn to God. Raging at God in prayer is a lot less abusive than verbally raging at another human being. God can handle rage!

I know people have difficulty praying these psalms. For me, they become safety valves. They provide a way of being honest in praying. If one is angry, these psalms provide a way of expressing it. And if there's one thing we must be in prayer, it's honest. The greatest mistake in wrestling with praying the Psalms is *quitting*. Avoid that! The best thing to do is to find a psalm or a portion of one that you are comfortable with, and live with it for a while. Done regularly, the Psalms will become a habit. Before long you find that they have seeped into your bones and, like the very marrow of these bones, they will provide new blood and nourishment for the life of the spirit.

For Discussion

1. Which Psalms are your favorites? Why? Do you ever sing the Psalms?
2. How do the Psalms express the emotions of the Psalmist? Can you identify with these feelings?
3. How do the major psalm types—hymn, lament, and thanksgiving—express different relationships to God and different forms of prayer?
4. Have you ever raged with God? How do the "cursing psalms" (imprecatory) help you with your prayer life?
5. How do the "penitential psalms" help you to reflect on your need to acknowledge sinfulness and seek God's forgiveness?

6. For an interesting and challenging experience, try comparing the translations of the Psalms in various Bibles. How does this comparison help you to better appreciate the biblical Book of Psalms?

For Further Reading

Brueggemann, Walter. *The Message of the Psalms: A Theological Commentary*. Minneapolis: Augsburg Publishing House, 1984.

Brueggemann, Walter. *The Psalms and the Life of Faith*. Minneapolis: Augsburg Fortress, 1995.

Brueggemann, Walter. *Praying the Psalms*. Winona, MN: St. Mary's Press, 1982.

Gunkel, Hermann. *Introduction to the Psalms: The Genes of the Religious Lyric of Israel*. Macon, GA: Mercer University Press, 1995.

Holliday, William L. *The Psalms Through Three Thousand Years: Prayerbook of a Cloud of Witness*. Minneapolis: Fortress Press, 1993.

Murphy, Roland E. *The Psalms Are Yours*. Mahwah, N.J.: Paulist Press, 1993.

Stuhlmueller, Carroll. *Psalms* (Old Testament Message, vols. 21 and 22). Wilmington, DE: Glazier, 1983.

9 | WISDOM LITERATURE

There IS AN ANCIENT ADAGE THAT STATES: "WHO is wise? The person who can learn from anyone." True wisdom is a way of life, a personal philosophy. As a matter of fact, the word "philosophy" means "love of wisdom." All cultures, both ancient and modern, have treasuries of wisdom that have been gleaned from experience, have survived the test of time, and have been handed down through generations. The earliest rules and codes of proper living developed in the family. For family life to prosper, rules were necessary. In these rules the wisdom tradition originated. Many wisdom sayings in the Old Testament point to family origin. Some examples of this are found in the Book of Proverbs:

> *Discipline your children, and they will give you rest;*
> *they will give delight to your heart* (Proverbs 29:17).

Better is a dry morsel with quiet
than a house full of feasting with strife (Proverbs 17:1).

Wisdom and the Monarchy

In addition to the family, wisdom is also related to the court and the monarchy. Every nation of the ancient world had its court schools. Here the sons of the aristocracy were trained in the skills of reading and writing. The method of education was to copy and memorize. Israel's neighbors, Egypt and Mesopotamia, had such schools, and they influenced the Israelite wisdom tradition.

When the monarchy developed in ancient Israel, wisdom moved from the home and family to the court. The sages of the court drew upon the wisdom of the surrounding cultures. Ancient Israel's early wisdom tradition contained very little that is specifically Israelite. Since the monarchy was linked to the temple in Israel, there was exchange among the sages, priests, and prophets. The priests preserved rituals and the various codes of law prescribed for the temple. The prophets were charismatic messengers who were sent to communicate God's message to his people. Sages used experience to explain how one was to live correctly. Sages freely chose experiences which people could readily understand and used them to explain the proper ways of living. For example, when we change our mode of action people may be thrown off. The sages used the example of clouds appearing. When the clouds appear with no rain, that is unusual. Applying that to human experience, the sage pointed out that when a person speaks, yet has not accomplished everything he said, it is like clouds appearing without rain. "Like clouds and wind without rain is one who boasts of a gift never given" (Proverbs 25:14).

King Solomon: Patron of Wisdom

When ancient Israel's monarchy was not reestablished after the exile, the sages did not disappear. Wisdom continued to exist outside the royal court. Much of the wisdom literature was compiled during this period. Since Solomon had emerged as the prototype of the wise man (see 1 Kings 3:4), many of these compilations were attributed to him. The Book of Proverbs begins: "The proverbs of Solomon son of David, king of Israel" (Proverbs 1:1). This may be because in 1 Kings 4, Solomon is said to have authored thousands of proverbs. Song of Solomon (Song of Songs) begins, "The Song of Songs, which is Solomon's" (Song of Solomon 1:1). One wisdom book, the Book of Wisdom, is specifically attributed to Solomon.

Just as the Psalms were ascribed to King David because of his skills as a harpist, much of the wisdom literature is credited to king Solomon. Even though Solomon did not personally write all the wisdom literature, he remains its patron.

The sages of ancient Israel equated wisdom with the virtue of fear of the Lord: "The fear of the LORD is the beginning of wisdom" (Job 28:28; Psalm 111:10; Proverbs 1:7; 9:10; 15:33). This Hebraic idiom does not mean to be scared to death of God. Rather, "fear of the LORD" means to hold God in awe. For the sages, success and happiness becomes knowing one's place before God. This means living according to practical common sense, avoiding bad companions, jealousy, and pride, and, most of all, a real reverence for the awesome presence of God. This constituted real wisdom.

Old Testament Wisdom Literature

The wisdom literature of the Old Testament includes the books of Proverbs, Job, Ecclesiastes (Qoheleth), Song of Solomon (Song of Songs), the Wisdom of Solomon, and Sirach. Several psalms have been designated as wisdom psalms (1; 37; 49; 73; 91; 112; 119; 127; 128; 133; 139). The wisdom books deal with general questions of human life, welfare, value, and destiny.

The Book of Proverbs

Proverbs is the earliest of the Old Testament wisdom books. It is composed of short sayings meant to edify. The brevity of the sayings made them easy to memorize. Each statement in the Book of Proverbs is a two-part verse. Like the Psalms, there is often some kind of parallelism; for example, "Let your eyes look directly forward, and your gaze be straight before you" (Proverbs 4:25). There are several collections of proverbs that make up the book. Two of these collections, Proverbs 10:1–22:16 and 24:1–29:27, trace their origins to the court of Solomon. Both begin with a specific reference to Solomon. Other collections date from the time of king Hezekiah and the postexilic period. Three sections of the book are attributed to sages: ("Sayings of the Wise" in 24:23–24; "Sayings of Agur" in 30:1; and "The Words of Lemuel" in 31:1–10). Nothing is known about the aforementioned sages.

The introduction to the Book of Proverbs provides a succinct summary of the nature and purpose of wisdom.

> ¹*The proverbs of Solomon son of David, king of Israel:*
> ²*For learning about wisdom and instruction,*
>   *for understanding words of insight,*
> ³*for gaining instruction in wise dealing,*
>   *righteousness, justice, and equity;*
> ⁴*to teach shrewdness to the simple,*
>   *knowledge and prudence to the young —*
> ⁵*Let the wise also hear and gain in learning,*
>   *and the discerning acquire skill,*
> ⁶*to understand a proverb and a figure,*
>   *the words of the wise and their riddles.*
> ⁷*The fear of the* LORD *is the beginning of knowledge;*
>   *fools despise wisdom and instruction.* (Proverbs 1:1–7)

For the sage who wrote Proverbs, the purpose of wisdom is to teach first the young and then anyone else who will listen. A healthy respect for God's power, presence, and will is the beginning point of making a successful and godly journey through life.

One of the many teachings of the Book of Proverbs is that blessings come to the good; misfortune and unhappiness are the lot of the wicked.

The house of the wicked is destroyed,
 but the tent of the upright flourishes (Proverbs 14:11).

In the house of the righteous there is much treasure,
 but trouble befalls the income of the wicked (Proverbs 15:6).

The fear of the LORD *is life indeed;*
 filled with it one rests secure
 and suffers no harm (Proverbs 19:23).

Another characteristic of the Book of Proverbs is sound advice on living life more meaningfully. Here is an anthology of proverbs on the topic.

But the path of the righteous is like the light of dawn,
 which shines brighter and brighter until full day
 (Proverbs 4:18).

Hatred stirs up strife,
 but love covers all offenses (Proverbs 10:12).

A soft answer turns away wrath,
 but a harsh word stirs up anger (Proverbs 15:1).

Those who are hot-tempered stir up strife,
 but those who are slow to anger calm contention
 (Proverbs 15:18).

Pride goes before destruction,
 and a haughty spirit before a fall (Proverbs 16:18).

Gray hair is a crown of glory;
 it is gained in a righteous life (Proverbs 16:31).

Those who mock the poor insult their Maker;
 those who are glad at calamity will not go unpunished
 (Proverbs 17:5).

A cheerful heart is a good medicine,
 but a downcast spirit dries up the bones (Proverbs 17:22).

The mouths of fools are their ruin,
and their lips a snare to themselves (Proverbs 18:7).

Train children in the right way,
and when old, they will not stray (Proverbs 22:6).

¹Do not boast about tomorrow,
for you do not know what a day may bring.
²Let another praise you, and not your own mouth . . .
(Proverbs 27:1–2).

While the Book of Proverbs offers some of the best advice on the eternal values of humility, hard work, charity, and wisdom, the book also offers some of the worst advice:

Those who spare the rod hate their children,
but those who love them are diligent to discipline them
(Proverbs 13:24).

Do not withhold discipline from your children;
if you beat them with a rod, they will not die
(Proverbs 23:13).

For centuries these verses have been used to justify parents spanking, the school principal's paddling, the nun's rap on the knuckles with a ruler, and even more severe and at times hideous forms of corporal punishment.

The best modern interpretation of these texts is that what was once acceptable in a primitive culture is no longer the case. Just as we no longer keep slaves, or stone adulterers, society can no longer tolerate the physical punishment of children. Discipline is crucial for every child, but beatings are unacceptable. In the current era of commonplace child abuse, even hinting that the Bible condones such behavior is a grievous mistake. It is a sacrilegious and abusive use of the Bible.

Personification of Wisdom

Finally, with regard to the Book of Proverbs, mention needs to be made of the personification of "wisdom." The Hebrew word for

268

"wisdom" is *hocmah* (or *hokmah*), a feminine word in that language. The noun for wisdom in Greek is *Sophia*, also feminine. In Proverbs 8, the figure of Woman Wisdom is that of the one who was with God at creation. In Proverbs 9, the author personifies wisdom and foolishness as two different kinds of women, representing the choice one must make between two ways of life, a wise one or a foolish one. Lady Wisdom is portrayed as someone who lives in a proper house and sets a proper table—of wisdom, knowledge, and wine. The result of choosing this option portrayed by Dame Wisdom is long life and happiness. The opposite is Dame Folly (see Proverbs 9:13–18). She tries to imitate Lady Wisdom but cannot do so. Her advice is absurd, but unfortunately there are those who listen to her. In latter wisdom books, the Book of Sirach and the Book of Wisdom, the figure of Lady Wisdom is also found personified (see Sirach 24:7–11; Wisdom 10:1–12:27).

The Book of Job

We turn our attention now to the classic of all Old Testament wisdom literature, the Book of Job. Some scholars have referred to Job as the "Shakespeare of the Old Testament." The British poets Tennyson and Carlyle praised it for its poetry, and the playwright Archibald MacLeish made a play out of it entitled *J.B.: A Play in Verse.*

Yet the Book of Job suffers from misunderstanding and ignorance on the part of many, most specifically, those who refer to the allegedly proverbial "patience of Job" (James 5:11). In this popular misconception, Job is a model of piety—a man who patiently and serenely suffered without losing his faith. But this portrait holds true only in the prologue (Job 1:1–2:13) and epilogue (Job 42:7–17), both of which are written in prose. The main part of the book is in poetic form, and here Job is anything but a paragon of patience.

The Book of Job sets out to explain the mystery of why the righteous must suffer—or in modern terms, why bad things happen to good people. Based on an ancient folk tale set in the land of Uz in the southeast desert regions of Israel, it is about a saintly man—never identified as a Jew—who suffers unthinkable pain and tragedy after Satan challenges God to a bet. While the precise date of the composition of the Book of Job is unknown, it supposedly dates from the time of the exile in Babylon (597/87–537 B.C.E.) or soon after the return to Jerusalem.

Written when Jewish society was seen as divided between the pious and the unfaithful, the Book of Job does not set out to explain the problem of evil and disease in the world, but specifically addresses why righteous believers must suffer if God is truly just. Written in both prose and poetry, the forty-two chapters are divided as follows.

OUTLINE/DIVISION OF THE BOOK OF JOB

Prologue (in prose)	1:1–2:13 (God and an adversary named Satan agree to test Job)
Dialogue section (in poetry)	3:1–26 (the lament of Job)
Triple dialogue section (in poetry)	4:1–14:22 (first set of dialogues)
between Job and his friends,	15:1–21:34 (second set of dialogues)
Eliphaz, Bildad, and Zophar	22:1–28:28 (third set of dialogues)
	29:1–31:37 (closing lament of ob)
Elihu's speeches (in poetry)	32:1–37:44
God's responses (in poetry)	38:1–42:6 (two dialogues between God and Job)
Epilogue (in prose)	42:7–17

Plot Summary of the Book of Job

God is boasting about how faithful servant Job is when Satan (which in Hebrew means "the Accuser" or "Adversary") says: "Sure he's a good guy. He has everything. Take it all away and see how good he is." Accepting Satan's dare, God allows Satan to do his work.

Satan, fulfilling his job description, sees that God has Job losing everything, including his ten children, who die when their house collapses in a windstorm (Job 1:18–19). Despite this terrible calamity and personal tragedy, Job stands strong.

SATAN

What does the word "Satan" conjure up in your mind? An image of a demon with horns, dressed in a red suit, and having a tail, who tortures people gleefully in the fires of hell? Or does it present the picture of a fallen angel who personifies an evil presence wandering the world looking for people to tempt and corrupt? If these are your images of "Satan," they are not what the Book of Job (1:6–12; 2–17) or Zechariah (3:1) have in mind. In these passages, Satan is working for God, he is part of God's heavenly court. In fact, the word "Satan" is best understood as a job description rather than a name; it means "adversary." As a member of God's court, Satan's responsibility is to go around accusing or testing humans before God.

Challenged a second time, God allows Satan to further test Job by covering his body with painful sores (Job 2:7). When Job's wife tells him, "Curse God, and die" (Job 2:9)—in other words, put an end to your misery—Job faithfully answers that he must take the good and the bad from God.

> But he said to her, "You speak as any foolish woman would speak. Shall we receive the good at the hand of God, and not receive the bad?" In all this Job did not sin with his lips (Job 2:10).

That's how most people thought the story ended, with a dutiful obedient Job refusing to question the Lord. But it is really just the beginning.

Three of Job's friends—Eliphaz, Bildad, and Zophar—arrive to offer sympathy and wise counsel, or at least to discuss the subject of divine justice. Job and his friends sit in silence for seven days (Job 2:13). Silence is often the wisest position in relationship to a life-numbing tragedy. When the friends finally speak, the consoling friends quickly assume that Job must have done something wrong to deserve the punishment he is receiving. Angrily protesting his innocence and railing against his fate, Job curses the day he was born (Job 3:1–3), no longer appearing as quite the faithful, patient servant of God accepting his situation. Another character arrives, Elihu (Job 32:1–37:44), and attempts to promulgate and vindicate his own view of God's mysterious ways, but Job counters each of his arguments with continuing protests of innocence, pointing out how evil people just always seem to prosper.

Ultimately, God arrives to speak directly to Job from a whirlwind (Job 38:1–7), telling him that for humans to discuss how God functions is presumptuous, since God is utterly beyond all mortal understanding. At the same time, God's showing up for a face-to-face encounter with this mere mortal is supposed to demonstrate how much God cares for Job. In a sarcastic and cutting way, God says to Job throughout chapters 38 and 39 that Job doesn't even comprehend what a big task being God is, from ordering the heavens to "who has let the wild ass go free" (Job 39:5). God has lots of balls to juggle. Somewhat enraged by Job's questioning, God ends his whirlwind speech with:

> *Shall a faultfinder contend with the Almighty? Anyone who argues with God must respond* (Job 40:2).

Chastened by God's unanswerable questions to him, Job is repentant: "See, I am of small account; what shall I answer you?" (Job 40:3). Instead of getting a clear answer to the questions he had posed to God, Job recognizes God's awesome power and realizes that he can never comprehend God's purpose. He repents for his weakness in questioning God.

> *²I know that you can do all things, and that no purpose of yours can be thwarted. . . . ³Therefore I have uttered what I did not understand, things too wonderful for me, which I did not know. . . . ⁵I had heard of you by the hearing of the ear, but now my eye sees you; ⁶therefore I despise myself, and repent in dust and ashes* (Job 42:2–6).

In the presence of God, Job, who has been doing a lot of talking throughout the book, is simply quiet. He has become a listener. He has become wise.

Just as the character Job learns there are no easy answers, so do we, for the "character Job" represents every man or woman. Job is every one of us, especially in the questions that he asks and ponders of himself and of God. Further, the fact that those who put the Bible together decided to include a book with so many unanswered questions is a living witness ("testament") of their recognition of God's mysterious ways and the legitimacy of wondering about them. This is not a book that celebrates blind faith. Its message still seems a bit subversive, leaving behind an uneasy sense that this somewhat capricious God of Job offers his "servant" the trite but time-honored, thoroughly frustrating response so many children receive from their parents: "Because I said so."

The Book of Ecclesiastes (*Qoheleth*)

Looking at the title of this book, it is easy to see the word "ecclesial" in it. The Hebrew name for the book is *Qoheleth,* the Hebrew word for "the preacher," the one who calls the people into assembly and addresses them. The Greek title, Ecclesiastes, is a translation of that Hebrew word.

In our lives, almost all of us have bumped into a pessimist. The resident pessimist of the Old Testament is the author of Ecclesiastes. Listen to this litany of negativity and pessimism:

There is nothing new under the sun (Ecclesiastes 1:9).

Sorrow is better than laughter (Ecclesiastes 7:3).

Whether or not we agree with Ecclesiastes' pessimism, he does cause us to think. Among the questions he wants us to think about are: Why do wise people perish just like fools? (Ecclesiastes 2:12–17) Why is it that bad people live longer than good people? (7:15–16) And why is it that the most deserving do not get what they really had worked for? (9:11–12). The answers provided to these questions by Ecclesiastes do not always leave the reader cheerful. Ecclesiastes is always seeing the negative side of things. He is similar to the cynics of Greek philosophy.

What do we make of such a book? *Qoheleth*/Ecclesiastes was a sage who marched to a different drum and had a different voice among the crowd of wisdom teachers who were his contemporaries when the book was written in the third century B.C.E. He never avoided telling things the way he saw them.

> *²Vanity of vanities, says the Teacher, vanity of vanities! All this is vanity! ³What do people gain from all the toil at which they toil under the sun? ⁴A generation goes, and a generation comes, but the earth remains forever. . . . ⁹What has been is what will be, and what has been done is what will be done; there is nothing new under the sun* (Ecclesiastes 1:2–4, 9).

In the above passage the use of the English word "vanity" is an inadequate translation, for the English word conveys a sense of pride. The Hebrew word used here is *havel*. It is the Hebrew word for emptiness or something hollow. Like steam in the air, it is there but you cannot capture it. Or like a breath or a breeze, it is there but not for a long time.

Somewhat resignedly, we have to admit that *Qoheleth*, the teacher, is right. In fact, one generation does pass away only to be replaced by another. Like all sages, *Qoheleth* tells the truth. That is wisdom. With regard to "nothing new under the sun," granting technological developments, he is right again. Human nature does not change, technology does. People still love, hate, are born, and die. *Qoheleth* tells us the truth. His purpose, of course, is to cause the reader of every generation to reflect, react, and respond, which is the purpose of any good teacher.

Possibly the most famous passage of the Book of Ecclesiastes is the passage that reflects on the ways in which we use our time on this earth.

> *¹For everything there is a season, and a time for every matter*
>   *under heaven:*
> *²a time to be born, and a time to die;*

a time to plant, and a time to
   pluck up what is planted;
³*a time to kill, and a time to heal;*
a time to break down, and a time to build up;
⁴*a time to weep, and a time to laugh;*
a time to mourn, and a time to dance;
⁵*a time to throw away stones,*
   and a time to gather stones together;
a time to embrace, and a time to
   refrain from embracing;
⁶*a time to seek, and a time to lose;*
a time to keep, and a time to throw away;
⁷*a time to tear, and a time to sew;*
a time to keep silence, and a time to speak;
⁸*a time to love, and a time to hate:*
a time for war, and a time for peace (Ecclesiastes 3:1–8).

Qoheleth's interests in this passage are not about clock-watching the way a trainer watches the clock for a long-distance runner or a racehorse. The word "time" here does not refer to hours and minutes or even months and years. It refers to time that makes a difference, time that really changes us. Not a chronological measurement of time, like having to be at work by 9 A.M. The Bible has a word for this nonchronological time; it is the Greek word *kairos*. The date of our birth indicates our chronological time of arrival in the world, nothing more. What really matters is the lives and destinies we live while on earth. They will change. Therefore our lifetime is significant. *Qoheleth* is not only reminding us that there are many significant moments in our lives, but asks us to be wise enough to discern them.

Unquestionably, the Book of *Qoheleth* is a book for our times when so much time, energy, and effort are placed on what we gain, how important our job is, how big and luxurious are our cars and homes, how impressive our clothing, and how large our bank accounts might be. He reminded the assembly of his day and he reminds us that in the end things don't matter. He encourages us to find value in what we do and in who we are at the present moment.

> *Rejoice, young man, while you are young, and let your heart cheer you in the days of your youth. Follow the inclinations of your heart and the desire of your eyes, but know that for all these things God will bring you into judgment* (Ecclesiastes 11:9).

Qoheleth is a truth-teller. Unchecked self-fulfillment is not wise. It is, on the other hand, wise to enjoy life and realize it is experience that makes us wise. Ecclesiastes reminds us of the transitory nature of material wealth and calls every generation to examine its conscience on how life is being lived. For Ecclesiastes, true wisdom is not how much you know, but, rather, how well and responsibly you live life.

The Book of Sirach

The Book of Sirach is one of the books included in Catholic Bibles but not in Jewish or other Christian denominations' Bibles. Such books are called *deuterocanonical* by Catholics and *apocryphal* by other Christians. In Catholic versions of the Bible the Book of Sirach is found between the books of Wisdom and Isaiah. This book also goes by the name of *Ecclesiasticus*, which stems from the Greek word for church, suggesting the book's early usage as "the church's book." Since the name Sirach is used by most English translations of the Bible, we will use it here.

The earliest title for the book was the "Wisdom of Ben Sira." The book was written sometime between 200 and 175 B.C.E. Its author was Jesus ben Eleazar, ben Sirach (Sirach 50:27). The book shares many similarities with the Book of Proverbs. It may be viewed as an updated book of wise instruction for a later situation in Israel. Written during the growing challenge of Hellenism, the author tries to convince his fellow Jews that true wisdom is to be found in the religious traditions of Israel. Ben Sira seeks to show all, whether Jew or Greek, that true wisdom resides in Israel because the origin of true wisdom is none other than God himself.

The best example of this is found in chapter 24, often labeled the hymn to wisdom, and is similar in content to Proverbs 8. Yet Sirach adds his own spin or take on wisdom. Wisdom now comes from the mouth of the Most High, sings her own praises, and searches for a dwelling place.

After an introduction (Sirach 24:1–2), the hymn falls into two parts. Wisdom's speech (Sirach 24:3–22) and Sirach's commentary (Sirach 24:23–34). The speech of Wisdom narrates how Wisdom came from the mouth of the Most High and dwelt on a pillar of cloud. She roams the universe seeking a place to dwell. Finally, she finds a dwelling place in Jacob (Israel), ministering in the holy tent before the creation.

The commentary (Sirach 24:23–24) applies all that has been said concerning Wisdom in the speech to the book of the Most High's covenant, the law or Torah, equating Torah and Wisdom to show that it is through the law that people achieve wisdom. And it is by the practical living out of the law that a person becomes truly wise. In sum, for the author of Sirach, the greatest treasure of Wisdom is the revelation granted by God to his own special people.

The Book of Wisdom (Wisdom of Solomon)

The Book of Wisdom is attributed to King Solomon, but it was written long after his death. It is perhaps the last of the Old Testament books to be written dating from the first century B.C.E. The author appears to be a Jew of the Diaspora living in Alexandria in Egypt. He wrote the book in Greek rather than in Hebrew. Further, he wrote the book to defend his Jewish religion against the pagan ideas that were infiltrating from the Hellenistic philosophical milieu. Jews living in Alexandria were being lured away from their ancestral faith by the cultural appeal of Hellenism, with its emphasis on philosophy, language, literature, and sporting games. With sagelike skill, the anonymous author of the Book of Wisdom transmits the glory of the Hebrew tradition to a group of fellow Jews who had grown skeptical of it. A magnificent example of this is the personification of wisdom and "her" role in the great events of salvation, especially the exodus. A careful reading of Wisdom 10:1–12:27 will quickly convey this.

The central issue that the Book of Wisdom deals with is good versus evil. The author is convinced that there will be a final judgment, in which good people "will stand with great confidence," and evil people will shake "with dreadful fear" (Wisdom 5:1, 2). What is more, the good will live forever (5:15), whereas the evil will disappear without a trace (4:18–19). The Book of Wisdom sees life after death as the answer to the troubling question: Why do innocent people suffer when God is good and just? Using the concept of the soul, which the author borrowed from Greek philosophy, he provides the final Old Testament solution to the question of human immortality and divine retribution.

> ¹*But the souls of the righteous are in the hand of God,*
> *and no torment will ever touch them.*
> ²*In the eyes of the foolish they seemed to have died,*
> *and their departure was thought to be a disaster,*
> ³*and their going from us to be their destruction;*
> *but they are at peace.*
> ⁴*For though in the sight of others they were punished,*
> *their hope is full of immortality.*
> ⁵*Having been disciplined a little, they will receive great good,*
> *because God tested them and found them worthy of himself;*
> ⁶*like gold in the furnace he tried them,*
> *and like a sacrificial burnt offering he accepted them.*
> ⁷*In the time of their visitation they will shine forth,*
> *and will run like sparks through the stubble.*
> ⁸*They will govern nations and rule over peoples,*
> *and the Lord will reign over them forever.*
> ⁹*Those who trust in him will understand truth,*
> *and the faithful will abide with him in love,*
> *because grace and mercy are upon his holy ones,*
> *and he watches over his elect* (Wisdom 3:1–9).

To be wise is to realize that suffering is not without purpose. There is a final reward for virtuous life. It is eternal life with God. Along with the Book of Daniel, the Book of Wisdom gave the Jews a new theology of personal immortality, a theology which was to function as the final transfer point from the Old Testament to the New Testament.

Song of Solomon (Song of Songs, Canticle of Canticles)

As any marketing manager for a retailer will tell you, sex sells. The advertising world knows this. Advertisers love to take advantage of our natural fascination with sex. Whether it be a curvaceous woman scantily clad getting out of a sports car or a bare-chested, flat-stomached man popping open a can of soda pop, we are bound to take notice. From an advertiser's point of view, the Song of Solomon, a collection of ancient love poems, is a well-kept secret of the Bible. How many advertising agency executives are aware of its explicit sexual images? Consider this sampling of verses:

> *Let him kiss me with the kisses of his mouth!*
> *For your love is better than wine* (Song of Solomon 1:2).

> *³Your lips are like a crimson thread,*
>   *and your mouth is lovely . . .*
> *¹¹your lips distill nectar, my bride . . .* (Song of Solomon 4:3, 11).

> *¹. . . Your rounded thighs are like jewels,*
>   *the work of a master hand.*
> *²Your navel is a rounded bowl*
>   *that never lacks mixed wine.*
> *Your belly is a heap of wheat,*
>   *encircled with lilies.*
> *³Your two breasts are like two fawns,*
>   *twins of a gazelle.*
> *⁴Your neck is like an ivory tower. . . .*
> *⁷You are stately as a palm tree,*

> and your breasts are like its clusters.
> *8I say I will climb the palm tree
> and lay hold of its branches.
> Oh, may your breasts be like clusters of the vine . . .*
> (Song of Solomon 7:1–4, 7–8).

Some people who read the Bible find these images so surprising that they steam up their bifocals. Others wonder why the Song of Solomon is found in the Bible at all. As a matter of fact, its place in the canon was still being argued in the first century C.E., because, like the Book of Esther, it never mentions God and doesn't deal with laws, prophecy, or religion. The question is, how did such a sexual poem, richly luscious in erotic imagery, and not overly concerned with marriage, make it into the Bible in the first place?

Scholars believe that the naming of King Solomon in the Song's first verse is most likely the main reason the book was preserved and eventually included with the books of the Old Testament. Although written long after Solomon's death, this book, like the books of Proverbs and Ecclesiastes, was attributed to him to give it authority.

The traditional interpretation of this book in Judaism and Christianity is that these juicy love poems represent God's love for Israel. For Christians, the Song of Solomon supposedly expresses the love of Christ for his church. Given the sheer eroticism of the poetry, both interpretations require quite a reach. Such an allegorical interpretation of the love of God and God's people fails to present the high regard in which the Bible holds physical love and sexuality. A more literal understanding of the Song of Solomon affirms that sexuality is one of the gifts God gave us for our enjoyment.

Further, the portrait of the woman in the Song of Solomon is exceptional for literature from a patriarchal and male-centered society. This is not the image of a sexually naïve and passive woman, dependent on a man for protection and sustenance. Quite the contrary, it is the woman who takes the initiative in this romantic pursuit. She utters almost twice as much of the erotic poetry as does the man. She shatters any stereotypes that suggest that women may be romantic but they are not sexually inclined. The Song of Solomon is devoid of male dominance and female subordination. The woman is an independent person. She has her own vineyard (Song of Solomon 1:6) and is encouraged to pasture her flocks (1:8), occupations normally assigned to men. This wisdom book clearly teaches that human passion is both noble and ennobling. Finally, its attraction and vitality are natural to both men and women.

Summary

Wisdom literature has something for everyone. The words and reflections of the sages cover all possible interactions that people could have with one another and with God. All of it causes the reader to reflect and ponder their own sagacity: how to get along in life; how to relate to God; how to ponder existence through the lenses of reason; how to develop hope in immortality; how to affirm healthy sexuality.

For Discussion

1. What does it mean to be truly wise?
2. What is meant by the "personification" of wisdom?
3. How do you react to the feminine image for Wisdom?
4. What point does the Book of Job make about: suffering? friends? God language?
5. How is human sexuality a gift from God to be celebrated?

For Further Reading

Bergant, Dianne. *What Are They Saying About Wisdom Literature?* New York: Paulist Press, 1984.

Ceresko, Anthony R. *Introduction to Old Testament Wisdom.* Maryknoll, NY: Orbis Books, 1999.

Habel, Norman C. *The Book of Job: A Commentary.* Philadelphia: Westminster Press, 1985.

Murphy, Roland E. *The Tree of Life: An Exploration of Biblical Wisdom Literature.* New York: Doubleday, 1990.

Von Rad, Gerhard. *Wisdom in Israel.* Nashville: Abingdon Press, 1962.

10

SHORT STORIES AND HEBREW HEROINES OF THE OLD TESTAMENT

There ARE FIVE "SHORT STORIES" IN THE OLD Testament: Ruth, Jonah, Esther, Tobit, and Judith. Each of these stories is concerned with the relationship between God's people and the Gentiles. Several are written to assure the reader of God's superiority to pagan divinities and the religious supremacy of God's people over all the races of the earth. At the same time, however, the stories display either an underlying emphasis on God's compassion and mercy for non-Israelites or a conviction that God's actions embrace the lives of *all* people.

In four of the stories women are either the chief character or play major roles. This emphasizes the theoretical social equality of all Israelites, as well as the fact that charismatic leadership was a gift bestowed by God on persons—namely, women—otherwise ignored by then-prevailing social patriarchal hierarchies. The predominance of women, a powerless and disenfranchised group in Israelite society, emphasizes that it is God who is the deliverer, not mortal human beings. All but Jonah are concerned with one or more related themes: widowhood, the single state, marriage, remarriage, ancestry, and family succession.

The thread that binds all of these stories together is the importance of the Israelites as a people. Each of the five books recounts the story of some important communal tradition and how that tradition is subjected to peril—either of a natural or human origin. Each story follows that thread to its point of greatest conflict—and then to resolution. Thus, in each case, the ongoing life of the community is enhanced. In each narrative God is present, moving the events along, whether openly or secretly, toward a conclusion that preserves the integrity and well-being of his people as well as the integrity of his own name and personhood.

The Book of Ruth

The Book of Ruth comes from about the same time period as the composition of the early books of the Old Testament—some time between the tenth and eighth centuries B.C.E. The author of Ruth was concerned with Davidic ascendancy when he wrote this charming account of King David's Moabite great-grandmother, Ruth.

In the Christian Old Testament, Ruth follows Judges. It is placed after Judges to maintain chronological continuity. The date of its composition is uncertain. The Hebrew Bible places Ruth among its third section, called "Writings," or *Kethuvim*.

An ancient Hebrew short story, probably based on an earlier folk tale, the Book of Ruth is ostensibly set in the days of Judges, but it has little in common with that book. Ruth, the main character, is from neighboring Moab, not Israel. The opening verses tell of Ruth's marriage to a Hebrew man and how she chose to return to Judah with her mother-in-law, Naomi, after her husband's death. Her loyalty and kindness are rewarded by God.

The Plot of the Book of Ruth

This brief four-chapter book has a marvelous plot to it. During a famine in the time of the Judges, a woman named Naomi, from the ancient town of Bethlehem, takes refuge in the neighboring land of the Moabites, who occupied the land east of the Dead Sea. According to Israelite tradition, the Moabites were descended from one of Lot's daughters. While there, Naomi's sons both marry Moabite women. When her husband and two sons die, the grieving, bereaved Naomi decides to return to Bethlehem and she urges her two daughters-in-law, Orpha and Ruth, to remain in Moab. Ruth loyally insists on returning with Naomi in the famous passage:

> *¹⁶But Ruth said, Do not press me to leave you or to turn back from following you! Where you go, I will go; Where you lodge, I will lodge; your people shall be my people, and your God my God. ¹⁷Where you die, I will die—there will I be buried. May the LORD do thus and so to me, and more as well, if even death parts me from you!"* (Ruth 1:16–17).

The two women reach Bethlehem at the beginning of the barley harvest. While there, Naomi sees some marital possibilities for Ruth in Boaz, a distant relative, and she suggests Ruth go and lie next to Boaz and "uncover his feet" (Ruth 3:4, 7), a biblical euphemism for the male sex organ. Ruth takes Naomi's advice, and when Boaz awakens to discover Ruth cuddled up nearby, she tells him to spread his cloak over her (Ruth 3:9), another euphemism suggesting more than just getting cozy under the blankets. Boaz is definitely interested, but under the law another kinsman has the right of first refusal (this is based on the levirate law of Deuteronomy 25:5–10). When the man passes Ruth up, Boaz marries her. Despite the fact that Ruth is a foreigner, she becomes the great-grandmother of King David. Besides its importance to Jewish tradition, this line of descent is doubly significant because Jesus was also born from this lineage, a fact noted in the genealogy given at the beginning of the Gospel of Matthew (see Matthew 1:5).

As a literary character, Ruth has been viewed in two compelling lights. First of all, despite aggressively climbing into the sack with Boaz and seducing him, she is otherwise the model of a virtuous, loyal woman who does what is right. Although the Old Testament "bad girls"—Eve, Bathsheba, Delilah, Jezebel—have received most of the publicity from male interpreters, many of the "good girls" were far more significant in Israelite history. Ruth belongs to this group who, unfortunately, have often been interpreted to have taken a backseat to the more familiar male heroes. Sadly, women in ancient Israelite society were little more than slaves with few legal rights. But the roster of Hebrew heroines who took matters into their own hands is impressive: Deborah of Judges; Rachel, whose quick thinking when she sat on her father's idols in Genesis saves her husband Isaac; Miriam, who rescues her brother, the infant Moses, and then helps lead the exodus; Zipporah, Moses' wife, who saves his life; Rahab, the prostitute who helped capture Jericho; and Tamar, who played the resourceful prostitute to win her just due from Judah and was, like Ruth, an ancestor of King David, Israel's greatest king—and, by extension, an ancestor of Solomon and Jesus as well.

So far removed from and different than the violence and warfare of the Book of Judges, the simple, folksy Ruth has been interpreted in various ways. Although it is set before the Babylonian exile, some scholars believe it was written after the exile in Babylon, and its message was aimed at the harsh decrees opposing Jewish intermarriage in the period after the exile when Jewish men were urged to divorce their foreign wives (see the Book of Ezra). The clear emphasis on the fact that Ruth is a foreigner, her acceptance by Boaz despite this fact, and her place in the genealogy of King David all seem to underscore the acceptability of foreign wives.

On the other hand, the Book of Ruth can be seen as a much simpler "virtue" tale that proves that God is open to those outside Israel, just as God was open to bless Israel through the foreign prophet Balaam (Numbers 22:1–24:45) and to bring the people back to Jerusalem after the Babylonian exile by the decree of the foreigner Cyrus (2 Chronicles 36:22; Ezra 1:8; Isaiah 44:28–45:13).

Ruth is the first piece of Israelite literature written about a woman who triumphs as a result of her own assertiveness. Ruth is the first "liberated" woman whom we meet in these short stories. She and her later Israelite sisters saw liberation as a means of making themselves available for greater service to God and the entire Israelite community. They also saw themselves as partners to men, complementing men's talents with their own and, through the wise use of their feminine virtues, enabling men to bring out the best of their masculine virtues.

As is brought out clearly in these five short stories, the truly liberated human being is the person who maximizes his or her own talents through service to the community. Each of these stories is a story about personal freedom—and how that personal freedom is fulfilled by using it for the greater good of the entire Israelite family. There are no better models today for true personal liberation than the figures portrayed in these five stories.

The Book of Jonah

While often listed as one of the minor prophets, the Book of Jonah, in fact, is not a prophetic oracle but, rather, a short story.

Here the theme of personal liberation is displayed in spite of the often humorous actions of the hero of the Book of Jonah. Written in postexilic times, possibly in the mid-fifth century B.C.E., this book stars an arch-traditionalist prophet completely set in his ways. The thing Jonah feared most was an overturning of the status quo. In particular, Jonah didn't want anyone to tamper with his long-established picture of God.

To Jonah, God was the special possession of the Israelites. Furthermore, God operated according to certain set formulas, one of which stated that good people prosper on account of their virtue and bad people suffer because of their wickedness. The Book of Jonah is like the Book of Job in this respect: both were written in reaction to the

narrow, traditionalist viewpoint which equated prosperity with righteousness and suffering with wickedness. Jonah was also written in
reaction to exclusivist thinking, namely, that God had concern only
for Israelites and not for Gentiles.

In opposition to popular thought, the author of Jonah dared to
write that God's mercy is universal. To dramatize this, he sets his story
in the kingdom of the Assyrians—a people whose wickedness and
cruelty were legendary. The implication is that if God can forgive the
Assyrians, he can forgive anybody. Conversely, if the Assyrians can
avail themselves of God's mercy, anyone can.

The Book of Jonah is primarily theological in character, rather than
historical. There was a prophet named Jonah, but it is doubtful that he
ever experienced any of the events described in the book bearing his
name. Jonah, son of Amittai (2 Kings 14:25), certainly didn't convert
the Assyrians to God. Nor did anyone else, for that matter. The
Assyrians were perfectly horrid people right to the end of their history.

This acknowledgement of the historical inaccuracy of the Book of
Jonah leads to one of the most popular questions about the entire
Bible: "Did Jonah really get swallowed by a great fish?" My response:
Probably not! Keep in mind that the author was writing religious
fiction. And while anything is possible—particularly where God is in
charge—the author of Jonah used the story about the fish for a
different purpose than to demonstrate God's power over great sea
creatures. His purpose was to show how one man—the prophet
Jonah—experienced the utter deprivation of God's presence and
through God's merciful salvation was brought to a new state of
religious consciousness.

Jonah tried to flee from God, thinking that by escaping from him
he would find freedom and independence. God had to show Jonah
that human freedom is found only by submitting in trust to God's
guidance and protection. Like the slaves Moses led from Egypt, God
had to lead Jonah through a desert experience.

Unfortunately for the author, desert land was scarce in the middle
of the Mediterranean. Therefore, he had to find another means by

which God could bring Jonah to a change of heart. Hence, the great fish. Jonah's transformation from man-relying-on-himself to man-dependent-on-God takes place in the belly of the fish. It was there that God lifted Jonah from the "pit" (Jonah 2:7) of his own self-assurance to the liberation of his reliance on God.

The lesson learned in the belly of the fish was unfortunately forgotten as soon as Jonah reached the city of Nineveh, capital of the Assyrian empire. In Nineveh, Jonah was his old self—narrow-minded and prejudiced; he was outraged when God forgave the sins of the Ninevites.

God's free act of love and mercy flew in the face of Jonah's preconceived notion of how God *should* act. God then intervened to teach Jonah the true divine nature. Through the use of the castor-oil plant, God drove home the message that his love is universal and that Jonah's fellow human beings are of more importance in God's eyes than human traditions concerning divine retribution.

Jonah's reaction to God's forgiveness of the Ninevites reminds us of Elijah's reaction to God's defeat of Baal on Mount Carmel (see 1 Kings 18:1–19:18). Both men grew angry that God did not follow through according to script. Jonah wanted to destroy the wicked Ninevites and Elijah wanted God to stamp out Baalism—the worship of the Canaanite gods—in Israel for good. God did neither. The author of Jonah thus implies that Jonah's end would be like Elijah's: after a brief period of separation, Elijah came to know God even more intimately than before. Since the short story known as the Book of Jonah does not describe this happening to Jonah, one can only conjecture whether or not Jonah accepted God's control over his life.

The Image of God in the Book of Jonah

Jonah occupies center stage in his book. And yet the story is basically about God and how we understand (or misunderstand) the divine nature. Jonah won't give up some hallowed ideas. The God of Israel (that is, the God of the Old Testament) is in Jonah's worldview a wrathful God, intent upon destroying the sinner. Isn't this self-evident in the prophets, who continually condemn sin and proclaim divine retribution? They frequently announce the devastation of the nation by foreign powers as divine punishment for sinfulness (see Isaiah 8:6–8; 9:7–20; Jeremiah 4:5–8; 5:15–17; 6:22–26; Ezekiel 5:5–10; 7:1–27). They also announce the chastisement of other nations because of their wickedness (see Isaiah 13:23; Jeremiah 46–51; Ezekiel 25–32; Amos 1:3–2:3). But where is this image of God to be found in the Book of Jonah?

It is true that God's first words in the story seem to fit the pattern of an angry and just God committed to punish the wicked city of Nineveh: "Go at once to Nineveh, that great city, and cry out against it; for their wickedness has come up before me" (Jonah 1:2). God specifically mentions the evil of the city, an evil that demands a divine response. The sinfulness of Sodom and Gomorrah (Genesis 18:20–21) and the oppression of the house of Israel by the Egyptians (Exodus 2:23–24) similarly claimed God's attention and received a divine response. So it is reasonable to assume that the wickedness of Nineveh provoked the divine wrath and was liable to divine punishment. Why else would Jonah have been sent to the city to "preach against it"? Nineveh, the capital of an evil empire, was a symbol of oppression and injustice in the ancient Near East. It deserved divine retribution.

However, the story of Jonah is full of surprises. The first surprise is the prophet's response to God's command. One would think that a fervently nationalistic prophet such as Jonah would be delighted with the task of condemning a wicked enemy city. However, he boards a ship heading away from Nineveh, and God has to send a storm in order to turn back the stubborn prophet. But neither wind nor wave nor the threat of shipwreck changes Jonah's mental habits. His only response is a death wish: "Pick me up and throw me into the sea; then the sea will quiet down for you; for I know it is because of me that this great storm has come upon you" (Jonah 1:12). Jonah prefers death over the loss of his hallowed ideas.

It would seem appropriate for God to be angry with Jonah and to punish him. Drowning in an angry sea would be a fitting end for such a recalcitrant and faithless prophet. Yet that is not what happens. We are surprised by God's reaction. Jonah does not drown. Neither is he eaten—in the sense of digested—by the large fish that God sent to rescue the prophet from certain death. Our habits of logic may convince us that Jonah had every "right" to die. He even seems to prefer it! But the Lord rescued him by means of the fish, which vomited Jonah safe and sound—as well as wet and slimy—onto the shore: "Then the Lord spoke to the fish, and it spewed Jonah out upon the dry land" (Jonah 2:10).

When Jonah is commissioned the second time to go to Nineveh, he finally obeys. His message to the city, however, could hardly be shorter: "Forty days more, and Nineveh shall be overthrown!" (Jonah 3:4)—only five words in Hebrew. To our surprise, these few words inspire the speediest and most thorough conversion that the world has ever witnessed. And with that conversion comes a change in the divine will. "God changed his mind about the calamity that he had said he would bring upon them; and he did not do it" (Jonah 3:10). The anger, which we assume motivated the divine actions up to this point, suddenly disappears.

Is divine wrath really a part of the story? In the Book of Jonah, only human beings ascribe anger to God. The king of Nineveh mentions the divine wrath (Jonah 3:9), and Jonah is upset when it does not materialize (Jonah 4:2). However, God never mentions divine wrath and refrains from angry responses to Nineveh and Jonah. The prophet is by far the more irascible of the two. Four times the text mentions the prophet's anger (Jonah 4:1, 4, 9 [two times]). Jonah is even angry enough to die! Instead of divine wrath and human understanding, we have a story of human wrath and divine understanding.

Jonah is bold enough to quote God as a protest against divine mercy. He is upset with ". . . a gracious God and merciful, slow to anger, and abounding in steadfast love, and ready to relent from punishing" (Jonah 4:2; see Exodus 34:6; Numbers 14:18; Psalms 86:15; 103:8; 145:8; Joel 2:13). This citation aptly describes the image of God in the Book of Jonah. Then why is the prophet so angry? Because he feels that God is unfair. Jonah cannot accept divine mercy for the wicked, especially when Israel suffers so much. Why should God be patient with an evil city? For Jonah, justice requires divine wrath and retribution.

Nevertheless, there is no divine wrath—not even when Jonah gets angry with God. Patient with the stubborn prophet, God attempts to teach him a lesson in mercy. God rescues Jonah a second time by providing a fast-growing plant that protects him from the burning sun. Jonah neither deserved this favor nor earned it. The sulking prophet had not planted it, had not watered it, and had not cared for it. Yet he became angry when it withered. Jonah feels he has a right to be angry—over major as well as minor injustices. We don't know if Jonah ever learned the lesson about divine mercy. It seems unlikely, however, since he is so caught up in his own anger.

The Book of Jonah portrays a powerful deity. Wind and wave, fish, worm, and plant are all obedient to divine commands. Human response to divine power, however, is more complicated, more subtle. The sailors make vows when they recognize the power of God. The Ninevites repent after a simple message from God's prophet. But the prophet himself is less than pliable. He eventually accomplishes the divine will, but he remains angry with God. Jonah appreciates God's mercy when it is directed toward him, but he does not appreciate it when it is directed toward other sinners. Yet this is precisely the lesson that Jonah needs to learn: The God of Israel is a caring, gentle, patient God—who prefers mercy to wrath and punishment.

The Book of Jonah portrays God as patient and merciful rather than as angry and vindictive. Instead of allowing Jonah to drown, God sends a fish to rescue him. Instead of destroying Nineveh, God relents when its inhabitants repent. Instead of becoming angry with Jonah, God tries to teach the recalcitrant prophet a lesson. In the entire book, only human beings get angry, yet ascribe anger to God. Perhaps this is because humans have the bad habit of assuming that God is just like us—only bigger. So divine anger must be even greater than our own. The Book of Jonah challenges such an assumption and attempts to teach us something about God.

The story of Jonah can also teach us something about ourselves. The prophet symbolizes our own stubbornness, our own bad mental habits, our own limitations. Like all the characters in the story, we are challenged to respond positively to God's mercy and love when these are offered to us. Like Jonah, we may need to learn some lessons about God's mercy and love for sinful outsiders. God is patient and compassionate toward us and toward others. The challenge is to imitate the divine patience and compassion when we deal with those who are different from us, perhaps even hostile toward us.

The Book of Esther

The next short story to appear in the Old Testament is the Book of Esther. Known to Jewish readers as the source of the Purim festival—and unfamiliar to many Christians—the Book of Esther has a distinction shared with only one other Bible book—Song of Solomon. It never mentions God! Perhaps as a reaction to this omission, later editors, writing in Greek, added a lot of "God-talk" to the Hebrew original, thus making it appear to be a more "spiritual" book than when it first appeared. The *Jerusalem Bible* prints the Greek verses in italics. These Greek passages stand in clear contrast to the original Hebrew passages, which seem on first glance very secular in character. Since the Greek additions in a sense detract from the purpose of the original Hebrew author, we will not consider them here.

Set in the time of the Persian empire, the Book of Esther is the story of a brave Jewish heroine, Esther (*Hadassah* in Hebrew), who saves her people from a genocidal plot. The story goes like this. The Persian king, Ahasueras, gives a grand banquet at his capitol, Susa, and decides to publicly display his beautiful queen, Vashti. But Vashti, apparently uninterested in being put on display like a prize heifer, refuses to attend. The king issues a decree that all women must obey their husbands (we know a man wrote that!), and Vashti is deposed as queen. Deciding a new wife is in order, the king orders all of the beautiful young virgins of the kingdom collected for what essentially became the only beauty contest recorded in the Bible.

Concealing her Jewish identity, the beautiful Esther, a young woman brought up by her cousin Mordecai, was chosen as the new queen of Persia. Esther and Mordecai then helped foil a plot against the king's life. But cousin Mordecai refused to bow in deference to the king's chancellor, Haman. Completely infuriated at this show of disrespect, the enraged Haman determined to seek revenge on the Jewish Mordecai by eliminating all the Jews in the empire. He persuaded the king to decree death to the Jews.

Learning of Haman's plot, Mordecai prompted Esther to invite King Ahasuerus and Haman to a banquet. There she told the king that she was under threat of death from the king's decree and that it was Haman's doing. The horrified king rescinded his decree and ordered Haman and his sons to be hanged on the very same gallows that had been set up for the Jews. Mordecai was promoted to chancellor and the Jews were given license to take revenge on their enemies in the empire.

Traditional Jewish literature had always been careful to spell out humanity's insignificance before God and God's dominion over the events of history. The author of Esther, by contrast, pushed God's control of events into the background and brought human ingenuity and independence into the foreground.

The principal Jewish characters in the book—Mordecai and Esther—succeed through their own initiative, skill, cunning, and bravado. God never intervened to help them—at least not openly. Thus, Esther is very different from previous Old Testament writings we have considered, in which we found God personally involved with his people, and often sending angels to assist them.

Because Esther is so human-centered, it barely made it into the Jewish canon (official list) of scripture. Nevertheless, Esther is there, giving us a remarkable teaching still very relevant today. That teaching revolves around the age-old question: How much does the devout believer rely on God and how much on self?

The Book of Esther clearly tips the balance in favor of human activity. It was perhaps written in reaction to the unhealthy piety of postexilic Jews who imagined that strict observance of the details of ritual and nothing else assured them of God's protection. This attitude is still with us.

The message of Esther is clear: The devout believer is called to participate actively in the struggle against evil by confronting injustice and oppression openly rather than waiting for God to win the battle by himself.

The teaching of Esther is not godless, however. God is nowhere mentioned by name, but he is nonetheless present—in the actions of loyal Jews who asserted themselves in favor of righteousness. Without mentioning God, the author demonstrates that God operated behind the scenes in Esther, stage-managing events so that Mordecai and Esther could triumph over the wicked Haman. Why else did King Ahasuerus suffer from insomnia precisely on that fateful night (Esther 6)? Or was it simply a coincidence that Haman showed up at the very moment when the king decided to honor Mordecai for his loyalty?

The implication is obvious. God, while never mentioned by name, unobtrusively intervened on the side of his people, complementing their activity with his own. The message is that God helps those of his good and loyal people who help themselves. God does not regard his people as robots who are to sit around trancelike while he does all the work.

The Book of Esther thus sees human liberation coming to fulfillment only in the context of partnership: God will do his part, but human beings must at the same time assert their own creativity in doing theirs.

The Books of Tobit and Judith

Our two final short stories, the books of Tobit and Judith, repeat themes presented in Ruth and Esther. Like Ruth, Tobit is concerned with the sacredness of marriage and the preservation of family succession. Like Esther, Judith is concerned with the role a strong woman plays in saving her people from annihilation by a pagan power. Tobit is like Ruth, a gentle book; while Judith, like Esther, leads to a violent climax.

Both books were written to assure Jews living under *Greek* domination of God's constant protection, although the setting of both books is in the time of Assyrian domination, centuries before the books were written. Each book contains historical inaccuracies which in no way detract from the power of the books' respective teachings.

Tobit is the earlier work, written around 200 b.c.e. Judith was written a century or so later.

The more aggressive tone of Judith is due to the fact that the Maccabean struggle was in full bloom during the time of the book's composition. Judith is more militant than Tobit, more so even than Esther.

Tobit and Esther, like the first six chapters of Daniel, present a view of Jewish-Gentile relationship which allows for much accommodation between the two ways of life. Like the author of Daniel, the authors of Tobit and Esther would permit Jewish integration into Gentile culture, so long as Jews remain loyal to their faith. The author of Judith, on the other hand, presents the Gentiles as implacable enemies and sees no compromise possible between Jewish and Gentile ways.

Judith is the female version of Judas Maccabeus. The heroine of the book is presented as a female counterpart to the Maccabean hero, Judas. Like Judas Maccabeus, Judith was a courageous warrior for Judaism, even though she subdued her enemy through subtlety and scheming rather than by battle.

Tobit, on the other hand, is a more traditional book. The author of Tobit broke little new ground and made no radical departure from traditional Jewish thought. As in Ruth, the importance of marrying within the family unit and preserving family continuity is the core of the Tobit story. Liberation, as seen by Tobit's author, takes place fully within the context of attunement to the Law. Tobit, Tobias, and Sarah all submitted themselves to God's will as revealed in his Law.

When Tobias and Sarah married, they did so fully conscious that they were participating in a greater event than simply their own union. They were fulfilling God's plan—revealed in the Law—through which his people were to continue their bonds of family and kin in perpetuity. Tobias and Sarah found the fulfillment of their individual interest in their concern for the overall interest of the community. Because of their righteousness, they removed the curses which had plagued their families. The demon who had killed Sarah's seven previous husbands was driven away and Tobit's sight was restored. As in our previous stories, the author places human liberation in the context of submission to God's will.

This theme is continued by the author of Judith. Like the central characters of the previous stories, Judith too was challenged by critical events to choose between her own interests and those of the community. Judith's choice was spontaneous; the community's interests took precedence over her own.

In Judith, like no other short-story character in the Old Testament, we find a more harmonious blend of submissiveness to God and human assertiveness. Judith was a strong, dominant character, capable of making clear and immediate decisions. While the Jewish men in the story groveled in fear and confusion before the besieging Assyrians, Judith knew at once what she must do and set out boldly, without male assistance, to save the imperiled community. Yet she was not totally without assistance. She submitted her entire scheme to God, acknowledging God as the source of her strength and success:

> *¹²Please, please, God of my father, God of the heritage of Israel, Lord of heaven and earth, Creator of the waters, King of all your creation, hear my prayer! ¹³Make my deceitful words bring wound and bruise on those who have planned cruel things against your covenant, and against your sacred house, and against Mount Zion, and against the house your children possess. ¹⁴Let your whole nation and every tribe know and understand that you are God, the God of all power and might, and that*

there is no other who protects the people of Israel but you alone!
(Judith 9:12–14).

What a beautiful blend of submissiveness and assertiveness! Judith typifies true human liberation. She knew that God rules history, but that he does so only through human instruments who are willing to use their skills and talents in concert with God.

Judith avoided two extremes of the spiritual life: She neither passively waited for God's miraculous intervention nor charged ahead, self-assured and autonomous. She submitted her human talents to the will of God and asked God to use her talents for the common good of the people. That God did indeed use Judith in the story to preserve his people from annihilation demonstrates clearly for us today the Old Testament's conclusive message concerning the idea of human freedom.

Women in the Old Testament
Having looked at three outstanding leadership women of the Old Testament—Ruth, Esther, and Judith—one could get the impression that these are the only Hebrew heroines. Such an impression is false and a disservice to the myriad of women who were a profoundly important part of God's revelation contained in the Old Testament. Space does not permit an in-depth treatment of all of them, but the following chart will help acquaint one with these important women.

HEBREW HEROINES

In the entire Bible there are over two hundred named women, and in excess of six hundred unnamed women. In relation to just the Old Testament, there are many Hebrew heroines, women who were great leaders and profoundly faithful in the practice of their religion. This chart attempts to summarize the lives of the more important ones. There is no intention whatsoever to exclude any of the other leadership women—named or unnamed—that are mentioned in the Old Testament. Some women included in the list may not merit the title "heroine," but they are included anyway because of their importance in the Old Testament.

Eve (Genesis 2–3; 4:1–2, 8, 16, 25; 5:1–2)

In the recorded history of Jews and Christians, she is the first woman with a name and an identity. She was wife of Adam and mother to many sons and daughters, including Cain, Abel, and Seth. As the "original woman," Eve continues to be the symbol of both domination and liberation of women.

Sarah (Genesis 11:27–32; 12; 13; 16:1–18:15; 20:2–21:12; 22:1–14; 23; 24:36; 25:10; 49:31; Isaiah 51:2)

Born in Ur of the Chaldeans, Sarah married her half-brother, Abraham. She left Ur to settle in the land of Canaan. Sarah was childless until the age of ninety, when she bore a son, Isaac. She was the first matriarch.

Hagar (Genesis 16:1–6; 16:7–16; 17:1; 21:1–4, 8–21; 25:5–6, 12–17)

The Egyptian slave of Sarah, Hagar became Abraham's concubine when Sarah did not bear children. Hagar twice fled to the wilderness with her son, Ishmael, because of the hostilities she suffered in Abraham's household. Each time, God's messenger comforted her and intervened to save her life.

Milcah (Genesis 11:26–29; 22:20–23; 24:15, 24, 47)

Milcah was Sarah and Abraham's niece, the daughter of their brother Haram. Her granddaughter, Rebekah, married Sarah and Abraham's grandson, Jacob.

Rebekah (Genesis 22:20–23; 24; 25:19–34; 26:1–11, 17, 23, 34–35; 27:1–46; 28:1–5; 29:1–35; 30:1–43; 31:14–35; 34; 35:16–20; 49:31)

Rebekah was the wife of Isaac and mother of twin sons, Jacob and Esau. She helped her second-born and favored son, Jacob, conspire against his father to win Esau's birthright and blessing. She also secured Jacob's safety in the face of Esau's wrath.

Deborah, Rebekah's Nurse (Genesis 35:8)

A faithful servant of Rebekah who is known for her care of Rebekah's children and grandchildren.

Leah (Genesis 29:15–36; 30:1–21; 31:4–55; 32:22–24; 33:1–7, 12–14; 34:1; 35:23, 26; 46:8–18; 49:31)

Leah was the elder sister of Rachel, whom Jacob had worked seven years to marry. Leah tricked Jacob into marrying her by taking Rachel's place on their wedding night. Jacob ultimately married both sisters. She had six sons who become six of the Israelite tribes.

Rachel (Genesis 28:1–5; 29:1–31:55; 32:22–24; 33:1–7, 12–14; 35:16–21, 24–25; 46:19–22; 48:7; Jeremiah 31:15)

Leah's sister, the younger daughter of Rebekah's brother Laban. Jacob worked seven years to win the right to marry her. She was the mother of Joseph and

Benjamin. She was the ancestress of the northern kingdom, which was called Ephraim, after Joseph's oldest son. After Ephraim and Benjamin were exiled by the Assyrians, Rachel is remembered as the classic mother who mourns and intercedes for her children. The prophet Jeremiah over one hundred years after the fall of the Northern Kingdom had a vision of Rachel still mourning (Jeremiah 31:15–21).

Bilhah and Zilpah (Genesis 29:24, 29; 30:3–7; 32:22–23; 33:1–3; 35:22; 37:2; 46:25)

These women were the maidservants of Leah and Rachel who, while at times were pawns in the hands of men, nonetheless were mothers of one-third of the tribes of Israel.

Shiphrah and Puah (Exodus 1:15–22)

Shiphrah and Puah were Hebrew midwives in Egypt. They defied the orders of Pharaoh to kill all male Hebrew children and as midwives may have delivered Moses. The Hebrew midwives resisted oppression so their people would live.

Jochebed (Exodus 2:1–10; 6:20; Numbers 26:59)

Jochebed, a daughter of Levi, was the mother of Miriam, Aaron, and Moses. She and her husband, Amram, were both of the priestly tradition by birth. Jochebed saved the life of Moses with the help of Miriam and the Pharaoh's daughter.

Miriam (Exodus 2:1–10; 15:19–21; Numbers 12; 20:1–2; Deuteronomy 24:8–9; 1 Chronicles 6:1–3; Micah 6:3–4)

Miriam was the sister of Moses and Aaron and shared leadership with them during the exodus from Egypt. She led the women in song and dance after the parting of the Sea of Reeds. She saved Moses' life by convincing Pharaoh's daughter to take him into her household after he was weaned.

Pharaoh's Daughter (Exodus 2:1–20)

Pharaoh's daughter took pity on the three-month-old male Hebrew child, Moses, and gave him to his own mother to nurse. She acted contrary to her father's law, which said male Hebrew children must die. In solidarity with the midwives and Miriam, she chose life over death. This led to the liberation of the Hebrew people.

Zipporah (Exodus 2:15–22; 4:19–26; 18:2–6; Numbers 12:1)

The wife and "savior" of Moses, Zipporah played a key role in preserving Moses from God's wrath.

Hannah (1 Samuel 1; 2:1–11, 18–21)

The wife of Elkanah, Hannah was childless until God heard her intense prayer to become a mother. She gave birth to Samuel, whom she consecrated to God, and who became a great prophet.

Gomer (Hosea 1:2–9; 3; 4:1, 5–6, 10)

Gomer, a prostitute, was the wife of the prophet Hosea. Hosea's marriage, divorce, and remarriage to Gomer, the naming of their children, and his indictments against his wife's promiscuous behavior are all a metaphor for Israel's relationship with God.

Huldah (2 Kings 22:11–20; 2 Chronicles 34:22–28)

Huldah was a prophetess who lived in Jerusalem during the time of the prophet Jeremiah. She was consulted by King Josiah when a book of the Law was found in the temple. She foretold God's wrath upon the nation as well as God's mercy toward its king, Josiah.

Micah's Mother (Judges 17:1–6)

Micah's mother is an example of a syncretic time for the Hebrew people, when there was no king in Israel. Many religious practices were incorporated with the Hebrew faith. Micah's mother built a molten silver memento (idol) to show her gratefulness to God when her son returned eleven hundred pieces of silver which he had stolen from her.

Tamar (Genesis 38:6–30; Ruth 4:12; 1 Chronicles 2:3–6)

Tamar was betrayed several times over by Judah and his family. However, by patience and cleverness she secured her rights. In the Book of Genesis she is described as righteous. She had twin sons, Perez and Zerah, with Judah, whom she seduced after disguising herself as a prostitute. Perez was the ancestor of David.

Rahab (Joshua 2:1–24; 6:1–2, 15–25)

Rahab, a prostitute in the city of Jericho, was cunning. She harbored and bargained with Joshua's spies and took charge of her own life. As a result, she and her family were spared when Joshua's army destroyed her city.

Deborah, the Judge (Judges 4:1–22; 5:1–31)

Deborah was a judge, a warrior, and a prophetess in Israel during the time of the judges. She brought victory to the people of Israel during a national effort against the Canaanites during the time of the judges. She wrote a Hebrew heroic poem, similar to Psalm 68, which was filled with many female images.

Jael (Judges 4:1–3, 14–22; 5:1, 6, 24–27)

Jael enticed Sisera, the general of the Caananite army, to seek refuge in her tent, and then killed him. She was the wife of Heber, the Kenite, a descendent from Jethro, the father-in-law of Moses. Deborah celebrated this event with a song.

Samson's Mother (Judges 13:2–24; 14:1–9; 16:30–31)

Samson's mother waited a long time for a baby after many years of infertility. She was the wife of Manoah of Zorah. After a heavenly visitor announced she was to give birth, she was instructed to dedicate the child to God, to be raised as a Nazarite.

Delilah (Judges 16:4–31)

Delilah was probably a Philistine, a lover to Samson. She eventually found out the source of his amazing, destructive strength and informed upon him.

Ruth and Naomi (Book of Ruth)

Ruth was the daughter-in-law of Naomi, who migrated with her family to Moab when famine struck Bethlehem. When Ruth and Naomi both became widows, Ruth insisted they return to Bethlehem rather than to the Moabite people. Ruth married Boaz and was great-grandmother to David.

David's Mother (1 Samuel 22:3–4)

David's mother is not mentioned by name. She was the wife of Jesse. The lineage of David is traced through his father, Jesse, his grandfather, Obed, his great-grandparents, Ruth and Boaz, and on through his patriarchal ancestry instead of through his mother's Jewish heritage.

Michal, One of David's Wives (1 Samuel 18:20–29; 19:11–17; 25–44; 2 Samuel 3:13–16; 6:16, 20–23; 21:8–9).

Michal was the daughter of Saul, and was given to David as a wife; she loved him very much and protected him from death at the hands of Saul. Later she mocked David for dancing before the Ark (2 Samuel 6:16–23), and as a punishment she remained childless to her death.

Abigail (1 Samuel 25:39–43; 27:3; 30:3, 5, 18; 2 Samuel 2:2; 3:3).

The second wife of David, known for her good manners and diplomatic strategy, she preserved her first husband, Nabal, from being murdered by David.

Bathsheba (2 Samuel 11:1–18, 25–27; 12:1–25; 1 Kings 1:1, 11–40; 2:13–25; 1 Chronicles 3:5)

Bathsheba epitomizes the dependence upon men and also the strength to assert her wishes. She fell under David's control but in turn secured power for her son, Solomon. David and Solomon respected her and granted her favors.

Queen of Sheba (1 Kings 10:1–13; 2 Chronicles 9:1–12)

The Queen of Sheba is claimed by Arabs and Ethiopians and much mythology surrounds her. The scripture describes her as a contemporary of Solomon in the tenth century B.C.E., who visited him for a length of time. They are believed to have had an equal intellectual rapport and are reported to have had a fruitful sexual relationship before she returned to her country.

Jezebel (1 Kings 16:29–34; 18:1–20, 38–40; 19:1–3; 21:1–25; 22:51–53; 2 Kings 9:1–13, 21–37)

Jezebel was a princess, queen, queen mother, and interim ruler of Israel around 850 B.C.E. She was a worshiper of Baal and Asherah and threatened the prophets of Israel, most especially Elijah. While not a Hebrew woman, but a foreigner, she exercised great power and influence over her husband, King Ahab.

Athaliah (2 Kings 8:16–18, 25–26; 10:13; 11:1–21; 2 Chronicles 21:4–6; 22:1–3, 9–12; 23:12–15, 20–21; 24:1–2, 7)

Athaliah continued the cruelty of her mother, Jezebel. She secured the throne after the death of her son, Ahaziah, by slaughtering all male heirs. One grandson, Joash, was spared by hiding in the temple. During her reign, she restored the worship of Baal.

Esther (Book of Esther)

Esther was a Jew in the kingdom of Medea and Persia. She was raised by her relative, Mordecai, after her parents died. Because of her beauty, she was conscripted into the harem of King Ahasuerus and eventually became queen. She used her position to help her people. Their victory against slaughter gave rise to the feast of Purim. Her Jewish name is known as Hadassah.

Judith (Book of Judith)

Judith, daughter of Merari, wife of Manasseh, was a beautiful, wealthy courageous woman who lived in the town of Bethulia. She liberated her people from an Assyrian siege by seducing the Assyrian general, Holofernes, and chopping off his head.

Shelomith (Levi 24:10–23)

Shelomith could be considered an invisible woman in scripture. She is named as a mother of a son who blasphemed against God. She was a member of the tribe of Dan, married to an Egyptian. Moses used this occasion to show that justice is meted out to Hebrew and alien alike.

Jewish Mother (2 Maccabees 7:1–43; 2 Maccabees 8–18)

Jewish mother is a narrative about a mother and her seven sons during the time of the Maccabees. She exhorted her children to stand firm in the practice of Judaism. They endured extreme horrors of the Seleucid persecution. All seven sons were tortured and slaughtered before she herself was killed. She is admired as a martyr along with her sons by the Catholic Church. In Syriac Christian accounts, she is called Shamone/Maryam.

Wisdom (Sophia) (Proverbs 8:1–3; 8:22–31; 9:1–5; 31:10–31; Sirach 24:1–27; 51:13–30; Wisdom 7:22–8:1)

In the Wisdom books, we find an image of God personified as Wisdom/woman. She is beautiful and desirable and promises life to all who seek her. She is present with God at creation and in speaking of her, we speak of God.

Susanna (Daniel 13:1–59)

The story of Susanna is attached to the Book of Daniel and is written in Greek. She is presented as a virtuous woman who trusts God with her life. She makes two speeches in which she declares her commitment to remain faithful to God and her husband (Daniel 13:22–23), and cries to God for help in a desperate situation (Daniel 13:42–43).

Medium of Endor (1 Samuel 28:7–25).

Saul consults this woman, who is in some Bible translations called a "witch," to conjure up the ghost of Samuel, which she does, so that Saul can converse with it. While a foreign woman, the medium is used by Saul to bring Samuel back.

For Discussion

1. How is Ruth a liberated woman for her time?
2. How did Jonah make God over into Jonah's own personal image and likeness of God? What couldn't Jonah stand about God's behavior?
3. In the Book of Esther, since God is not overtly active in the actions of Esther and Mordecai, how is God involved in the book? Explain.
4. How is the Book of Tobit similar to the books of Ruth and Esther?
5. How is the Book of Judith similar to the books of Maccabees?

For Further Reading

Ceresko, Anthony R. "Jonah," in the *New Jerome Biblical Commentary*. Edited by R.E. Brown, J.A. Fitzmyer, and R.E. Murphy. Englewood Cliffs, NJ: Prentice Hall, 1990, 580–84.

Craghan, J. *Esther, Judith, Tobit, Jonah, Ruth*. Wilmington, DE: Michael Glazier, 1981.

Myers, Carol, ed. *Women In Scripture*. Grand Rapids, MI: Eerdmans, 2000.

McKenna, Megan. *Not Counting Women and Children*. Maryknoll: Orbis, 1994.

Nowell, I. *Women In the Old Testament*. Collegeville, MN: Liturgical Press, 1997.

Nowell, I., T. Craven & D. Dumm. "Tobit, Judith, Esther," in the *New Jerome Biblical Commentary*. Edited by R.E. Brown, J.A. Fitzmyer, and R.E. Murphy. Englewood Cliffs, NJ: Prentice Hall, 1990, 568–79.

Sasson, J. *Jonah: A New Translation with Introduction, Commentary and Interpretation*. New York: Doubleday, 1990.

11

JUDAISM, THE GREEKS, AND THE CLOSING OF THE OLD TESTAMENT

The HISTORY OF JUDAISM DURING THE PERIOD OF Greek domination (ca. 300–70 B.C.E.) was haunted by the temptation of the Jews to dilute their faith in God by mixing pagan elements into their religion. We have seen this pattern in operation throughout Israel's history, as narrated in other books of the Old Testament. In this chapter, we will find the Old Testament Jews undergoing the final test of their faith.

One could easily imagine how Old Testament writers who lived during this period were affected by the national crisis of the arrival of the Greeks and the temptation to compromise their faith. Like the patriots of the American Revolution, Jewish patriots of late Old Testament times knew that their lives were at stake. They knew also that their nation was locked in a struggle whose outcome would bring either life or death for the Jewish faith. To understand how this moment of great crisis was reached, let us look for a moment at the history of the ancient Near East.

The Arrival of the Greeks

In the year 333 B.C.E., the history of the ancient world was pointed in a new direction. A young warlord from Macedonia, Alexander the Great, defeated the Persians at the battle of Issus, and consolidated his hold on Asia Minor. He then set out to conquer the known world, following his desire to form all peoples into a single Greek empire. Alexander died ten years later in Babylon, weeping over the fact that there were no more worlds to be conquered. During his brief military career, he brought all of Asia Minor under the domination of Greek power.

Empire-building was nothing new in ancient history. What distinguished Alexander from his power-hungry predecessors was the way in which his conquest influenced the people he subdued. All previous conquerors had been Asian. Alexander was a European. Previous conquerors had come from cultures based on the supremacy of mystery over reason and religion over science. Alexander, who studied at the feet of the great philosopher Aristotle, believed in the triumph of rationalism over religion, and human individualism over the angry power of the gods.

This, of course, is a great generalization and somewhat an oversimplification. Alexander and the Greeks had their gods and mystery cults, too. But compared to the Asians, the Greeks stood for a bold new type of thinking which could best be summarized by saying that, in Greek thought, human reason was more important than religious faith.

Just as after World War II the modern world entered the "American Era," so after the death of Alexander the ancient world entered the "Greek Era." (The technical term for this is "Hellenism," which refers to the imitation or adoption of ancient Greek language, thought, architecture, arts, customs, etc.) Just as many countries liberated by the Americans during the Second World War rushed to adopt various aspects of American culture, so too many ancient peoples became enamored with the new Greek culture which Alexander's soldiers left behind.

Not everyone, of course, was attracted to the new ways. Just as many modern Europeans began to detest the corruption of their ancient customs by the American hot-dog and drugstore culture, many ancient peoples likewise began to wonder whether Greek ways were good for them after all. Nowhere was the conflict between new and old ways more noticeable than in Judah. Like their pagan neighbors, many Jews were entranced by the new Greek ideas. Rationalism, science, philosophy—these were heady topics for a people whose entire life was bound up with religious Scripture and the temple liturgy. Many young Jews in particular became intoxicated by these new ideas.

A serious cleavage in Jewish religious practice thus developed during the period following Alexander's conquest. One group of Jews insisted on the old ways, and looked upon Greek ideas as perverse. Another group went wholeheartedly over to Greek culture, repudiating their Jewish faith and Jewish ancestry all together. A third group—the "Hellenizers"—tried to compromise, maintaining their need to have no conflict between Judaism and Greek culture. This latter group even included some of the Jewish high priests.

When Alexander died, his empire was divided into four parts, with a different Greek family appointed to rule each part. The two ruling families that affected our story were the Ptolemies and Seleucids, whose respective capitols were Alexandria in Egypt and Antioch in Syria. The Ptolemies controlled Judah (and all of Palestine) until 201 B.C.E., when the Seleucid king, Antiochus III, defeated the Ptolemies in battle and assumed control of Palestine. This was to have drastic consequences for the Jews.

The Ptolemies had never insisted that the Jews adopt Greek culture. With the coming into power of the Seleucids, however, this began to change, if only in subtle ways at first. Jews were increasingly forced by the Hellenization programs of the Seleucids to choose between their ancient faith and the new Greek ways. More and more Jews renounced their Judaism—or tried to compromise it—by becoming good citizens of the Seleucid kings.

The Jews began to change their names from traditional Hebrew names like *Joshua* to Greek names like *Jason*. Jewish athletes, before competing in the Greek games, in which everyone competed naked, had their circumcision covered by surgery—that is, they renounced the ancient sign of the Abrahamic covenant (see Genesis 17:9–14), which they carried on their bodies. This was but one example of how Jews betrayed their allegiance to God.

Just as the American nation at the time of the Civil War could not exist half-slave and half-free, neither could the Jewish state long continue half-Jew and half-Greek. Matters came to a head with the accession to the Seleucid throne of King Antiochus IV (175–164 B.C.E.), nicknamed *Epiphanes*, or "God Manifest." Antiochus was not content to let some of the Jews choose Greek ways and some remain faithful to the old ways. He began an aggressive policy of Hellenization, forcing Jews under penalty of death to renounce fundamental elements of their faith. Offering sacrifice in the temple, circumcision of newborn boys, and reading the Pentateuch were among the many traditional Jewish observances declared capital offenses. Antiochus Epiphanes virtually declared war on Judaism. Left unchallenged, he no doubt would have wiped the Jewish faith from the face of the earth.

But challenges there were—on two fronts: one military and the other theological. The conservative Maccabee family rallied Jews to oppose Antiochus with force of arms. The writer of the Book of Daniel wrote to each of his compatriots the theological significance of Antiochus's attack on the Jewish faith and to assure them that even Antiochus's persecution was a part of God's universal plan.

The Book of Daniel

The Book of Daniel has always captured the imagination of its readers with such stories as the three youths who survived the fiery furnace (chapter 3); and Daniel, who reads and interprets the writing on the wall (chapter 5) and who survived death in the lions' den (Daniel 6:16–24).

The book was written around 169 B.C.E. By this time, the Persian empire had been swept away by Alexander the Great, who had died, and his surviving generals had divided up his conquests. Judea and Jerusalem were under the control of a Greek-speaking regime in Syria, descended from one of these generals.

Antiochus IV Epiphanes, the emperor at the time, brought war and persecution to Judea. In 169 B.C.E., he attacked and seized Jerusalem. Subsequently, he initiated a harsh persecution of the Jews. He ordered all copies of the Torah (the first five books of the Bible) be burned. He banned the practice of circumcision, stopped the sacrifices in the temple, and desecrated it by placing in the holy of holies a statue of Zeus, chief deity of the Greek pantheon. His persecution lasted until Judas Maccabeus (see 1 and 2 Maccabees) led a revolt, retook Jerusalem, and purified the temple in 164 b.c.e.—an event the Jews to this very day remember as the feast of Hanukkah.

The book centers on a great hero, Daniel, who gives people hope during this time of persecution. However, when one opens the Book of Daniel, one does not find explicit reference to these events. As a book, Daniel is *not* a chronological history but an anthology of stories and visions. Chapters 1 through 6 present six stories of Daniel and three friends living their faith during the Babylonian exile.

In some of the stories Daniel cooperates with the pagan rulers. These stories are illustrations of how faithful Jews could be both good Jews and productive citizens in a non-Jewish state. In other stories, Daniel stands up to pagan rulers who oppose the Jews' faithfulness to God. These stories speak particularly to Jews who were suffering persecution.

The second half of the Book of Daniel (chapters 7 through 12) presents Daniel's four visions about the empires that dominated Israel after the exile: Medea, Persia, and Greece. As you read these chapters, you will encounter a type of writing known as "apocalyptic." In

Greek, the word *apokalypsis* can mean "revelation" but more literally means "uncovering." Apocalyptic writings uncover hidden things; they especially uncover the hidden meaning of history. In the time of Antiochus's persecution, the Book of Daniel uncovers the real meaning of what is taking place. It is not merely a battle between Antiochus and faithful Jews, but a battle being fought in heaven between Michael, the guardian angel of Judea/Israel, and the evil forces behind Antiochus.

There are certain common characteristics of apocalyptic literature. It usually contains accounts of visions sent by God that require an angel to explain them. It uses the language of symbols: symbolic beasts (Daniel chapter 7), symbolic numbers, symbolic clothing. They often seem to speak of the distant future, but are really speaking first of all about the present. More important than these literary elements is the purpose of apocalyptic writing. It assured the people of Israel that God would triumph and the present evil would eventually pass away. It was one way to reinforce the belief that evil would be punished and good rewarded, even when it didn't look that way at the moment.

The most famous set of apocalyptic symbols is found in Daniel 7:1–9, the four beasts. The author meant by these symbols four specific pagan kingdoms: Babylonia, Medea, Persia, and the Seleucids. The last "beast"—the Seleucid kingdom of Antiochus—was worse than all the rest in its perversity and wickedness. Out of these arose ten horns, symbolizing the ten kings who ruled before Antiochus. Antiochus is the "little horn" (Daniel 7:8) which supplanted the ten horns or kings who went before him.

Out of this collection of beastly symbols suddenly arises a new vision, made up of hopeful, consoling symbols. "An ancient one" (Daniel 7:9), God himself comes to judge the nations. The power of Antiochus and his wicked cohorts is broken and is replaced by the power of a new figure, "one like a human being [son of man]" (Daniel 7:13):

> *To him was given dominion and glory and kingship, that all*
> *peoples, nations, and languages should serve him. His dominion is*
> *an everlasting dominion that shall not pass away, and his kingship*
> *is one that shall never be destroyed* (Daniel 7:14).

Who is this "one like the son of man"? Placed as it is in opposition to the symbols of the four beasts, the symbol of the son of man stands for a nation of righteousness which supplants the reign of the wicked nations. The son of man symbolizes victorious Israel, heir to the ancient messianic throne promised long ago in David's time. He assumes the throne held up in faith to the Jews by the great prophets for generations. The symbol further stands for Israel's angelic protector, Michael, who is appointed by God to fight for Israel against the spiritual foes who serve the Gentile nations. In a sense, the symbol of the son of man as people and as the angel Michael means the same thing, since it was believed that a nation's protective angel summarized in his person the entire body of the people.

Through the use of symbolism, therefore, the author in Daniel 7 through 12 encourages the faith of his fellow persecuted Jews. The effect of the symbols he used would have been powerful. Jews reading these passages could not have remained depressed about their condition for long. God would eventually triumph, and all history would end on that triumphant note, leaving the Jews as masters of the nations.

The last two chapters of Daniel (13 and 14) are a later addition. These chapters, as well as some additional material in chapter 3, are written in Greek, and are accepted as inspired and part of the Bible by the Catholic Church and Orthodox Christians, but not by Protestants. Further, since chapters 1 and 8 through 12 of Daniel are composed in Hebrew and chapters 2 through 7 in Aramaic, while the rest of the book is composed in Greek, Daniel is the only book in the Catholic Bible that is written in three languages.

Daniel is one of the books of the Bible which appears in different forms and with different verse numbers in various modern English translations. We have been referring to the longer form recognized by the Catholic Church. Any version of the Bible published under Catholic auspices, such as the *New Jerusalem Bible* and the *New American Bible*, will contain the longer version of Daniel.

Some Protestant editions of the Bible, for example, the *Revised Standard Version*, or the *New Revised Standard Version*, place these additional parts of Daniel along with other material between the Old Testament and New Testament in a section called "Apocrypha." If your Bible is arranged this way, you may need to do some flipping back and forth between Daniel and the "Apocrypha" section.

The Books of 1 and 2 Maccabees

The rather passive theology of Daniel did not require the Jews to take any action to advance their own cause. This stands in marked contrast to the worldview advanced by 1 and 2 Maccabees. The authors of these two books must have looked upon the Book of Daniel as pie-in-the-sky theology. Instead of counseling the Jews to wait patiently for God to take control of things, these writers urged the Jews to take up arms and fight their oppressors. Instead of looking forward to an age of an ethereal "son of man," they believed that the best hope for the Jews lay in allying themselves with the Maccabee family, whose history these books recount, and in supporting the Maccabees' aggressive tactics.

The books of 1 and 2 Maccabees, like several other books in the Old Testament, are very easy to put down. At times, they are boring. Catholics reading these books should be able to sympathize with the Protestant reformers who excised these books from the Old Testament because they often read more like political propaganda than "holy writ." Nevertheless, 1 and 2 Maccabees do help us round out our understanding of late Old Testament writing.

Different authors wrote 1 and 2 Maccabees. The second book is not a continuation of the first, but a separate work in itself. Both, however, are concerned with the same general theme: the rise to power of the Maccabee family and its leadership in the Jewish struggle against the Seleucid persecution.

1 Maccabees was written originally in Hebrew and 2 Maccabees in Greek. The first Book of Maccabees begins with the first days of King Antiochus Epiphanes (175 B.C.E.) and ends with the ascension to the Jewish high priesthood of John Hyrcanus (134 B.C.E.). The historical period covered in 2 Maccabees is the same, but the story cuts off a little earlier, in the year 161 B.C.E. There is some overlap in the two books, particularly in 1 Maccabees 3–7 and 2 Maccabees 8–15, which essentially recount the same details.

In broad outline, the two books can be viewed as follows. When Antiochus Epiphanes began his terrible persecution of the Jews in 167 B.C.E., many loyal Jews refused to capitulate to his demands to compromise their Jewish faith. Chief among these were the Maccabee family of Modein. Mattathias, the patriarch of this family, triggered a Jewish revolt when he refused to offer sacrifice to a Greek god and killed the king's official in the process (1 Maccabees 2:23–26). Mattathias was supported by five sons. Upon Mattathias's death in 166 B.C.E., the leadership of the revolt passed to his son, Judas.

Both 1 and 2 Maccabees make it clear that the Seleucid persecution was facilitated by the treason and infidelity of the Jewish Hellenizers—Jews sympathetic to Greek ways. There were even high priests among this latter group, the most famous of whom was Menelaus, who had attained his office by bribing Antiochus. The authors are particularly harsh in their condemnation of these Jewish traitors. In 2 Maccabees, Menelaus is called "the chief enemy of his fellow citizens" (2 Maccabees 4:50). Thus, the Maccabean wars were not just military ventures against Gentiles. They also represented an attempt by conservative Jews to purge Judaism of those elements which stood for compromise with Greek culture.

Judas Maccabeus won victory after victory during his tenure as Jewish commander-in-chief. When Antiochus died in 164 B.C.E., claimants to the Seleucid throne regularly murdered each other off and destroyed the internal cohesion of Seleucid power. As a result, the Maccabees were able to play one rival Seleucid faction against another.

315

Jonathan Maccabeus succeeded to Maccabee family leadership in 160 B.C.E., upon the death of his brother Judas. During Jonathan's tenure of leadership (160–142 B.C.E.), the Maccabees were able to hold their own with the Seleucids. Antiochus's successor, King Alexander Balas, had to admit the growth in Maccabean power and even appointed Jonathan as Jewish high priest. Thus began a new era in Maccabean family history.

When Jonathan was succeeded by his brother Simon, the Jews at last entered an era of stability and independence from foreign domination. Under Simon, the various Jewish factions accepted the Maccabean claim to the high priesthood and the Maccabean hold on this office became hereditary. Simon served as high priest from 143 to 134 B.C.E. and was followed in office by his son John Hyrcanus. At that point, 1 Maccabees terminates its history.

This brief outline ignores many details of the story which are quite sacred in Jewish memories. One of the high points in all of Jewish history is found in 1 Maccabees 4:36–60, where we read of Judas Maccabeus rededication of the temple. The scene described is the first Hanukkah celebration, a feast which would become as important to Jews as Passover. The climax of 2 Maccabees is the martyrdom of seven Jewish brothers (see 2 Maccabees 7), an example of courage and religious fidelity which exceeds anything like it in the entire Old Testament.

The theological message of 1 and 2 Maccabees appears on virtually every page of these books: that Jews must resist religious persecution by force and, if necessary, lay down their lives to keep Judaism undefiled by paganism. The two books differ, however, on the issue of the final outcome of Jewish resistance.

A Bridge to the New Testament

The author of 1 Maccabees sees Jewish resistance leading to the establishment of an independent Jewish political state led by the Maccabean family. The author of 2 Maccabees, while not opposed to the establishment of such a state, holds out an even greater reward to loyal Jewish resisters, that reward is a personal resurrection from the dead. This is a belief 2 Maccabees shares with the Book of Daniel. The optimistic conclusion of Daniel 12 is that the good will rise from the dead and somehow share the glorious life of God's holy angels. This first unequivocal assertion of belief in personal resurrection in the Old Testament is echoed in 2 Maccabees 7, the story of the seven brothers. This is the famous story of a Jewish mother and her seven sons who refused to embrace foreign religion, and in it 2 Maccabees talks about the resurrection of the dead. Further, 2 Maccabees insists that whenever God's faithful people suffer, they can be assured of receiving justice—if not in this life, then in the resurrection (see 2 Maccabees 7 and 8). Finally, 2 Maccabees teaches the efficacy of the faithful praying for the dead (12:39–45), and that these prayers make atonement for the sins of the dead.

The respective authors of 2 Maccabees and Daniel (12:2) held up to their persecuted brothers and sisters a greater hope than mere political supremacy or military might. If you remain steadfast to the end, these authors urge their fellow Jews, you will win an eternal reward greater than anything that mere political or military power can achieve. "Many of those who sleep in the dust of the earth shall awake, some to everlasting life, and some to shame and everlasting contempt" (Daniel 12:2).

With this idea, Old Testament theology was on the verge of passing into New Testament theology. For soon on the dawn of the horizon would be encountered one of Israel's greatest rabbis, Jesus ben Joseph, from the town of Nazareth, and whom Christians proclaimed as:

> [25]*I am the resurrection and the life. Those who believe in me, even though they die, will live,* [26]*and everyone who lives and believes in me will never die* (John 11:25–26).

For Discussion

1. How was the religion of Judaism countercultural to the dominant Greek culture of the day?

2. Explain the Book of Daniel's theological response to Hellenization.

3. What is apocalyptic literature? What is its purpose and how is the Book of Daniel an example of it?

4. How is the content of the books of Maccabees different in their response to Hellenization from that of the Book of Daniel?

For Further Reading

Buchanan, George W. *The Book of Daniel*. Edwin Mellen Press, 1999.

Collins, John J. *Daniel, With an Introduction to Jewish Apocalyptic Literature*. Grand Rapids, MI: Eerdmans, 1984.

Doran, Robert. "The First Book of Maccabees: Introduction, Commentary, and Reflections" and "The Second Book of Maccabees: Introduction, Commentary, and Reflections." In *New Interpreter's Bible*, edited by Leander E. Keck, et al., 4:1–178, 179–299. Nashville, TN: Abingdon Press, 1996.

Harrington, Daniel J. *Invitation to the Apocrypha*. Grand Rapids, MI: Eerdmans, 1999.

Harrington, Daniel J. *The Maccabean Revolt: Anatomy of a Biblical Revolution*—Collegeville, MN: Liturgical Press, 1988.

AFTERWORD

In OUR STUDY OF THE OLD TESTAMENT WE HAVE SEEN how these varied and multifaceted books came into being within the life experience of the Hebrew people. We have also encountered the Old Testament as a record of the love affair between a people and their God. Like any loving relationship, it has its ups and downs, its agony and ecstasy, its experiences of faith and sinfulness and reconciliation.

What does that record have to do with our lives today? And what does it say to us? Is the Old Testament a dead transcript of events, having no relevance to modern times? Is it a museum piece? Or is there a timeless transcultural element in this story that speaks with great force to humanity at the dawn of the twenty-first century?

We will find the response to these questions only by approaching the Old Testament in the same way that the Psalmist approaches daily prayer—"Your face, LORD, do I seek" (Psalm 27:8). Studies of Sacred Scripture such as this book are helpful to lead us to a knowledge about the Word of God, but really to know the Word of God as the Psalmist did we must pick up the Old Testament in the same prayerful spirit which moved the Psalmist.

To understand the Old Testament we must acknowledge that yearning deep within ourselves for intimate knowledge of the only One who can still our restlessness and bring us to fulfillment. We will be able to know the relevance, meaning, and challenges of the Old Testament in our lives only when we can say with the Psalmists:

As a deer longs for flowing streams,
  so my soul longs for you, O God (Psalm 42:1).

The conclusion of this book is a challenge—a challenge for the reader to get to know and love and live with the Old Testament from the inside out, by reading it daily in a spirit of wonder, receptivity, and yearning:

- Standing with God at creation as God's holy breath brings order out of chaos, and embracing God's original blessing.

- Climbing Mount Moriah with Abraham and Isaac as Abraham leads his son to be sacrificed to God and experiencing the surprise of God's intervention in denial of such a sacrifice.

- Crossing the Sea of Reeds—the Red Sea—with our ancestors in faith as we leave behind the comfort of the known for the unknown, following God who calls us through the waters of chaos—a leap of faith.

- Standing at the foot of Mount Sinai with Moses as God calls each of us to become a member of his covenantal and consecrated nation.

- Wandering with the people of God in the wilderness as we seek to clarify God's presence in our own life and to find out what commitment to God really means in the covenant.

- Learning from the desert experience of the Hebrew nomads as you walk through your own daily desert.

- Embracing holiness and Sabbath rest as articulated in the Old Testament and as countercultural to our own time.

- Rejoicing before the Lord and accepting the refreshments of his forgiveness as King David did.

- Being spokespersons for God, like the biblical prophets who screamed for true monotheism and who championed the poor and disenfranchised by calling all to practice social justice.

- If necessary, venting our anger at God, like Jeremiah in his lamentations, or declare to him that we have "had enough," as did the prophet Elijah.

- Sensing the strength that comes from devotion to God's law as experienced in the lives of Ruth, Esther, and Judith.

- Being like Job, surrendering to the mystery of suffering and the mystery of God's power and majesty.

- Praying with the Psalmist in times of joy, sadness, anger, and rage.

- Embracing our sensuality and sexuality as lyrically proclaimed in the Song of Solomon.

- Seeking true wisdom—fear of the Lord—truly holding God in awe, as found in the Wisdom literature of the Old Testament.

- Being willing to embrace martyrdom as the Jewish mother and her seven sons did in the Book of Maccabees.

- Believing in the resurrection.

In short, relive the pages of the Old Testament in your own life and consciousness. This book is meant to give you ample suggestions on how to begin.

Follow your own desires and preferences and allow them to lead you where they will. If you're the active type, you may want to start with a passage from 1 Kings. Or if you are more introspective, you may want to look at Proverbs or Sirach as a beginning point. If you're lyrical and full of music, you may want to begin with the Psalms. If you're an environmentalist, you may want to start with the creation stories. If you want to learn how to keep your promises, look at the ways in which God keeps promises in the covenant, and try to imitate him. Regardless, be sure to appropriate into your own life the wonderful models, values, and challenges found in the Old Testament. Wherever you start, keep at it. Come back daily in a spirit of adventure, quest, and challenge. It won't be long before you discover the marvelous ability of the Old Testament to enlighten your own life and your own times, wherever you may live or be, so that you can pray with the Psalmist:

> [12]Blessed are you, O LORD;
>   teach me your statutes.
> [13]With my lips I declare
>   all the ordinances of your mouth.
> [14]I delight in the way of your decrees
>   as much as in all riches.
> [15]I will meditate on your precepts
>   and fix my eyes on your ways.
> [16]I will delight in your statutes;
>   I will not forget your word
> (Psalm 119:12–16).

SCRIPTURE INDEX

INDEX